CANNIBALS

CANNIBALS

Shocking True Tales
of the Last Taboo
on Land and at Sea

EDITED BY
JOSEPH CUMMINS

THE LYONS PRESS

Guilford, Connecticut
An Imprint of The Globe Pequot Press

The Lyons Press is an imprint of The Globe Pequot Press.

Printed in the United States of America.

10 9 8 7 6 5 4 3 2 1

Design by Compset, Inc.

Library of Congress Cataloging-in-Publication Data

Cannibals : shocking true tales of the last taboo on land and at sea / edited by Joseph Cummins.
    p. cm.
    ISBN 1-58574-217-1
    1. Cannibalsim. I. Cummins, Joseph.

GN409 .C37 2001
394′.9—dc21

2001050434

"The cauldron was a-
bubbling
the flesh was lean
and the women moved forward
like piranhas in a stream."

— "Summer Cannibals"
f. smith/p.smith

Contents

Introduction

"The primal command," writes anthropologist Christy Turner, "is, do not eat people." Eating humans is a viscerally powerful taboo—the ultimate, the final, taboo.

And yet, we do eat each other.

As this book shows, we eat each other to survive, we eat each other for revenge, we eat each other in war, we eat each other because we like the taste, we eat each other through madness and sexual sadism—we even eat each other out of love.

The true stories and eyewitness accounts collected here range from 1150 A.D. to the last decade of the twentieth century, but the story of cannibalism is as old as mankind. In October 2000, the journal *Science* presented findings on the discovery of the remains of six Neanderthals who had been devoured by their fellows around 100,000 years ago. The Greek historian Herodotus, writing around 450 B.C., describes cannibalism among the Scythians, who supposedly killed and ate the elderly of their tribe. (Herodotus also reported the widespread custom of using dead men's skulls for drinking cups.) Chinese records from well before the birth of Christ speak repeatedly of humans eating other humans during periods of famine. It's even in the Bible: "Because of the suffering that your enemy will inflict on you during the siege, you will eat . . . the flesh of the sons and daughters the Lord your God is giving you. Even the most gentle and sensitive man among you will have no compassion on his own brother or the wife he loves or his surviving children, and he will not give to one of them any of the flesh of his children that he is eating." (Deuteronomy 28:53)

While the practice of cannibalism is age-old, the term is relatively new. During the fall of 1492, as Columbus sailed among the lustrous isles of his New World, he began to hear troubling tales of a fearsome, red-painted tribe called the Caribs. Supposedly, these terrifying warriors and extraordinary seamen were not only conquering the gentler Taino and Arawak tribes, but literally devouring them as well. Columbus himself, it is said, entered a Carib dwelling and there found baskets full of human skulls and bones. The Spanish word for Caribs, *caribales*, came to be pronounced *canibales*, and thus this tribe gave their name not only to the Caribbean Sea, but to practice of eating human flesh.

Over the next five hundred years, explorers brought home hair-raising, flesh-crawling tales of cannibalism. It was said to be a common practice among the Mayan and Aztec peoples; among both North and South American Indians; in the Congo basin and other parts of Africa; in New Guinea and the Solomon Islands; and among the Maori and the Fiji Islanders (the latter possessed a particularly fierce reputation, as can be seen in Garry Hogg's startling "Cannibalism Among the Fiji Islanders"—one Fijian chief was reported to have eaten nine hundred people).

But—is any of this true? Was ritual cannibalism a fact of life for primitive peoples, right up to the 1960s? (Michael Rockefeller, adventurous son of Nelson, is widely believed to have been killed and eaten in November of 1961 by a Stone Age New Guinea tribe, the Otsjanep people.)

Many anthropologists believe that primitive people ate each other as a common practice, for reasons ranging from wanting to acquire the qualities of a brave enemy to seeking to destroy his spirit so utterly that he might never come back to haunt you. In cases of so-called mortuary cannibalism, wherein a dead relative is being eaten, this "affectionate cannibalism" was due to a desire to incorporate the deceased individual back into the life of the tribe. A minority group of anthropologists even speculates that tribal cannibalism emerged as a cultural response to chronic protein shortages. (The actor Errol Flynn, of all people, lived on a coconut plantation in New Guinea when he was seventeen and later wrote that raiding headhunters from the Highlands could be prevented from killing and eating others by giving them salt!)

In *The Man-Eating Myth*, a highly influential book published in 1979, anthropologist William Arens argued firmly that cannibalism in human societies almost never existed in any ritualistic way. Credulous Europeans, he claims, were duped time and again by tribes pointing over the next hill—to that *other* tribe who ate babies for breakfast.

The debate will undoubtedly go on. But since the publication of *The Man-Eating Myth* over twenty years ago, physical evidence has accrued which indicates that ritual cannibalism among primitives did occur, although how frequently is still anybody's guess. Traces of human myoglobin, a protein found in the human heart and skeletal muscles, has been discovered in cooking pots and fossilized human feces in the ruins of Anasazi villages in the American Southwest. Preston Douglas's chilling "Cannibals in the Canyon" makes a highly compelling case that cannibalism as a deliberate tool of terror may have helped destroy a flourishing civilization.

That humans in extreme conditions eat other humans, however, has never been in doubt. "By far the most common reason for human beings eating one another is what we would expect: hunger," writes Hans Askenasy in his excellent study, *Cannibalism: From Sacrifice to Survival*. As can be seen in the true stories collected in this volume, stranded or shipwrecked people, wasting away from starvation, almost always eat their dead.

These dire situations affect different human beings differently—cannibalism, like so much else, becomes a matter of style. In the infamous case of the Donner Party (depicted in Peter Limburg's "The Forlorn Hope"), some ate human flesh reluctantly, but others prowled with sharp knifes, barely waiting for their fellows to take their last breaths (one woman watched her newly dead husband's heart torn out before her eyes).

For the highly religious survivors of the Uruguayan plane that crashed in the Andes in 1972 (immortalized in Piers Paul Read's classic *Alive*) consuming their frozen dead had Eucharistic overtones: "When Christ died he gave his body to us so that we could have spiritual life," one of them said. "My friend has given us his body so that we can have physical life."

Eating those already dead under these desperate circumstances is understandable, but what if no one dies fast enough to keep the others from starving? What about murder?

In the eighteenth and nineteenth centuries, "the custom of the sea"—drawing lots in order to pick an unfortunate to be sacrificed for the good of the shipwrecked group—was considered acceptable. "Given the cruel mathematics of survival cannibalism," writes Nathaniel Philbrick in his bestseller *In the Heart of the Sea,* "each death not only provided the remaining men with food but reduced by one the number of people they had to share it with." In the case of the crew of close-knit

Nantucketer whalers, whose ship, the *Essex,* was stove in by a whale, the young man chosen at random to die gave up the ghost with relatively good grace—almost with a sacrificial air.

But Edward E. Leslie's "The Ownership of a Plank" portrays a nightmarish situation that, one suspects, is probably closer to what usually occurred. In 1765, the American colonial merchant sloop *Peggy* became disabled in the Atlantic during a storm. Her crew had no food, but their cargo was rum and brandy, and they began to drink it copiously. After some days, a black slave was chosen to die (often, in these instances, the lottery was rigged to make sure that blacks or foreigners went first). Despite the man's piteous pleas, he was quickly killed, gutted and roasted. Another man was then chosen to die and given overnight to think about his fate. By 4 A.M., he was stark raving mad. The next day, the crew was miraculously rescued and the man's life saved, but he never recovered his sanity.

Probably the most fascinating, and yet most horrible, cases of cannibalism belong to our twentieth century. It is one thing to read of the rituals of primitive tribes, or of starving, half-mad survivors devouring each other, entirely another to learn of government-sanctioned cannibalism in 1967 during China's Cultural Revolution (as described in journalist Zheng Yi's "The Slaughter at Wuxuan"). Or to watch the cruelty with which Japanese soldiers kept Allied prisoners as human cattle during World War II (a dark rumor now finally exposed in Yuki Tanaka's "Judge Webb and Japanese Cannibalism").

And, of course, where would our age be without serial cannibal killers? Reading Albert Fish's letter to the mother of a child he ate . . . seeing the row of heads in Jeffrey Dahmer's refrigerator . . . learning of the strange case of the art student Issei Sagawa, who killed and ate a beautiful young Dutch woman but is now a celebrity in his native Japan . . . well . . . the mind begins to tune out the reality of these terrible tales and seeks relief in the unconscious.

But that is precisely where the cannibals have been hiding all along, sneaking out at night to appear in our darkest myths and fairy tales. The Algonquian-speaking Indians of northeastern Canada were haunted by windingo monsters, grotesque and spectral creatures who hid in the primeval forests and feasted on the flesh of unwary humans. In *Hansel and Gretel,* the witch admonishes Gretel to "cook food for your brother. I wish to make him nice and fat and then I will eat him up." (Interestingly enough, Issei Sagawa dreamt at age three of being cooked along with his brother. He also thought that *Sleeping Beauty* was a fairy tale of a cannibal witch.)

These days, our bogeyman of choice is the civilized gourmand, Hannibal Lecter, who combines horror with good wine. Millions have flocked to see him, have—dare we say it?—rooted for him as he approaches his victims, mouth bared. Odd, indeed. The peculiar intensity of our fascination with *canibales* suggests a disturbing thought—that it is not the cannibal without we need fear, but the one who lurks within.

Joseph Cummins
Summer, 2001

Part One
Primitive Cannibalism and Human Sacrifice

Cannibals in the Canyon

About the year 1150, in the American Southwest, the flourishing Anasazi civilization—marked by immense stone structures called Great Houses, some up to four stories high—collapsed completely. One anthropologist now claims to have found the answer to this ages-old mystery—the evidence strongly points to marauding gangs of cannibals who turned the windswept canyons into places of "hideous evil."

More than a century ago, American travellers in the Southwest were astounded to find ruined cities and vast cliff dwellings dotting the desert landscape. Surely, they thought, a great civilization had once flourished here. It looked to them as if the people who created it had simply walked away and vanished: the ruins were often littered with gorgeous painted pottery and also contained grinding stones, baskets, sandals hanging on pegs, and granaries full of corn. The Navajo Indians, who were occupying much of the territory where this lost civilization once existed, called them the Anasazi—a word meaning "Ancient Enemy"—and they avoided the ruins, believing they were inhabited by *chindi,* or ghosts.

Not surprisingly, American archeologists focussed on the Anasazi and their great works, and they became the most intensely studied prehistoric culture in North America. A standard picture emerged, based on wide-ranging excavations of sites and on detailed ethnographic research among the Hopi, Zuni, and other Pueblo Indian tribes, who are the Anasazi's descendants. The Anasazi were—so the findings suggested—peaceful farmers, and they attained astonishing results in engineering, architecture, and art. The center of this cultural flowering, from the tenth century to the twelfth, seems to have been Chaco Canyon,

New Mexico, a windswept gulch in the apparently endless sagebrush desert of the San Juan Basin. Chaco is marked by immense stone structures, some up to four stories high, called Great Houses. The largest, Pueblo Bonito, contains some six hundred and fifty rooms, and its construction required more than thirty thousand tons of shaped sandstone blocks. The Chaco Anasazi also built hundreds of miles of roads that stretched out from Chaco Canyon across the landscape in arrow-straight lines—an engineering marvel achieved without compass, wheel, or beast of burden. They erected shrines, solar and astronomical observatories, irrigation systems, and a network of signalling stations. They constructed more than a hundred Great Houses outside Chaco Canyon, spreading them over fifty thousand square miles of the Four Corners region of the Southwest. Many of these outlying Great Houses seem to have been connected to Chaco by the radiating pattern of roads. Archeologists today call this cultural explosion "the Chaco phenomenon." But the phenomenon ended abruptly around 1150 A.D., when a vast collapse apparently occurred, and Chaco, along with some of the outlying sites, was largely abandoned.

Equally remarkable was the Chaco society. It seemed to be almost utopian. The Anasazi, the traditional view held, had no absolute rulers, or even a ruling class, but governed themselves through consensus, as the Pueblo Indians do today. They were a society without rich or poor. Warfare and violence were rare, or perhaps unknown. The Anasazi were believed to be profoundly spiritual, and to live in harmony with nature.

As a result, the Anasazi captured the fancy of people outside the archeological profession, and particularly those in the New Age movement, many of whom see themselves as the Anasazi's spiritual descendants. The ruins of Chaco Canyon have long been a New Age mecca, to the point where one of the sites had to be closed, because New Agers were burying crystals and illegally arranging to have their ashes scattered there. During Harmonic Convergence, in 1987, thousands gathered in Chaco Canyon and joined hands, chanting and praying. People have also flocked to the villages of the present-day Pueblo Indians—the Hopi in particular—seeking a spirituality outside Western civilization. The Hopi themselves, along with other Pueblo Indian descendants of the Anasazi, feel a deep reverence for their prehistoric ancestors.

In 1967, a young physical anthropologist named Christy Turner II began looking at the Anasazi in a new light. He happened to be examining Anasazi teeth in the Museum of Northern Arizona, in Flagstaff, attempting to trace a peculiar trait known as the three-rooted first molar. On the last day of his research, he asked the curator to pull down a large, coffin-shaped cardboard box from a top shelf. The accession record said that the box contained remains from a remote area along Polacca Wash, an arroyo situated below First Mesa, on the Hopi Indian Reservation. The remains had been excavated in 1964 by an archeologist named Alan P. Olson. Turner removed the lid and found himself gazing at a bizarre collection of more than a thousand human bone shards. Thirty years later, when he described the experience to me, the memory was still vivid. "Holy smokes!" he recalled having exclaimed to himself. "What happened here? This looks exactly like *food* trash." The fragments reminded him of broken and burned animal bones that he had found in prehistoric Anasazi garbage mounds. As he looked more closely, another thought struck him. Like many physical anthropologists, he had sometimes done forensic work for police departments. Once, in California, the police had asked him to examine some remains that had been found in the Oakland Hills—a skeleton still wearing a pair of boots. Turner had informed the police that the person had been savagely beaten to death. "Now," he told me, "I could see the same violence done to the Polacca Wash bones."

Turner borrowed the bones from the museum and took them to Arizona State University, where he was a professor. In 1969, he presented his findings in a paper he read at an archeological meeting in Santa Fe. Word of what the paper would say had got around, and the room was packed. Co-written with a colleague of Turner's named Nancy Morris, the paper was entitled "A Massacre at Hopi." Turner informed the audience that the bones belonged to a group of thirty people—mostly women and children—who had been "killed, crudely dismembered, violently mutilated," and that the heads, in particular, showed extreme trauma: "Every skull is smashed, chiefly from the front, and massively so. . . . The faces were crushed while still covered with flesh." Most of the skulls had received a number of "blunt, heavy, club-like fracturing blows." The bone material had still been "vital" at the time the blows were struck. "The many small pieces of unweathered teeth and skulls and post-cranial scrap suggest, but do not prove, that the death of these people occurred at the burial site." Moreover, "every skull, regardless of age or sex, had the brain exposed." Heads had been placed on flat rocks and smashed open, apparently so that the brain could be removed.

He went on to say that most of the bones—not only the skulls—also showed marks of cutting, chopping, dismemberment, butchering, "defleshing," and roasting. The larger bones had been broken apart and the marrow scraped out, or, in the case of spongy bone, reamed out. Turner and Morris concluded that the Polacca Wash bones represented "the most convincing evidence of cannibalism in all Southwest archaeology."

Turner said that Olson, the original excavator, had been wrong in assuming that the bones were prehistoric, for Turner had had the bones radiocarbon-dated, and the results had come back as 1580 A.D. plus or minus ninety-five years. Given the date, Turner wondered whether some record or legend might still exist relating what happened.

When he talked with me, he said, "We knew who the bods were. There were a certain number of kids and females. We looked at dental morphology. We got a good match with Hopi. So we asked ourselves, 'What is there in oral tradition about a whole bunch of Hopi being killed and eaten, or massacred, of this age and sex composition, at this date?' "

Turner eventually concluded that the Polacca Wash site was a place known in Hopi legend as the Death Mound. Hopi informants had first described the legend to an anthropologist at the end of the nineteenth century. According to the story, sometime in the late 1600s a Hopi village called Awatovi had been largely converted to Christianity under the influence of Spanish friars. In addition, the people of Awatovi practiced witchcraft, which the Hopi considered a heinous crime. Eventually, five other Hopi villages decided to purge the tribe of this spiritual stain. An attack was organized by the chief of Awatovi himself, who had become disgusted with his own people. Warriors from the other villages attacked the errant village at dawn, surprising most of the men inside the kivas—sunken ceremonial chambers of the Pueblo Indians—and burning them alive. After killing the men, the warriors captured groups of women and children. As one of these groups was being marched away, a dispute broke out over which village would get to keep the captives. The argument got out of hand. In a rage, the warriors settled it by torturing, killing, and dismembering all the captives. Their bodies were left at a place called Mas-teo'-mo, or Death Mound. "If the stories are correct," the anthropologist who first collected these legends wrote, "the final butchery at Mas-teo'-mo must have been horrible."

Turner recalls that the lecture room was quiet when he finished arguing that the bones were the remains of a cannibal feast. "You could *smell* the disbelief," he said. Most of his colleagues felt that there simply had to be another explanation for the strange bone assemblage. To suggest that the Hopi could have deliberately tortured, murdered, mutilated, cooked, and eaten a defenseless group of women and children from their own tribe seemed to make a mockery of a hundred years of cautious, diligent scholarship. The paper was looked upon with deep skepticism by many of Turner's peers, and the Hopi objected to what they considered a crude slur on their ancestors.

Over the next thirty years, Turner looked deeper into the archeological record for signs of cannibalism—going all the way back to the Hopi's Anasazi ancestors. To his surprise, he discovered that a number of claims of Anasazi violence and cannibalism had been published by archeologists, but the profession, perhaps blinded by the conventional wisdom, had ignored the reports, the notes, the evidence, the very bones.

Turner has identified many Anasazi sites that he believes represent "charnel deposits"—heaps of cannibalized remains. The University of Utah Press published the results of his work, under the title *Man Corn: Cannibalism and Violence in the Prehistoric American Southwest*. The term "man corn" is the literal translation of the Nahuatl (Aztec) word *tlacatlaolli,* which refers to a "sacred meal of sacrificed human meat, cooked with corn." (The book had a co-author, in Turner's wife, Jacqueline—also an anthropologist—who died in 1996.)

Man Corn reëxamines seventy-two Anasazi sites at which violence or cannibalism may have occurred. Turner claims that cannibalism probably took place at thirty-eight of these sites, and that extreme violence and mutilation occurred at most of the others. He calculates that at least two hundred and eighty-six individuals were butchered, cooked, and eaten, with a mean of between seven and eight individuals per site. As a test to see how widespread cannibalism might have been, Turner also examined a collection of eight hundred and seventy Anasazi skeletons in the Museum of Northern Arizona. He found that eight percent—one skeleton in twelve—showed clear evidence of having been cannibalized.

Turner's book does more than attack the traditional views of the Anasazi. It also addresses one of the great unsolved problems of American archeology: What caused the collapse of the Chaco culture around

1150? There was a severe drought at the time, but most researchers don't believe that it alone could have brought about such a cultural implosion. Other, unknown factors must have played a role.

After the Chaco collapse and abandonment, many Anasazi moved into deep, remote canyons, building their dwellings in cliffs or on high, often fortified, mesas. A century later, they abandoned even these defensive positions, leaving almost the entire Four Corners region uninhabited. To some archeologists, it seemed as if the Anasazi had been seized with paranoia—that they were protecting themselves from some terrible enemy. But, no matter how hard archeologists looked, they could find no such enemy.

Bone Cakes

I have been following Turner's work for about ten years. He is one of the country's leading physical anthropologists and has a reputation for being something of a loner—brilliant, arrogant, even intimidating. When I heard rumors that he was finishing his monumental treatise on cannibalism, I paid him a visit at Arizona State University, in Tempe, just outside Phoenix. The door to his office led me into a dim dogleg space created by the backs of shelves and filing cabinets that stood in the middle of the room. At one end of a scarred oak table lay an untidy heap of plastic bags containing broken human bones, including skulls. Dental picks, a tiny magnifying glass, and other instruments rested nearby. The far wall was covered with photographs of skulls, of a grimacing mummy head, and of Hopi medicine men, among other things. A crude photocopy of an old sideshow bill was taped on another wall, near a computer terminal. The bill read, "The Head of the Renowned Bandit Joaquin! Will be exhibited for one day only, April 19, 1853. Plus the hand of the notorious   robber and murderer Three Fingered Jack."

Turner sat behind an old desk next to a window, which overlooked a pleasant courtyard with two palm trees. He is sixty-four, and has sandy hair and bleached, watery brown eyes behind large glasses. His skin is rough and leathery from years of outdoor work in the sun.

Turner was born in Columbia, Missouri, and grew up in Southern California. "I was baptized without being consulted," he told me. "Presbyterian. I hated it so much it turned me quickly to Darwin." He had been a premedical student at the University of Arizona, but he switched to anthropology. Best known for work he has done on dental morphology—the shapes of human teeth—he has spent most of his academic life attempting to trace the various waves of human migration from Asia to America by looking at teeth.

I spent three days with Turner. He is a mercurial man, who can be by turns gracious, witty, charming, aggressive, and vituperative. It is perhaps a good thing that he has surrounded himself with the dead, because in dealing with the living he is legendarily difficult. "I have no friends, but I have no scars," he told me. He seems to relish being on the unpopular side of an academic fight. According to his daughter, Korri, "He loves it, being branded politically incorrect."

After chatting with Turner for a while, I asked him about the heap of bones on his table. He said that they were from a site called Sambrito Village, on the San Juan River, in New Mexico. It had been excavated thirty-five years before, when the area was to be drowned by Navajo Reservoir. The excavating archeologist had concluded that cannibalism had occurred there, but his finding was ignored. Turner was now reëxamining the bones for his book.

"All the makings of cannibalism are here," he said enthusiastically, pointing to the charnel heap. He lifted a plastic bag holding a piece of skull, and slid the piece into his hand, cradling it gently. "This is a good one to illustrate the roasting of the head. A lot of the heads have this burning pattern on the back." He indicated a patch on the skull where the bone was crumbling and flaking off. He handed it to me, and I took it gingerly. "Clearly," he continued, "they were decapitating the heads and putting them in the fire face up."

"Why?" I asked. "To cook the brain?"

"It would have cooked the brain, yes," he said, rather dryly.

"What happens when a brain is cooked?"

"Thinking stops. Except among some of my students."

Turner pointed to the broken edge of the skull, which showed several places where sharp blows had opened the brainpan: small pieces of broken skull were still adhering to the edges. "These are perimortem breaks. This cannot happen except in fresh bone," he said. "Perimortem" refers to events at the time of death. Most of the bones, he said, showed numerous perimortem breaks; the crushing, splintering, and breaking of the bones had thus occurred just before, at, or just after death.

"How old was this person, and of what sex?" I asked.

Turner took the skull and flipped it over. "No signs of sutural closing. I'd put it at eighteen to twenty years. Sex is female. There are very light brow ridges, orbit is sharp, mastoid is relatively small, bone is light. I couldn't rule out a very light male."

He rummaged through the pile and showed me other bones. Some had cuts and marks of sawing near the joints, caused by dismemberment with stone tools. He pointed out similar cuts where the muscles had been attached to the bone—evidence that meat had been stripped off. He showed me percussion marks from stone choppers used to break open bones for marrow and to hack through the skulls.

Turner was the first person ever to quantify what a set of cannibalized human remains looks like. Eventually, in the course of his work, he identified five characteristics that he felt had to be present in a bone assemblage before one could claim that the individual had been cooked and eaten:

(1) Bones had to be broken open as if to get at the marrow.

(2) Bones had to have cutting and sawing marks on them, made by tools, in a way that suggested dismemberment and butchering.

(3) Some bones had to have "anvil abrasions." These are faint parallel scratches, which Turner noticed most often on skulls, caused when the head (or another bone) is placed on a stone that serves as an anvil, and another stone is brought down hard on it to break it open. When the blow occurs, a certain amount of slippage takes place, causing the distinctive abrasions.

(4) Some bone fragments had to be burned; heads, in particular, had to show patterns of burning on the back or top, indicating that the brain was cooked.

(5) Most of the vertebrae and spongy bone had to be missing. Vertebrae and spongy bone are soft and full of marrow. They can be crushed whole either to make bone cakes (something the Anasazi did with other mammal bones) or to extract grease through boiling. (Fresh bone is full of grease.)

While Turner was involved in his multi-decade project, Tim D. White, a well-known paleoanthropologist, made another discovery. In examining a six-hundred-thousand-year-old fossilized skull from Africa, he noticed some peculiar scratches. They looked as if someone had scraped and carved the flesh from the skull with a stone tool. He wondered whether the skull was evidence of cannibalism deep in the human fossil record.

To learn more about what cannibalism does to bones, White turned his attention to the American Southwest. In 1973, in Mancos

Canyon, Colorado, an archeological team had found the broken and burned remains of approximately thirty people scattered on the floors of a small ruined pueblo. White borrowed the bones in the summer of 1985 and studied them intensively for the next five years. He found all five of the indications of cannibalism that Turner had identified. But he also noticed another peculiar trait: a faint polishing and beveling on many of the broken tips of bones. White wondered if this polishing might have been caused by the bones' being boiled and stirred in a rough ceramic pot, to render their fat. To test the idea, White and his team performed an experiment. They broke up several mule-deer bones and put the pieces in a replica of an Anasazi corrugated clay cooking pot, partly filled with water, and then heated the mixture on a Coleman stove for three hours, stirring it occasionally with a wooden stick. The fat from the bones rose to the surface and coagulated around the water-line, forming a ring of grease about half an inch thick. They decanted the contents, and White took a bone piece and scraped off the ring of fat around the inside of the pot.

Under magnification, the deer bones showed the same micro-scopic polishing that White had observed on the Mancos bones. Furthermore, the bone used to scrape out the ring of fat showed a pattern of scratches that exactly matched that of one Mancos bone. White called this "pot polish."

On learning of White's discovery, Turner took a second look at many of his cannibalized assemblages. He found pot polish on most of them, including the Polacca Wash bones, and he added pot polish to his list. (For the most part, Turner and White communicate with each other via scholarly journals; they have no personal relationship.)

I asked Turner if there were any examples of pot polish among the bones in his office. He searched around and pulled out a tiny frag-ment. He went to his desk for a hand-held magnifier and examined the fragment in the brilliant Arizona light. "This is polishing," he said, with a grin, holding it up like a jewel. "I wanted you to see this. It's from Burnt Mesa, in New Mexico. Alan Brew is the excavator. The interesting thing is that the polishing occurs only on the ends of the fragments, not on the mid-portion. The physics of a pot prohibit it. We also don't get the polishing on the large pieces that won't fit into the pot."

He handed me the bone and the magnifier. As I examined it in the light, I could see a bright polished line along one fractured edge of bone.

"Just a delightful break," Turner said.

"Did you experiment with deer bones, like Tim White?" I asked, handing the bone back.

"We can't get deer in the grocery store," he said. "We used beef and chicken."

Sensitivities

Turner's work on Anasazi cannibalism took place during a much larger debate on cannibalism worldwide. In 1979, William Arens, a professor of anthropology at the State University of New York at Stony Brook, published an influential book entitled *The Man-Eating Myth*. The book questioned the very existence of cannibalism in human societies, and it was widely reviewed. (*The New Yorker* called it "a model of disciplined and fair argument.") Arens argued that there were no reliable, firsthand accounts of cannibalism anywhere in the historical or ethnographic record. He showed that published reports of cannibalism were mostly hearsay, from unreliable witnesses, who talked about something they had not seen personally. Despite a diligent search, he said, he had been unable to find even one anthropologist, living or dead, who claimed to have witnessed cannibalism. (Apparently, not even D. Carleton Gajdusek, who in 1976 won a Nobel Prize in Medicine for identifying a cannibalistic disease called *kuru* among the Fore tribe of New Guinea, had ever seen it.) Arens documented how some anthropologists in Brazil and elsewhere had badgered and hectored their informants until they finally "admitted" that their ancestors had been cannibals. He argued that vivid accounts of cannibalism collected by the Spanish in the Caribbean and in central Mexico were mostly written by people who were attempting to justify conquest, conversion, and enslavement.

Calling one's neighbor a cannibal, Arens went on to say, was the ultimate insult. It was always members of some tribe down the river or over the mountains who were cannibals. Or it was one's bad old ancestors, before contact with "superior" European civilization. Arens took his profession to task for not demanding more rigorous evidence before making such claims. "You have to ask anthropologists why they need cannibalism," he wrote, and he went on to give an answer: that anthropologists love cannibalism because they thrive on the exotic, the weird, the strange; they want to perpetuate the idea that some people are radically different from us and thus worth studying. Arens's book leaves little doubt that anthropologists have accepted, eagerly and uncritically, many dubious accounts of cannibalism. Naturally, when the book was published many anthropologists objected to it, but a surprising number of scientists (particularly archeologists) felt that Arens had made a valid point, which needed to be tested. *The Man-Eating Myth* bolstered Turner's critics and contributed to an atmosphere in which his assertions were regarded with suspicion.

I called up Arens to find out what he thought of Turner's work, twenty years later. Surprisingly, he turned out to be a Turner believer. Cannibalism, he said was "a possible interpretation, even a good interpretation," of Turner's bone assemblages. He worried, however, that most people would conclude that all the Anasazi were cannibals—and, by extension, all Native Americans. "There's a whole discipline in existence looking for 'savage' behavior among the people we have colonized, conquered, and eradicated. That point almost *has* to be made—that the people here before us were cannibals—to justify our genocide of Native Americans."

Turner still has many articulate detractors. One of the most outspoken is Kurt Dongoske, a white man who is the archeologist for the Hopi tribe. Dongoske doesn't take issue with Turner's analysis of how the bones were processed, but he objects to Turner's conclusion that any people were actually eating the cooked meat. There is simply no proof that the meat was consumed, he told me, nor does he believe that Turner has sufficiently considered other alternatives, such as bizarre mortuary practices. Leigh J. Kuwanwisiwma, who is the director of the Hopi Cultural Preservation Office, wonders why Turner assumed that the Polacca Wash bones, if they were cannibalized at all, represented Hopi-on-Hopi cannibalism. He points out that Navajo, Apache, and Ute all raided the Hopi, killing men and stealing women and children. He feels that it was unfair of Turner to pursue this research without the Hopi tribe's being involved. "Turner has never sat down with us," Kuwanwisiwma says. "There was an open invitation, back in 1993, to come before the Hopi people and see if he was able to explain his research to us, and he refused. He never made contact with us before or after." Turner, for his part, says that the invitation was extended for only one visit and that he couldn't come for personal reasons. He says he offered to come at another time but never received a response. As for the possibility that other tribes had carried out these acts against the Hopi, Turner said that the Awatovi story best fitted the facts.

Others have accused Turner of insensitivity in presenting such inflammatory findings. Duane Anderson, an archeologist who is the vice-president of the highly respected School of American Research, in Santa Fe, has said that Turner, in common with some other physical anthropologists, doesn't show much concern about how his work might affect living, related people. "There's a tendency when dealing with bones to treat the material as *objects,* rather than as *subjects.*"

Many of Turner's critics have proposed alternative explanations. J. Andrew Darling, the executive director for the Mexico-North Research Network, in Chihuahua, wrote a paper (not yet published) suggesting that the bones might be those of witches executed in a particularly grisly fashion. The utter destruction of the witch's body through dismemberment, defleshing, burning, boiling, and crushing was an attempt to efface his or her evil powers. He cites known instances of Pueblo Indian witches being killed, violently mutilated, and dismembered. Debra L. Martin, a professor of biological anthropology at Hampshire College, in Massachusetts, and an authority on Anasazi violence, also feels that Turner rejected other explanations out of hand. "I don't see why those bones couldn't have been stomped on, cut up, broken apart, and boiled ritually" without being eaten, she said. "And why isn't there anything about cannibalism in the ethnographic record? I would like to see just one clan history, one story, one early Spanish account, that confirms this." Martin herself examined some of Turner's bone assemblages. "Christy homogenizes all these assemblages in his publications," she pointed out. "He makes them all seem alike. But they're not. What if the explanation is a lot more interesting? What if it's something grander than this? Maybe some cannibalism, some witchcraft executions, and some really unusual or interesting mortuary practices?" She made another point. Because Turner did not collaborate with Native Americans, "they are making a special effort to reclaim and bury those bones," she said. "He'll have been the only person who's looked at them and that's too bad."

Others are even more blunt in describing Turner. "He's not nice," one colleague said. "He's a pain in the ass." Another called him "loud" and "a bully."

There is a high level of apprehension at some of the museums where Turner has done his research. At the Museum of Northern Arizona, his longtime hangout, I was firmly denied permission even to enter the collection area, let alone look at the bones Turner had worked on. "We're walking a tightrope here," Noland Wiggins, a collections supervisor, said apologetically. "Because, as you may imagine, the tribes are not too happy with Christy's research."

Turner doesn't shy away from responding forcefully to his critics. In a recent paper he accused one of them of "playing to the choir"
and called Dongoske "self-serving." He also considered it strange that
his critics and the Hopi were more exercised over cannibalism than over
violence and mutilation. "How can you tolerate killing, murder, and torture and then be so horrified by cannibalism? Why is it that the Hopi
can admit killing eight hundred at Awatovi as if it were nothing, but
then the whole universe falls apart when they are accused of cannibalism?"

I asked him why he felt that there had been so much opposition
to his ideas.

"There's a simple answer," he said, with a mirthless smile. "In our
culture, cannibalism is a food taboo. That's the essence of this whole
problem."

Although Turner admitted that he had no direct evidence that
human meat was eaten at any of the sites, he said that he based his fun-
damental conclusion of cannibalism on the scientific principle of
Occam's razor: the simplest explanation fitting the facts is probably the
right one. "There's still a chance," he said sarcastically, "that aliens are
doing this." Nevertheless, his critics continue to point out that he lacks
proof. In 1996, Kurt Dongoske was quoted in *National Geographic* as saying that Anasazi cannibalism would not be proved until "you actually
find human remains in prehistoric human excrement."

In the early 1990s, a firm called Soil Systems won a contract to
excavate a group of archeological sites at the base of Sleeping Ute
Mountain, in Colorado, on the Ute Mountain Ute Indian Reservation.
The Ute planned to irrigate and farm seventy-six hundred acres of land,
and the law required them to excavate any archeological sites that would
be disturbed. The project director at Soil Systems was a young man
named Brian Billman, who is now an assistant professor at the University of North Carolina at Chapel Hill.

He and his team began work in 1992, and at one unremarkable
site along Cowboy Wash, called 5MT 10010, he and two colleagues, Pa-
tricia Lambert and Banks Leonard, made a grotesque discovery. The results have not yet been published, but Billman was willing to talk to me
about them—up to a point. We spoke by telephone the day before he
was to go off to Peru to do fieldwork. Billman spoke slowly and carefully, weighing every word, and this is the story he told:

When the team began excavating, they uncovered what seemed at first a typical Anasazi site—some rooms, a trash mound, and, lined up in a row, three kivas. As the team dug out the first kiva, they found a pile of chopped-up, boiled, and burned human bones at the base of a vent shaft leading up and out of the kiva. It looked as though the bones had been chopped up and cooked outside, on the surface, and then dumped down the shaft. There were cut marks on the bones made by stone tools, and the long bones had been systematically broken up for marrow extraction.

In the second kiva, they found the remains of five individuals. In this case, it appeared that the bones had been processed inside the kiva itself. "Instead of boiling," Billman recalled, "it looked more like roasting going on." Here cut marks at muscle attachments suggested that the bones had been defleshed, and again they had been split open for marrow. The skulls of at least two of the individuals had been placed upside down on the fire, roasted, and broken open, and the cooked brains presumably scooped out. In that same kiva, the team found a stone tool kit such as was typically used in butchering a midsized mammal. The kit contained an axe, hammerstones, and two large flakes with razor-thin cutting edges. Billman submitted the tool kit to a lab, and the two flakes tested positive for human blood.

The third kiva contained only two small pieces of bone, which had apparently been washed down from the surface. In the dead ashes of the central hearth, however, the team made an "extremely unusual" find. It was a nondescript lump of some material, which was field-classified as a "macrobotanical remain"—a piece of an unidentified plant. A worker put it in a bag, and when the team had a chance to examine it more closely, back in the laboratory, they realized that it was a desiccated human turd, or coprolite. "After the fire had gone cold," Billman said, "someone had squatted over this hearth and defecated into it."

Billman sent the coprolite off to a lab at the University of Nebraska for analysis. The first oddity the lab noted was that it contained no plant remains; other tests indicated that the coprolite had formed from digested meat. From a pollen analysis, the lab could tell that the coprolite had been deposited in the late spring or early summer, at the same time of year that the site was abandoned.

In three nearby ruined sites, another group of excavators also found chopped-up, boiled, and burned bones scattered about. The four sites, which seemed to constitute a small community, contained a total of twenty-eight butchered individuals. Mysteriously, all four sites were filled with valuable, portable items, such as baskets, a rabbit blanket, pots, and ground-stone tools. Little, if anything, seemed to have been taken.

"This site has a frozen instant of time in it," Billman said. "You could almost read it." What he read was: The year was approximately 1150. Times were hard. The area was in the grip of a severe drought. Pollen samples showed that a crop failure had probably occurred the previous year. One late-spring day, the community was attacked. The people were killed, cooked, and eaten. Then, in an ultimate act of contempt, one of the killers defecated in a hearth, the symbolic center of the family and the household. Instead of looting the site, the invaders left it and its many valuables for all to see.

"When I excavated it," Billman told me, "I got the sense that it may have been taboo. We are proposing that this may have been a political strategy. One or several communities in this area may have used raiding and cannibalism to drive off people from a village and prevent other people from settling there. If you raided a village, consumed some of the residents, and left the remains there for everyone to see, you would gain the reputation of being a community to stay away from."

Billman, Lambert, and Leonard presented their findings at the 1997 Society for American Archaeology meetings, in Nashville, and they were subsequently reported by Catherine Dold in *Discover*. At the end of the Nashville symposium, a man came up to Billman, introduced himself as Richard Marlar, and said, "I'm a biochemist, and I think I can tell you if there is human tissue in that coprolite"—in other words, he could determine directly whether or not cannibalism had occurred. Billman sent some samples of the coprolite off to Marlar for analysis, along with some pieces of a ceramic Anasazi cooking pot found at the site.

I recently called up Richard Marlar, who is an associate professor of pathology at the University of Colorado Health Sciences Center, in Denver. "I heard his talk," Marlar said. "I said to myself, 'I can figure that out. We can answer that question.'" The basic problem, he realized, was that he needed a way to identify human tissue that had passed through the digestive system of another human being. He had to make sure he was not picking up traces of human blood in the intestinal tract (from internal bleeding) or cells naturally shed from the lining of the intestine. He finally decided to test the coprolite for the presence of human myoglobin, a protein that is found only in skeletal and heart muscle, and could not get into the intestinal tract except through eating. (As a control, Marlar tested many stool samples from patients in his hospital, to verify that none had traces of myoglobin in them.)

Marlar set up an immunological assay of the kind that is normally used in clinical medicine to determine whether someone has a disease. So far, he explained to me, he had performed several tests, each in triplicate, using twenty-one samples of the coprolite. He also ran six tests on the ceramic pottery to see if it had traces of human protein from cooking. All the results, he told me, were the same.

"And what were those results?" I asked.

He declined to answer. The Ute tribe had asked all the excavators to keep the results confidential until the paper could be published.

In the small world of Southwestern archeology, very little can be kept secret, and I soon began to hear rumors about the results. I tracked them down and established that the tests had been positive. All of Marlar's assays, I learned, had shown the presence of human myoglobin protein in the coprolite and on the interior walls of the cooking pot.

The Great Terror

For thirty years, Turner had been documenting cannibal sites, but for a long time he had not tackled the question "Why?" It is this question that he takes up in the last, and what is certain to be the most controversial, chapter of *Man Corn*. He advances a theory of who the cannibals were, where they came from, and what role the eating of "men, women, and children alike" may have played in Anasazi society. For this was not, he says, starvation cannibalism, such as befell the Donner party. Starvation cannibalism did not explain the extreme mutilation of the bodies before they were consumed, or the huge charnel deposits, consisting of as many as thirty-five people (that's almost a ton of edible human meat), or the bones discarded as trash. Furthermore, there was no evidence of starvation cannibalism (or any other kind of cannibalism) among the Anasazi's immediate neighbors, the Hohokam and the Mogollon, who lived in equally harsh environments and endured the same droughts.

A colleague of Turner's, David Wilcox, who is a curator at the Museum of Northern Arizona, had prepared a map showing the distribution of Chaco Great Houses and roads. Using Wilcox's map, Turner was able to chart charnel deposits in time and space. "When we found that Dave's Chaco maps coincided with my cannibalized assemblages," Turner recalls, "that's when it came together." Turner decided that the civilization centered in Chaco Canyon was probably the locus of Anasazi cannibalism.

The maps, Turner says, showed that the charnel deposits were often situated near Chaco Great Houses and that most of them dated from the Chaco period. The eating of human flesh seems to have begun as the Chaco civilization began, around 900; peaked at the time of the Chaco collapse and abandonment, around 1150; and then all but disappeared (Polacca Wash being a notable exception).

Turner theorized that cannibalism might have been used by a powerful élite at Chaco Canyon as a form of social control. "It was order by terrorism," he said to me. "Big-stick order." In *Man Corn* he writes:

> Terrorizing, mutilating, and murdering might be evolutionarily useful behaviors when directed against unrelated competitors. And what better way to amplify opponents' fear than to reduce victims to the sub-human level of cooked meat, especially when they include infants and children from whom no power or prestige could be derived but whose consumption would surely further terrorize, demean, and insult their helpless parents or community? . . . The benefits would be three-fold: community control, control of reproductive behavior (that is, dominating access to women), and food. From the standpoint of so-ciobiology, then, cannibalism could well represent useful behavior done by well-adjusted, normal adults acting out their ultimate, evolu-tionarily channelled behavior. On the other hand, one can easily look upon violence and cannibalism as socially pathological.

The second question Turner asked was "Who were these cannibals and where did they come from?" He looked around for a source. The Anasazi's immediate neighbors showed no evidence of being cannibalis-tic. "I couldn't find cannibalism in California or on the Great Plains, ei-ther," Turner said. "Where is it? In Mexico."

Turner directed his attention to central Mexico, to the empire of the Toltecs—the precursors of the Aztecs—which lasted from about 800 to 1100 A.D. Central Mexico, he writes, developed a very powerful, de-humanizing sociopolitical and ideological complex," centered on human sacrifice and cannibalism used as a form of social control. Fur-thermore, cannibalism spread from central Mexico "into the jungle world of the Mayas and the desert world of Chichimeca" in northern Mexico. Turner concludes, "It takes nearly blind faith in the effectiveness of geographical distance . . . to believe that this complex and its adherents failed to reach the American Southwest."

During the Toltec period, Turner hypothesizes, a heavily armed group of "thugs," "tinkers," or perhaps even "Manson party types" (as he put it to me in various conversations) headed north, to the region we refer to as the American Southwest. "They entered the San Juan Basin around A.D. 900," he surmises in *Man Corn,* and "found a suspicious but pliant population whom they terrorized into reproducing the theocratic lifestyle they had previously known in Mesoamerica."

In other words, the flowering of Chaco society that we have so long admired—in engineering, astronomy, architecture, art, and culture—was the product of a small, heavily armed gang from Mexico, who marched into the Southwest to conquer and brutalize.

Archeologists have long known that there was a strong Mesoamerican influence on the Anasazi. There was extensive prehistoric trade between Mexico and the Southwest. Turquoise from Santa Fe has been found throughout Mesoamerica, and tropical parrots and macaws brought up live from Mexico have been found in Chaco graves. Indeed, corn, pottery, and cotton originally came into the Southwest from Mexico. There is good evidence, Turner writes in *Man Corn,* that Mexicans did in fact make the journey northward. He notes that a skull found in Chaco Canyon had intentionally chipped teeth—a decorative trait thought to be restricted almost entirely to central Mexico. He also details many parallels between Hopi and Toltec mythology.

A number of Pueblo Indian myths seem to support Turner's cannibalism theories. For example, a Pueblo legend collected by the anthropologist John Gunn and published in 1916 describes a drought and famine in the past which reduced the people "to such an extremity that they killed and ate their children or weaker members of the tribe."

The Navajo tell many stories about Chaco Canyon that paint a very different picture from the popular Anglo view—stories that may also have been taken from the Pueblo Indians. While doing research for a book on the Navajo creation story, I was told a number of these stories. Chaco, some older Navajo say, was a place of hideous evil. The Chaco people abused sacred ceremonies, practiced witchcraft and cannibalism, and made a dreaded substance called corpse powder by cooking and grinding up the flesh and bones of the dead. Their evil threw the world out of balance, and they were destroyed in a great earthquake and fire.

Cannibalism seems to have peaked in the Southwest at the time of the Chaco collapse because the system of terror, Turner theorizes, could not be sustained. Terror begat social chaos. "The evidence is that cannibalism—and this chaos that ensued—started in the north and it rippled southward and it wiped the Southwest out," Turner told me. In other words, cannibalism and social terror may have been a factor—perhaps the *missing* factor—in the Chaco collapse. Turner doesn't reject the standard explanations of the Chaco implosion: he hypothesizes that social pathology and cannibalism, combined with one or more of the standard theories (drought, erosion, disease, famine), sparked chaos, violence, and the "near-extinction of the entire prehistoric Southwest population." The subsequent retreat of the Anasazi into inaccessible cliff dwellings and mesas now makes sense. The long-sought elusive enemy of the Anasazi was, in fact, themselves.

Turner gave me a paper he had just written and was planning to deliver at a conference. Entitled "The Darker Side of Humanity," the paper extends some of the ideas in the last chapter of *Man Corn*. Turner writes, "I can easily imagine the cancerous random fractals of social chaos branching all over the Southwest, starting in the north with the collapse of Chaco and like a wildfire erupting here and there in hot spots of human violence. . . . Think of the hundreds of thousands of socially pathological killings and mutilations committed in central Africa these last few years. Think about Pol Pot."

Cannibalism was not "normal" behavior among the Anasazi, he argues, even if it was widespread. It was the product of a few socially pathological individuals who whipped up the emotions of their followers, like the chief of Awatovi who plotted the grim extinction of his own village. Turner compares such men as the Awatovi chief to Adolf Hitler, Genghis Khan, and Joseph Stalin.

This argument leads Turner into even stranger territory. In his paper he calls on archeologists to give up the time-honored "concept of culture." The problem with archeology is that it is a science of generalization. The archeologist digs a site and then extrapolates the findings into a description of a culture. The orientation of the archeologist is always toward matters like "What was usual and customary in this culture?" and "What was the norm?" There is no provision for abnormality, for the charismatic or sociopathic individual—the deranged Great Man. "In my thirty-five years of teaching I have never heard of a graduate student specializing in archeology who had taken a course or a seminar in abnormal psychology," Turner writes. "Why should they? . . . The very idea of abnormal behavior is alien to Southwest archaeological thinking." He suggests replacing the paradigm of culture with a "Darwinian paradigm of evolutionary psychology" that "emphasizes identification of individuals and seeks to understand their actions wherever possible." Only through this paradigm shift, Turner asserts, will archeologists be able to understand the darker side of human nature in the archeological record.

Place of Ghosts

On my last day with Turner, he decided to visit a cannibal locale in Monument Valley, straddling the border of Utah and Arizona.

We left the cool ponderosas of Flagstaff on a June morning. By three o'clock, we had arrived at the escarpment that looks down on Monument Valley—surely one of the most dramatic landscapes on earth. We descended into the valley on a rutted dirt road, our two cars kicking up corkscrews of red dust, and after a few miles the Three Sisters came into view on the right, three spires of rock. According to a photograph that Turner had of the site—his only clue to where it was—it lay less than a mile from this valley landmark. As we bounced along the valley floor, the spires began to move into the alignment seen in the photograph.

Turner lurched off the road to follow a track in the bottom of a dry wash. We skirted the base of a large mesa, stopped, backtracked, and stopped again. Turner finally got out, squinting in the brilliant sunlight and clutching the photograph. "This is it," he said. "This is it, exactly."

We scrambled up the sandy rise above the wash. The site lay about twenty feet above the valley floor, on the talus slope of Thunderbird Mesa. It was a small patch of sand sheltered among giant plates of stone that had spalled from the cliff behind—a sheer wall of red sandstone four hundred feet high and streaked with glossy desert varnish. It was a breathtaking spot, commanding a sweeping view of Tse Biyi Flats, Rain God Mesa, the Three Sisters, Spearhead Mesa, and dozens of other buttes and mesas layered one against another, receding into vast distances. The afternoon sun was invading the valley, sculpting and modelling the buttes in crisp yellow light.

The site itself was covered with windblown sand and clumps of Indian rice grass and snakeweed. In the center lay a large, exquisite piece of a painted Anasazi pot, white with a black geometric design. Near the pot, the edge of a slab-lined hearth stuck up from the sand. The smashed, chopped, and burned bones of seven people had been found piled in this hearth. They were the remains of an old man and an old woman, a younger man, two teenage girls, a third adolescent, of undetermined sex, and an infant. Turner believed that they had been ambushed, killed, mutilated, dismembered, and cooked right there, for the hearth seemed to have been custom-built for that purpose. After it had been used, the cracked and burned bones were left there in the fire pit and the site was abandoned.

Turner poked around the site, scowling and squinting, with two cameras swinging from his neck. "Dogoszhi black-on-white," he said, glancing at the potsherd and referring to a common Anasazi pottery type. He took a careful series of photographs of the site and its surroundings.

"Do you think that potsherd was left at the time of the massacre?"

"Yes," he replied.

"Why here?"

"That's a bit of a mystery. It's not *at* anything. But I wouldn't be surprised if there was a Great House near here, and somebody got waylaid." He pointed to a wedge of green growth nearby. "There must be an intermittent spring there. That would be part of the story—perhaps this was a hunting camp for deer or antelope. Perhaps it was in wintertime. This is a nice place in the winter."

As we were tramping around the site, an old Navajo man came by in a pickup truck, which had two dazed, dust-covered tourists in the back. He was wearing a straw cowboy hat and was missing his front teeth. He stopped the truck.

"Any Anasazi ruins around here?" Turner called out.

"Over there," the man said, his hand waving obscurely across thousands of desolate acres. He seemed reluctant to talk more about the Anasazi, and drove on.

"That fellow was vague about ruins," Turner said to me. "But there must be some nearby. This is a *chindi* place"—a place of ghosts. He continued to move restlessly around the site—a skinny man with a potbelly and sticklike arms and legs—staring into every recess. Only the occasional click of his camera broke the stillness. I remembered my first interview with Turner, when I had asked him why he was investigating cannibalism. He had replied breezily, "I think it's interesting. It's fun. Here's an unsolved problem." As I looked at his face, I could see that he was indeed having a marvellous time.

Turner moved back to the car. I remained at the spot and looked around, trying to arrive at an understanding of what had happened here. The age and sex of the remains suggested that they might have been an extended family—two parents, three teenage children, a son-in-law, and a little grandchild, perhaps. I thought of my own family. The light deepened. A grasshopper began scratching among the dry stones, and a faint breeze brought with it the scent of sun-warmed sand.

Blood for the Gods
From *Flesh and Blood*

In her classic 1975 book *Flesh and Blood,* Scottish historian Reay Tannahill shows how legendary cannibals from the Caribs to the Aztecs found suste- nance both temporal and spiritual—in human blood.

By Renaissance times, the use of blood for magical purposes may have been found more often in the realm of private en- terprise than public endeavour—but only in the Old World. When the Spaniards began to colonise the New, they stum- bled on something they had never before encountered or even dreamed of, a whole civilisation founded on, and in the most literal sense sus- tained by the blood of its people.

Or so they said.

Most of the so-called civilised world believed them and went on believing them, because the more savage a people, the greater the glory of saving their souls for Christ—an ambition as dear to the Catholic Church of Columbian times as it was to be to the missionaries of Queen Victoria's day.

By an odd coincidence, however, just when, in the latter decades of the twentieth century, the world ran out of primitive tribes (and mis- sionaries and anthropologists out of gainful employment), the doctrine of white Christian supremacy was turned on its head and it became *de rigueur* to believe not the worst but the best of every tribal society as it had been in its 'pure' state, before it was contaminated by Western cul- tural imperialism.

Predictably, just as much humbug has been generated under the new dispensation as under the old, and humbug that is no less patronising. To deny the existence of, for example, human sacrifice and/or cannibalism in pre-Columbian America is simply another way of reaffirming the superiority of Western Christian morality. By rejecting, on behalf of others, what offends against their own ingrained beliefs, the revisionists are also rejecting the early Americans' entitlement to have minds of their own and a religious code that regarded human sacrifice and/or cannibalism not as the ultimate evil but as a means of saving the world from destruction.

As, during the last three decades, the star of the Native American has glowed ever brighter and that of the Dead White European Male dimmed to virtual invisibility in the politically correct groves of academe, Columbus and his successors have been demoted from legendary heroes to villains on a par with Adolf Hitler and Attila the Hun. In reality, of course, they were neither heroes nor villains but simply men of their time—tough men, certainly; men, equally certainly, with axes to grind; men whose perceptions were dulled by their own religious beliefs; but men who could not conceivably have foreseen the continent-wide avalanche of destruction that their exploits were destined to provoke. They were no angels, but if pre-Columbian America did not also have its due proportion of sinners, it must have been the only society in the whole of recorded history able to make such a claim.

The difference was that the Spaniards came armed with military technology which the Native Americans had nothing to match and diseases against which the Native Americans had no immunity.

It was the 1519 expedition of Hernando Cortés—described by a modern historian as 'a farsighted, courageous, well-educated and charming Spanish gentleman'—that was to be the catalyst of disaster. As he and his band of between five and six hundred conquistadors, with sixteen horses and a few cannon, marched from the coast towards the splendid capital city of the Aztecs (or the Mexica, as they are more correctly known), the cultural shock was profound. Nothing in the twenty-seven years since Spain's arrival in the Indies had prepared them for what they saw on the road to Tenochtitlán.

Victims of the Gods

Human sacrifice on the Aztec scale required a regular supply of victims in numbers that were far from negligible. As a result, the Aztecs lived in a state of almost perpetual war with their neighbours, though not the kind of war familiar elsewhere, its main purpose being to take prisoners, not to kill. When a battle began, archers and slingers first loosed their missiles and then the ranks broke and the warriors rushed in with spears. The battlefield disintegrated into innumerable separate duels as each man did his best to disarm another and hale him off to the sidelines, where noncombatants were waiting with ropes to tie him up. So deeply ingrained was the habit of capturing in preference to killing that the Mexica clung to it even when they found themselves fighting the Spaniards, who had no such inhibitions.

When serious war was impracticable, either because the economy could not stand it or because the nearest potential enemy was too far off, the old custom of the War of the Flowers was revived. This, which had been known since at least the mid-fourteenth century, was a friendly war between friendly states, a combat designed for the specific purpose of producing losers who could be sacrificed.

The best sacrifices, in general, were brave men of high rank, but slaves could be used instead. Indeed, there were two kinds of slave who almost invariably ended their lives on the sacrificial stone—well-bred prisoners of war who had escaped being sacrificed immediately after their capture, and barbarians paid as imperial taxes by cities in tributary relationship to Moctezuma. Of other slaves, only one category could be offered to the flint knife, workers who had been so unsatisfactory that three successive masters had been forced to get rid of them. Delinquents such as these could be bought for sacrificial purposes by tradesmen or artisans who had no opportunity of capturing prisoners of war for themselves.

Most victims appear to have gone to their deaths fairly philosophically, especially the military captives, who had been indoctrinated since birth with the knowledge that some day they might have to die so that the world could go on living. Nothing was born or could endure without the sacrifice of human blood and heart's blood, and the man whose blood and heart were sacrificed knew that his death was a divine necessity, however much he may have wished that someone else had been chosen. He went to his death, in most cases, dressed, painted and ornamented to simulate the god for whom he was intended; it was the god himself who was sacrificed, in re-enactment of that first occasion when all the gods had given themselves so that the sun might begin its passage across the heavens. Soldiers therefore went steadfastly to their deaths, while the civilian slaves, ritually bathed and luxuriously dressed for the occasion, were mercifully stupefied by the *pulque* they were given to drink beforehand.

The ceremonial cannibalism that sometimes followed was an extension of the sacrifice itself. The head of the victim was removed and hung on a skull rack, one thigh was presented to the supreme council and other choice cuts to various nobles and to the victim's captor. By eating this flesh, the great and the good of Aztec society not only identified themselves directly with the sacrifice and, through him, with the god, but also absorbed the strength and life force that would enable them to achieve the ends necessary if the god's requirements were to continue to be met. Not even the bonier remnants went to waste; they were given to the animals in Moctezuma's private zoo, which had a religious role to play as guardians of the temples.

The scale of sacrifice is generally (if not by revisionists) held to have been considerable, although it never again reached the peak claimed for 1486, when twenty thousand victims were reputedly sacrificed in four days at the dedication of the great temple of the war god at Tenochtitlán. The city's new monarch, assisted by the ruler of neighbouring Texcoco, is said to have begun the work with his own hand, teams of lesser dignitaries then taking over and working in relays through the two endless lines of victims. It has, however, been pointed out that if the victims were dealt with two at a time, as the records say, and if the entire ceremony took up all the daylight hours for four days, then the figure of twenty thousand may have been something of an over-estimate.[10] Assuming a rate of one victim per team per minute over a twelve-hour working day, not more than 5,760 victims could have been disposed of in the time. The question may be academic today, but it was far from academic to the 14,240 victims who did, or did not, perish in 1486.

The Conquest

More than thirty years had passed by the time Cortés and his men visited the temple that dominated what was now a thriving and disciplined city, but it still stank of blood and death.

Moctezuma welcomed the conquistadors on the open platform at the top of the great flight of one hundred and fourteen steps, and showed them a bird's-eye view of other temples and shrines, 'gleaming white towers and castles: a marvellous sight'. But it was here, said Bernal Diaz, 'that the great stones stood on which they placed the poor Indians for sacrifice. Here also was a massive image like a dragon, and other hideous figures, and a great deal of blood that had been spilled that day.'

The emperor also showed them images of the gods, including the war god himself with his 'huge, terrible eyes' and 'so many precious

stones, so much gold, so many pearls and seed pearls stuck to him . . .
that his whole body and head were covered with hem'. At his shrine,
'there were some smoking braziers of their incense, which they call
copal, in which they were burning the hearts of three Indians whom
they had sacrificed that day; and all the walls of that shrine were so
splashed and caked with blood that they and the floor too were black.'

In other shrines, too, 'all was covered with blood, both walls and
altar, and the stench was such that we could hardly wait to get out . . . In
that small platform were many more diabolical objects, trumpets great
and small, and large knives, and many hearts that had been burnt with
incense before their idols; and everything was caked with blood. The
stench here too was like a slaughterhouse, and we could scarcely stay in
the place.'

Emerging into the open air again, Cortés ill-advisedly made another attempt to convert the emperor. 'Lord Moctezuma,' he said with a
half-laugh, 'I cannot imagine how a prince as great and wise as Your
Majesty can have failed to realise that these idols of yours are not gods
but evil things. . . . Allow us to erect a cross here on the top of this
tower, and let us divide off a part of this sanctuary . . . as a place where
we can put an image of Our Lady, and then you will see, by the fear that
your idols have of her, how grievously they have deceived you.'

This extraordinary suggestion gave deep offence to Moctezuma
and his priests, and it says much for the emperor's strength of character
that he did not order the Spaniards sacrificed on the spot. Instead, he
banished them from the temple and they went off to see what other examples of barbarity they could find to disgust them. They found idols,
blood, smoke, skulls and bones, as well as great pots and jars and pitchers
in a house where 'they cooked the flesh of the wretched Indians who
were sacrificed and eaten by the priests. Near this place of sacrifice there
were many large knives and chopping blocks like those on which men
cut up meat in slaughterhouses. . . . I always called that building Hell,'
concluded Bernal.

Inevitably, the day came when it was not 'wretched Indians' but
Spaniards who had their hearts torn out in honour of the gods during
the last bitter battles that ended in the destruction of the whole of Aztec
civilisation.

Wounded and exhausted, a little group of conquistadors heard
from their temporary refuge the terrifying sound of the sacred drum,
conches and horns. 'When we looked at the tall temple from which it

came we saw our comrades who had been captured in Cortés' defeat being dragged up the steps to be sacrificed. When they had hauled them up to a small platform in front of the shrine where they kept their accursed idols, we saw them put plumes on the heads of many of them; and then they made them dance with a sort of fan in front of Huichilobos [the war god]. Then after they had danced the priests laid them down on their backs on some narrow stones of sacrifice and, cutting open their chests, drew out their palpitating hearts which they offered to the idols before them. Then they kicked the bodies down the steps, and the Indian butchers who were waiting below cut off their arms and legs and flayed their faces, which they afterwards prepared like glove leather, with their beards on, and kept for their drunken festivals. Then they ate their flesh with a sauce of peppers and tomatoes. They sacrificed all our men in this way, eating their legs and arms, offering their hearts and blood to their idols as I have said, and throwing their trunks and entrails to the lions and tigers [actually, pumas and jaguars] and serpents and snakes that they kept in the wild-beast houses.'

But in the end, after a siege in which the people of Tenochtitlán died like flies, the conquistadors experienced a faint twinge of doubt as to whether the Mexica were quite the unregenerate cannibals they had thought. The houses, streets and courts of the city, even the lake stockades, were strewn with corpses, and 'the stench was so bad that no one could endure it.'

But when Cortés agreed that the survivors might leave, 'for three whole days and nights they never ceased streaming out, and all three causeways were crowded with men, women and children so thin, sallow, dirty and stinking that it was pitiful to see them.' The city itself 'looked as if it had been ploughed up. The roots of any edible greenery had been dug out, boiled and eaten, and they had even cooked the bark of some of the trees.' Now, at very long last, Bernal Diaz had the grace to note that despite the famine in the besieged city, 'the Mexicans did not eat the flesh of their own people, only that of our men and our Tlascalan allies whom they had captured.'

Only, that was to say, the ritually acceptable flesh of enemies who had been sacrificed in a last despairing attempt to stave off the end of the Aztec world.

Cannibalism Among the Fiji Islanders
From *Cannibalism and Human Sacrifice*

BY GARRY HOGG

Where would cannibals be without missionaries? And vice-versa, for that matter? Gary Hogg's classic 1966 work *Cannibalism and Human Sacrifice* provides shocking firsthand reports from what might be called the front lines of nineteenth century missionary work.

In the heart of the South Pacific Ocean, between the Equator and the Tropic of Capricorn, and extending roughly the same distance east and west of the International Date Line, there lie a number of groups of islands, some containing a mere handful, others consisting of several hundred, large and small. These islands are generally referred to as the South Sea Islands and, as such, have come to be associated with romance and voluptuous ease, 'lotus-eating' and the simple life beneath a hot sun. There are other aspects than these to be considered.

The ethnographer, primarily concerned with the physical characteristics and the distribution of the various races of mankind, has divided the main body of these groups of islands according to the dominant physical characteristic of the races inhabiting them. The majority of the inhabitants of the islands lying to the east, such as the Marquesas, Samoa, Tonga Island, the Society Islands, Tahiti, and others less popularly known, have light brown skin and generally wavy hair. Ethnographers refer to the region they inhabit as Polynesia—'many islands'.

West of the International Date Line there is another group of islands, on the whole larger than those of Polynesia. They include the Solomon Islands, the New Hebrides, New Caledonia, the Ellice Islands and many others less familiar. Because the majority of the inhabitants of these islands are darker skinned, and have crinkly hair, the islands are known as Melanesia—'black islands'.

Lying literally astride of the International Date Line is a group of islands numbering in all not far short of three hundred and known generically as Fiji. The ambiguous position of this group of islands in the easternmost fringe of Melanesia and the westernmost fringe of Polynesia, has led anthropologists to refer to them sometimes as Melanesian, sometimes as Polynesian. The true ethnographer, however, makes no mistake: he recognises among the vast majority of the islanders the darker skin, the crinkled hair, of the true Melanesian; and as such he describes him.

It is in Melanesia that cannibalism was longest in dying. The islands already mentioned, like the vastly larger island to the west of them, New Guinea, just to the north of Australia, are peopled by inhabitants who clung obstinately to their ancient tradition of devouring human flesh long after the tradition had begun to fade, or had even been wholly stamped out, elsewhere. Indeed, it is likely that, away from the coastline, in the fastnesses of the mountains, cannibalism is still practised at the present day. For this reason, among others, it will be as well, perhaps, to examine the practice of cannibalism as reported and described by travellers who, within the last generation or two, have been familiar with this region of the South Pacific either as traders or as missionaries or skippers of coasting craft, or as travellers with some training in anthropology.

These are very numerous, and their reports can nearly always be substantiated or corroborated by comparison with those received from other sources which tally in regard to place and date. Among the countless reports that accumulated during the nineteenth century, the least suspect, of course, were those from missionaries in the field. Few missionaries anywhere in the world can have had to face greater horrors than those workers of the Methodist Missionary Society who established their missions in the Fiji Islands rather more than a hundred years ago.

On November 22nd, 1836, a pioneer in this noble organisation sent back to England—

AN APPEAL TO THE SYMPATHY OF THE CHRISTIAN PUBLIC ON
BEHALF OF THE CANNIBAL FEEGEEANS
Men and Brethren (it began), To your sympathy this Appeal is made, and your help is implored on behalf of a most interesting but deeply depraved people, the inhabitants of the group of islands called FEEGEE,

little known to the civilised world except for the extreme danger to which vessels touching at them are exposed, from the murderous propensities of the islanders, and for the horrid CANNIBALISM to which they are addicted, in which abomination they exceed the New Zealanders themselves.

In FEEGEE, cannibalism is not an occasional, but a constant practice; not indulged in from a species of horrid revenge, but from an absolute preference for human flesh over all other food.

It is on behalf of this cannibal race that we appeal to you. Let all the horrors of a CANNIBAL FEAST be present to your minds while you read. We appeal to you on behalf of FEEGEEAN widows, strangled when their husbands die, and on behalf of the FEEGEEANS enslaved by vices too horrible for minute description. Pity CANNIBAL FEEGEE, and do so quickly. Come, then, ye Christians, and teach the poor, idolatrous, war-loving, man-devouring FEEGEEANS better things. . . .

We spare you the details of a cannibal feast (the writer goes on to say, rather surprisingly in view of the customary reticence of these missionaries, when it comes to lurid detail): the previous murders, the mode of *cooking* human beings, the assembled crowd of all ranks, all ages, both sexes, Chiefs and people, men, women and *children,* anticipating the feast with horrid glee. The actual feast. The attendants bringing into the circle BAKED HUMAN BEINGS—not one, nor two, nor ten, but twenty, thirty, forty, fifty at a single feast! We have heard on credible authority of 200 human beings having been thus devoured on one of these occasions. The writer of this APPEAL has himself conversed with persons who have seen forty and fifty eaten at a single sitting—eaten without anything like disgust; eaten indeed with a high relish!

To gratify this unnatural propensity, they make war, assassinate, kidnap, and absolutely rob the graves of their inhabitants. I have myself known FEEGEEANS to be guilty of the latter abomination; and such is the indomitable appetite of the FEEGEEANS for human flesh, that individuals have been known to act thus towards their own deceased children. . . .

This complete lack of parental affection, of any love, however primitive, within the Fijian family, has been noted by an American anthropologist, A. P. Rice, who in a learned paper read before an American Anthropologists' Association, had this to say:

> Within the Fiji Islands group, Cannibalism is one of the established institutions; it is one of the elements of the Fijians' social structure, and is

regarded as a refinement which should, and indeed must, be cultivated to become a 'gentleman'. Flesh-eating is a definite part of the Fijians' religion, but they delight in human flesh for its own sake. For example, there is a record of a man living in Ruwai who actually killed his wife, with whom he had been living contentedly, and who even before their marriage had been of his own social standing; and ate her. He agreed that his act was the result of his extreme fondness for human flesh.

The appeal for support in the missionary field in Fiji was successful, and the successive volumes of the Methodist Society's *Missionary Notices* reveal the fervour and courage and indomitable persistence in the face of appalling hazard that the Society's missionaries displayed. Among them were such eminent Christians as Cross and Cargill and John Hunt, whose letters and reports from their mission stations back to their London headquarters make vivid and impressive, through all too often very uncomfortable, reading.

Some of the circumstances connected with the immolation of human victims (wrote the Rev. David Cargill in 1838) are most revolting and diabolical. The passions of the people during the performance of these horrible rites seem inflamed by a fiendish ferocity which is not exceeded by anything we have ever heard of in the annals of human depravity.

When about to offer a human sacrifice, the victim is selected from among the inhabitants of a distant territory, or is procured by negotiation from a tribe which is not related to the persons about to sacrifice. The victim is kept for some time, and supplied with abundance of food, that he may become fat.

When about to be immolated, he is made to sit on the ground with his feet under his thighs and his hands placed before him. He is then bound so that he cannot move a limb or a joint. In this posture he is placed on stones heated for the occasion (and some of them are red-hot), and then covered with leaves and earth, to be roasted alive. When cooked, he is taken out of the oven and, his face and other parts being painted black, that he may resemble a living man ornamented for a feast or for war, he is carried to the temple of the gods and, being still retained in a sitting posture, is offered as a propitiatory sacrifice.

These ceremonies being concluded, the body is carried beyond the precincts of the consecrated ground, cut into quarters, and distributed among the people; and they who were the cruel sacrificers of its life are also the beastly devourers of its flesh. . . .

The unnatural propensity to eat human flesh exists among them in its most savage forms. The Feegeans eat human flesh, not merely from a principle of revenge, nor from necessity, but from choice. Captives and strangers are frequently killed and eaten. The natives of Thakanndrove kidnap men, women and children to glut their appetite for human flesh; it is said that, as if they were human hyenas, they disinter dead bodies, even after they have been two or three days beneath the ground; and that, having washed them in the sea, they roast and devour them. The flesh of women is preferred to that of men, and when they have a plentiful supply the head is not eaten. In some cases the heart is preserved for months. The bones of those persons whose bodies have been eaten are never buried, but are thrown about as the bones of beasts, and the smaller ones are formed into needles. Recently a boat's crew from the vessel *Active* was attacked by the natives in the expectation of obtaining their clothing and belongings. The four unhappy men were cooked and eaten, and *their* bones have now been formed into needles for making sails.

One of the great names among the Methodist Missionary Society's workers in Fiji is that of the Rev. John Hunt. He had established his mission base at Rewa, and reported back at some length to his head office in June of the year following David Cargill's letter:

Having given you some account of our comfortable—(in the conditions prevailing this is surely a quite extraordinary word to use!)—circumstances, I shall now give some account of the difficulties which we meet with in the great work in which we are engaged. As we are come to Feegee to Christianise, and thus to civilise the people, I shall mention a few features in their character which appear to me calculated to retard the progress of Christianity.

The first which I shall mention is their *cruelty*. Cruelty is so natural to the Feegeeans that it has lost every part of its own hideous form, and appears more lovely than hateful to the minds of those who are truly without natural affection. I know but little of their religious cruelty. It is very uncertain whether the numerous murders which are perpetrated at the building of canoes, and god-houses, are connected with their religion, or with their politics. Whatever may be their motives, their horrid acts of barbarity, and cannibalism, on the finishing of canoes and god-houses, are as shocking to humanity as they are unparalleled in history. Rome produced its monsters of iniquity, as Caligula,

Domitian, Nero and Commodus; Grecian history furnishes examples, in the characters of Olympias and others, and English history in the acts of Henry and Mary. But cruelty in Greece, and Rome, and England bears its own name, and wears its own form; it is called a monster, and every man hates it, and dreads to be underneath the influence of those who are governed by its principles.

But in Feegee, some of those who are most esteemed, are esteemed partly on account of their obedience to the dictates of this monster; and not only Chiefs but the common people delight in treacherously murdering, and feasting on the bodies of their neighbours, as well as on their enemies. We have heard the most shocking things of Namusi Matua, the Chief of Rewa, who has lately embraced Christianity. If the whole were told, I should think his history would be unparalleled in the history of human depravity.

It is said that when he built a canoe, he used to make a point of killing a man for every plank. Sometimes he would do his work by wholesale, and kill a whole settlement for a feast for his canoe builders. Being an adept at this kind of business, he was often employed by Tanoa, another Chieftain, in this inhuman work. So it would be impossible to imagine the number of victims that this man has killed; not in times of war but merely to satisfy the cravings of cannibal appetites. . . .

John Hunt was not content, as his colleague in the field, David Cargill, was, in the letter quoted above, merely to describe what happened; he analysed to the best of his ability and evolved some sort of a theory. And having speculated, he ended his report from the mission field in Fiji on a more hopeful note:

The case would be far different if they were led on to these acts of barbarity by religious motives or persuasions. But this, I believe, is not the reason for the sacrifices they make. All the answer I can get from my inquiries on this subject is: 'That is our custom.' But this custom disappears where the Light of the Gospel shines, and where its influence is felt, even in a small degree. We know of *no instance* of cannibalism having happened in Rewa, since the Gospel came to Rewa. The Chief has had a new god-house built, and many new canoes, but we do not know that a single man has been killed, either from malice or for cannibal purposes.

The Rev. John Hunt's letter, ending on such a note of optimism, carried the date June 29th, 1839. Like many missionaries in many fields, he was too sanguine. Having effected a conversion, he persuaded himself that the conversion was permanent. It is possible, of course, that so far as this one individual chief was concerned, the conversion was total, and lasting. But it is very clear from a report written by David Cargill only four months later that the conversion was by no means general.

The report forms part of a day-to-day record, or diary, that he was able to maintain for a considerable period, in spite of the appalling conditions in which he was obliged to live. He writes much as journalists had to write when reporting back the scenes they witnessed in war-torn Europe both during and after the war. And the story he tells is a horror story that may well have been matched only by the tales of atrocities of recent times:

October 31st, 1839, Thursday. This morning we witnessed a shocking spectacle. Twenty (20) dead bodies of men, women and children were brought to Rewa as a present from Tanoa. They were distributed among the people to be cooked and eaten. They were dragged about in the water and on the beach. The children amused themselves by sporting with and mutilating the body of a little girl. A crowd of men and women maltreated the body of a grey-haired old man and that of a young woman. Human entrails were floating down the river in front of the mission premises. Mutilated limbs, heads and trunks of the bodies of human beings have been floating about, and scenes of disgust and horror have been presented to our view in every direction. How true is it that the dark places of the earth are full of the habitations of cruelty.

November 1st, Friday. This morning a little after break of day I was surprised to hear the voices of several persons who were talking very loudly near the front fence of the mission premises. On going out to ascertain the cause of the noise, I found a human head in our garden. This was the head of the old man whose body had been abused on the beach. The arm of the body had been broken by a bullet which passed through the bone near the shoulder, and the upper part of the skull had been knocked off with a club. The head had been thrown into our garden during the night, with the intention, no doubt, of annoying us and shocking our feelings.

These poor victims of war were brought from Verata, and were killed by the Bau people. 260 human beings were killed and brought away by the victors to be roasted and eaten. Many women and children were taken alive to be kept for slaves. About 30 *living* children were hoisted up to the mastheads as flags of triumph. The motion of the canoes while sailing soon killed the helpless creatures and silenced their piercing cries. Other children were taken, alive, to Bau that the boys there might learn the art of Feegeean warfare by firing arrows at them and beating them with clubs. For days they have been tearing and devouring like wolves and hyenas.

This entry in David Cargill's diary was followed not long afterwards by another, briefer but no less horrible in its content:

February 2nd, 1840. Immediately after our English Class at the Mission we were called to witness one of the most horrid scenes that our eyes have yet beheld in this land. Eleven dead bodies were dragged to the front of the old king's house, but a few paces from our own door, from the adjoining island of Lauthala, having been slain together with the people of one whole village on the morning of the Sabbath by order of Tuiilaila, the young king. The reason assigned was their having killed one of the Bau people living in this land.

The execution of the bloody massacre was committed to the people of a village situated nearer to the island of Lauthala than this. They fell upon them by break of day, while they were still asleep, and spared neither age nor sex. As far as we can learn, about 40 of them were slain, or very near that number, and among the rest the principal chief of that isle. The bodies, being all brought into the presence of the two principal chiefs and their people, were quickly given out one by one, to be roasted and eaten, and were severally dragged away on the ground like logs of wood by their respective owners. After a while the chiefs and people dispersed to their disgusting feast. The offensiveness of the bodies evidently diminished not their zest. Two bodies were dressed at a fire but a few paces from our fence.

The cold-blooded cruelty of the Fijians heightens the horror implicit in their cannibal practices. It is one thing, one might say, in the heat of battle to slay a man and, having returned in triumph, to roast and share him with one's companions in the successful foray. It is quite another—if it is permissible to look on this as a matter of degrees—to act as the Fijians seem consistently to have done. This is obviously the thought dominating the mind of another Methodist missionary, named Jaggar, reporting back to London in 1844, and by yet another of the courageous and unhappy workers in the field, the Rev. John Watsford, a couple of years later. Jaggar wrote:

One of the servants of the king a few months ago ran away. She was soon, however, brought back to the king's house. There, at the request of the queen, her arm was cut off below the elbow and cooked for the king, who ate it *in her presence,* and then ordered that her body be burnt in different parts. The girl, now a woman, is still living.

Two men that were taken alive in the war at Viwa were removed from thence to Kamba, to be killed. The Bau chief told his brother—who had been converted by our Mission—the manner in which he intended them to be killed. His brother said to him: "That will be very cruel. If you will allow them to live, I will give you a canoe." The Bau chief answered: "Keep your canoe. I want to eat men." His brother then left the village that he might not witness the horrible sight.

The cruel deed was then perpetrated. The men doomed to death were made to dig a hole in the earth for the purpose of making a native oven, and were then required to cut firewood *to roast their own bodies.* They were then directed to go and wash, and afterwards to make a cup of a banana-leaf. This, from opening a vein in each man, was soon filled with blood. This blood was then drunk, *in the presence of the sufferers,* by the Kamba people.

Seru, the Bau chief, then had their arms and legs cut off, cooked and eaten, some of the flesh being presented to them. He then ordered a fish-hook to be put into their tongues, which were then drawn out as far as possible before being cut off. These were roasted and eaten, to the taunts of "We are eating your tongues!" As life in the victims was still not extinct, an incision was made in the side of each man, and his bowels taken out. This soon terminated their sufferings in this world. The father of the present king was one of the greatest cannibals ever known. He used to say, when vegetables were set before him: "What is there to eat with these?" If they answered "Pig," he would then say: "No, that will not do." Fish, too, he would refuse, asking: "Have you not got an *ikalevu?*" This is the Feegeean's word for 'great fish', but when used it always means a *dead human body.*

A variant on this sinister euphemism is reported, not by a missionary, this time, but by a well-known and intrepid traveller, Alfred St Johnston, who seems to have had a predilection for making his temporary home among the fiercest primitive tribes he could locate. Obviously he survived his experiences, for at the end of the nineteenth century he published his memoirs under the pleasantly alliterative title, *Camping Among Cannibals.* In this book he wrote: "The expression 'long pig' is not a phrase invented by Europeans but is one frequently used by the Fijians, who looked upon a corpse as ordinary butcher's meat. They call a human body *puaka balava*—'long pig'—in contradistinction to *puaka dina*—'real pig'."

The missionary, Jaggar, completed his grim report of cannibalistic practices among the Bau tribes of his island:

> The Bau Chief used to feel his victims. If they were fat, he would say, "Your fat is good. I shall eat you." If they were lean, he would send them away to be fattened. He preferred human flesh to all else, especially in the morning, and if his sons did not eat the flesh with him he would beat them.
>
> Another chief ran away in battle but was captured in a tree, from which he was brought into the presence of Chief Tanoa, who was actually related to him. His hands were tied and he was made to sit before Tanoa, who *kissed* him while, *with his own hands,* he cut off one of his arms. Having drunk some of the blood that had been spilled, he then threw the arm upon the fire to roast, and afterwards ate it *in his presence.*
>
> The captured chief said to him: "Do not do this to me. Like you, I am a chief." Tanoa then cut off the other arm, and also both his legs; also as much of his tongue as he could. Then he divided up the trunk, leaving the parts to dry in the sun.

Two years later, the Rev. John Watsford wrote from Ono to announce that the war between Bau and Rewa had at last come to an end. He does not say what it was that brought hostilities to a close, and it is unlikely that it was as the result of any influence brought to bear upon the combatants by the Mission workers, for all their courage and perseverance. For there is continuous evidence throughout these reports that not only fighting but cannibal practices took place on the very threshold of the Mission. Thankfully reporting the cessation of these hostilities, Watsford wrote on November 6th, 1846:

> We cannot tell you how many have been slain. Hundreds of wretched human beings have been sent to their account, with all their sins upon their heads. Dead bodies were thrown upon the beach at Vewa, having drifted from Bau, where they were thrown into the sea, there being *too many* at Bau to be eaten. Bau literally stank for many days, human flesh having been cooked in every hut and the entrails having been thrown outside as food for pigs, or left to putrefy in the sun.

The Somosomo people were fed with human flesh during their stay at Bau, they being on a visit at the time. Some of the chiefs of other tribes, when bringing their food, carried a cooked human being on one shoulder and a pig on the other; but they always preferred the 'long pig', as they call a man, when baked. One woman who had been clubbed was left upon the beach in front of our house at Vewa. The poor creature's head was smashed to pieces and the body quite naked. Whether it was done by the heathen *to insult us,* or not, we do not know.

One Christian man was clubbed at Rewa, and part of his body was eaten by the Vewa heathen and his bones then thrown near our door. My lad gathered them up and buried them, and afterwards learned that they were the bones of one of his friends. After Rewa was destroyed, heaps of dead bodies lay in all directions; their bones still lie bleaching in the sun.

We do not, and we cannot, tell you all we know of Feegeean cruelty and crime. Every fresh act seems to rise above the last. A chief at Rakeraki had a box in which he kept human flesh. Legs and arms were salted for him and thus preserved in this box. If he saw anyone, even if of his friends, who was fatter than the rest, he had him—or her—killed at once, and part roasted and part preserved. His people declare that he eats human flesh every day.

At Bau, the people preserve human flesh and chew it as some chew tobacco. They carry it about with them, and use it in the same way as tobacco. I heard of an instance of cruelty the other day that surpasses everything I have before heard of the kind. A canoe was wrecked near Natawar, and many of the occupants succeeded in swimming to shore. They were taken by the Natawar people and ovens were at once prepared in which to roast them. The poor wretches were bound ready for the ovens and their enemies were waiting anxiously to devour them. They did not club them, lest any of their blood should be lost. Some, however, could not wait until the ovens were sufficiently heated, but pulled the ears off the wretched creatures and ate them raw.

When the ovens were ready, they cut their victims up very carefully, placing dishes under every part to catch the blood. If a drop fell, they licked it up off the ground with the greatest greediness. While the poor wretches were being cut in pieces, they pleaded hard for life; but all was of no avail: all were devoured.

Part Two
Cannibalism and Survival
on the High Seas

The Ownership of a Plank: David Harrison on the Wreck of the *Peggy*
From *Desperate Journeys, Abandoned Souls*

BY EDWARD E. LESLIE

In his fascinating book, *Desperate Journeys, Abandoned Souls,* Edward Leslie discourses on what happens when a ship is wrecked, her crew cast adrift—and suddenly the question of who is to live, and who is to die, becomes much more than a philosophical one.

Perhaps it was the sheer number of men on board the sloop *Peggy* or the cargo they hauled or the slow, maddening ordeal they experienced—or the combination of these—that made them base. They had sailed from the island of Fyal, bound for their home port of New York, on October 24, 1765. Five days out, they encountered rough weather, heavy seas, and violent winds. In the month that followed, the *Peggy* was struck by one terrible gale after another, and her sails were gradually torn away until only one remained.

[Captain] David Harrison's assessment of the situation was bleak. There was, he felt,

no prospect whatever before us but what was pregnant with the bitterest distress. For the conflict which our vessel had so long maintained against waves and winds had by this time occasioned her to leak excessively, and our provisions were so much exhausted that we found it absolutely necessary to come to an immediate allowance of two pounds of bread a week for each person, besides a quart of water and a pint of wine a day. The alternative was really deplorable, between the shortness of our provisions and the wreck of our ship. If we contrived to keep the latter from sinking we were in danger of perishing with hunger, and if

45

we contrived to spin out the former with a rigid perseverance of economy for any time, there was but little probability of being able to preserve our ship. Thus on either hand little less than a miracle could save us from inevitable destruction. If we had an accidental gleam of comfort on one hand, the fate with which the other so visibly teemed gave an instant check to our satisfaction and obscured every rising ray of hope with an instant cloud of horror and despair.

Several times they saw other vessels, but the weather was so bad that they could do nothing more than exchange signals with them. These tantalizing sightings only increased their misery.

Harrison lessened further their daily rations, but inevitably the food ran out. The liquor supply was depleted as well, and only two gallons of "dirty water remain[ed] in the bottom of a cask."

It was now nearly the end of December. The men, emotionally exhausted and experiencing the fatigue of an advanced state of starvation, were compelled to work frantically, incessantly, merely to keep their ship afloat and themselves alive.

In this desperate condition, it was not unnatural for them to seize the bulk of the *Peggy's* cargo, which happened to be a large quantity of wine and brandy. The liquor was the last thing they had in the world, they told the captain, and they might have added that it was possibly the last they ever would have. They drank it in copious amounts, cursing and blaspheming continually. Witnessing this sudden breakdown of discipline and self-control, Harrison became increasingly uneasy. A dedicated officer who took seriously his responsibility for the safety of his crew, he could only view their behavior with trepidation.

So it must have been with an extra measure of relief that on Christmas morning Captain Harrison descried a sail to leeward. The sight of it

suddenly transported [us] with the most extravagant sensations of joy. . . . Distress generally inspires the human mind with lively sentiments of devotion, and those who perhaps dispute or disregard the existence of a Deity at other times are ready enough in the day of adversity to think every advantageous turn in their affairs a particular exertion of the Divine benignity. It was, therefore, but natural for some of the people to think that the twenty-fifth of December was appointed for their preservation. Our thanksgivings, however, to Providence, though profoundly sincere, were not offered in any general form.

Instead the men crowded upon the deck and hung out the distress signal. Before noon they had the "unspeakable satisfaction" of seeing the ship approach. Harrison quickly informed the captain of their plight: the *Peggy* was wrecked, and her sailors, "every moment exposed to the mercy of the waves, as our leaks continually increas[ed]," declined "in their strength in proportion as the necessity grew urgent to employ them at the pumps." Harrison asked if the captain would take them off the *Peggy*. He would not. Even after Harrison swore that neither he nor any of his company would eat so much as a single morsel of his provisions, the captain remained obdurate. All he was willing to do for them, in fact, was to give them a little bread. Harrison was grateful nonetheless: "The promised relief was but small; [yet] the smallest to people in our circumstances was inestimable."

The intractable captain promised to have the meager food passed over as soon as he completed his noon nautical observation. Gullible in his optimism, David Harrison went below to lie down. He was weary, emaciated, and suffering from a severe flux. The malnourishment had considerably impaired his vision and aggravated his rheumatism.

He had barely lain down when some of his men burst into his cabin. They were so excited that he had trouble understanding them, but their faces bore expressions of profound despair. Their purported provider was sailing away from the *Peggy* as fast as he could.

Harrison tried to make his way up on deck and found himself so feeble that he could only crawl. Topside, he saw his crew transfixed by the sight of the departing vessel as she was propelled away by a favorable wind.

> As long as my poor fellows could retain the least trace of him they hung about the shrouds or ran in a state of absolute frenzy from one part of the ship to the other. They pierced the air with their cries, increasing in their lamentations as he lessened upon their view and straining their very eyeballs to preserve him in sight, through a despairing hope that some dawning impulse of pity would yet induce him to commiserate our situation and lead him to stretch out the blessed hand of relief.
>
> But alas! to what purpose did we exhaust our little strength in supplicating for compassion, or aggravate our own misfortunes with a fruitless expectation of such a change? The inexorable captain pursued his course without regarding us and steeled, as he undoubtedly must be, to

every sentiment of nature and humanity, possibly valued himself not a little upon his dexterity in casting us off.

Yet for all the animosity Harrison felt toward his "barbarous" colleague, he would not "hang him up to universal detestation or infamy by communicating his name to the reader. If he is capable of reflection his own conscience must sufficiently avenge my cause and God grant that the pungency of that conscience may be my only avenger."

As joyous as the sailors had been at the prospect of deliverance, they were now to the same degree dejected. Their captain saw desperate gloom on every face.

On board the *Peggy* were two pigeons and a cat. The birds went for Christmas dinner that very afternoon. The next day the men drew lots for parts of the cat. Harrison's draw was the head. Though he had pitied the creature, he was forced to admit that "in all my days I never feasted on anything which appeared so delicious to my appetite. The piercing sharpness of necessity had entirely conquered my aversion to such food, and the rage of an incredible hunger rendered that an exquisite regale which on any other occasion I must have loathed with the most insuperable disgust."

When the last of the cat's bones had been picked clean, the men went back to their drinking. Drunk, they cursed their fate with torrents of excoriation. In the steerage this rough crew heated their wine, while in his cabin their captain lay nauseated by the odor of the cooking spirits. He was trying to distract himself from their blasphemy and his own desire to give up, to die and experience the "moment of dissolution," by focusing on the memory of his wife and children.

> When the reader comes to consider our total want of necessaries, that my vessel had been for some time leaky, that I myself was emaciated with sickness and had but one sail in the world to direct her; when he considers that the men were either too weak or too much intoxicated to pay a necessary attention to the pump; when he likewise considers the severity of the season, that it blew 'black December,' as Shakespeare phrases it; and is told that we had not an inch of candle or a morsel of slush to make any, having long since eaten up every appearance of either which could be found; when the reader comes to consider all these things and is moreover informed that the general distress had deprived me of all command on board my own ship, he will scarcely suppose that I could sustain any new misfortune.

Such a supposition would be incorrect. On December 28, the *Peggy* was struck by the worst storm yet, and it tore away the last of her canvas, the mainsail. Now, thought Harrison, she had truly become a wreck. "Death became so seemingly unavoidable that even I gave up hope, that last consolation of all the wretched, and prepared for an immediate launch into the dreadful gulf of eternity."

Yet he did not die. He was so weak that he could no longer hold the pen he had been using to make journal entries, but he was still alive on January 13, when, with the *Peggy* being "tossed about at the discretion of the sea and wind," the entire crew filed into his cabin.

Most probably he knew why they had come before a word was said. But even if he did not, their facial expressions, so "full of horror, . . . indicated the nature of their dreadful purpose."

The cabin would have been damp and dark and its atmosphere thick with the odor of their bodies and the liquor on their breath.

Archibald Nicolson, who was the first mate and their designated leader, spoke up. Their tobacco was "entirely exhausted." They were starving. They had eaten the buttons off their jackets and all the leather they could find in the ship, including that which was part of the pump. They could hold out no longer. Their only chance was to cast lots and sacrifice one of their number for the "preservation of the rest."

Knowing they were drunk, Harrison tried to "soothe them from their purpose," to stall them, begging them to get some rest and bring the matter back to him in the morning.

They were furious. They told him that what needed to be done could not wait, and they did not care if he disapproved of the plan: they had been kind enough to inform him of what would take place and, having done so, would "oblige me to take my chance as well as another man, since the general misfortune had leveled all distinction of persons."

The captain, because of the "excesses of their intoxication," had been expecting the drunkards to attack him, and he had prepared for it by keeping his pistols close at hand. Bitterly he realized that his forethought had merely been an "idle precaution": there were just too many of them for him to make a fight of it. Having failed at persuasion, he told them that even if they pursued this course he would not order any man's death, and neither would he "partake by any means of so shocking a repast."

Belligerently they replied that they were not asking his consent, and as to eating or not eating, why he could follow the "bias of my own inclination." Then they filed out of his cabin and into the steerage—but very soon they returned. Not surprisingly, the lot had fallen on a black slave who was part of the cargo.

Considering how little time it had taken to perform the ceremony and that it had been done carefully out of his sight, Harrison was more than suspicious that the draw had been fixed against the "poor Ethiopian." He was surprised that they had even bothered with the subterfuge.

When the black man saw the pistol being loaded, he ran to the captain and begged for his life, but Harrison could only watch helplessly as they dragged him away to the steerage, where he was shot through the head. He was hardly dead before some of the sailors had gutted him and built a large cooking fire. One of the foremastmen, James Campbell, was too ravenous to wait, and he tore out the liver and ate it raw. He would die three days later, a raving madman, having "paid dear for such an extravagant impatience," and his body would be thrown overboard immediately rather than eaten, since the men feared that devouring his flesh would make them insane, too.

They stayed up most of the night of the murder, David Harrison noted with disdain, feasting on the slave whose body afforded them "a luxurious banquet." In the morning the mate came to the captain to ask mockingly what his orders were relative to the pickling of the corpse. Weak as he was, Harrison grasped a pistol, leveled it at his tormentor, and offered to send him "after the Negro" if he did not instantly quit the cabin.

The man left, muttering that the captain was no longer in charge of the ship and that he would call a council of the crew. Its unanimous vote was to cut the body into slices, which the cannibals thereafter referred to as steaks.

Harrison heard one man say, "Damn him, though he would not consent to our having any meat let us give him some." Immediately the speaker entered the cabin with a portion and an invitation to dine, but the captain still had his pistol. He pointed it at the bearer and expressed a desire to hear him make the offer a *second* time.

Harrison would later freely admit that principle was not the only motivation for his refusal to eat:

> In fact, the constant expectation of death, joined to the miserable state to which I was reduced through sickness and fatigue, to say nothing of my horror at the food with which I was presented, entirely took away my desire of eating. Add also to this that the stench of their stewing and frying threw me into an absolute fever and that this fever was ag-

gravated by a strong scurvy and violent swelling in my legs. Sinking under such an accumulated load of afflictions and being, moreover, fearful, if I closed my eyes, that they would surprise and murder me for their next supply, it is no wonder that I lost all relish for sustenance.

The suspicion that he would be their second victim was well founded. He frequently heard them speculating over who would be the next "supply" and agreeing that they should kill their captain before putting any of themselves at risk.

"Notwithstanding the excesses into which my people ran, they nevertheless husbanded the Negro's carcass with the severest economy and stinted themselves to an allowance which made it last for many days." Even so, the time for another lottery was drawing close, and his awareness that the number of steaks was diminishing kept David Harrison from sleeping very much. He found that in "proportion as the Negro grew less, so in proportion my apprehensions were increased, and every meal which they sat down to I considered as a fresh approach to destruction."

In the end, his subordinates declined to murder him brazenly. (This refusal may be attributable to the vestiges of the old discipline they had once worked under, or to the captain's readiness to flourish his pistol, depending on your estimation of human nature.) Again the mate came leading a procession of the famished to propose casting lots. The Negro had been all eaten up days before, he told Harrison, and they preferred to die one at a time from a pistol shot rather than from starvation. They knew the captain must be hungry, too, Nicolson conciliated, but added that he would have to take his chances with the rest.

Again Harrison tried to dissuade them. Another death would be futile since killing and eating the black had done them no good: now that he was devoured they were as "greedy and as emaciated as ever." Submit to Providence, he counseled them, offering to pray with them for a quick rescue or a quick death.

They would not listen. Brusquely they dismissed his piety. There was no time for prayer; they were hungry *now*, and they would cast lots with or without his consent.

Seeing how stubborn they were, and having just cause to think that if he did not oversee the lottery it would certainly select him, Harrison got out of his bunk, tore pieces of paper into slips, and marked one with ink. Ever a man for doing things properly, he followed the procedure used at the Guildhall lottery drawing.

This time the loser was a foremastman named David Flatt, the only man of the crew the captain thought at all reliable. He was respected by his fellows as well, and when he drew the marked slip they fell into a long, unhappy silence broken only by Flatt himself.

"My dear friends, messmates and fellow sufferers," he said to them, "all I have to beg of you is to dispatch me as soon as you did the Negro and to put me to as little torture as you can." He then appointed James Doud as his executioner, as Doud had been for the black.

The fire was burning in the steerage and the pistol was loaded, yet they hesitated. When Flatt asked for a few minutes in which to prepare himself for death, they readily agreed. Harrison thought, in fact, that they were in a mood to spare Flatt altogether—until they resumed their drinking. "A few draughts of wine, however, soon suppressed all these dawnings of humanity." Well, not entirely: they regarded Flatt so highly that they agreed to put off his execution until eleven o'clock the next morning, in the hopes that in the interim "the Divine Goodness" would provide a rescuer. For now they asked—*begged*—Harrison to read prayers, which they joined in with the "utmost fervency."

As he read, he had the satisfaction of seeing his men behaving for the first time in a long time with "tolerable decency." He led them in religious observance while his strength lasted, and then he fell back on the bed, utterly wearied by those slight exertions. Yet even in a semiconscious state he heard the sailors trying to comfort the wretched Flatt with hope. Although they had been singularly unsuccessful at catching fish, they promised that at dawn they would put their hooks into the water and try once more to pull something in and thus "mitigate their distresses [and] avert the severity of his sentence."

There could be no solace for this unlucky man. He who at his selection had asked only that he not be tortured found the stress of waiting unbearable. By midnight he had become completely deaf. By four A.M. he was raving.

Lying on his bunk, David Harrison heard the men debate whether or not to put Flatt out of his misery *immediately* as an act of humanity. In the end they decided to keep to the agreed timetable.

It was eight o'clock the next morning when two men burst into the captain's cabin. Without a word they seized his hands. Their faces were contorted. He knew instantly why they were there: they were going to murder him. They would not risk insanity by devouring Flatt. They would kill and eat him. He wrestled one hand free and snatched up a pistol. He would sell his life as dearly as he could. But before he shot either one of them, they managed to blurt out that a sail had been descried. There was a ship to leeward! Here came the rest of their comrades, crowding in to jubilantly confirm the sighting.

> It is impossible to describe the excess of my transport upon hearing that there was a sail at any rate in sight. My joy in a manner overpowered me and it was not without the utmost exertion of my strength that I desired them to use every expedition in making a signal of distress. Our vessel, indeed, itself was a most striking signal; but as there was a possibility for the ship in view to suppose that there was not a living creature on board I judged it absolutely expedient to prevent the likelihood of so dreadful a mistake.

Now that salvation was at hand, discipline began to return. The crew followed their captain's instructions with alacrity. He heard the men cry, "She nighs us . . . she nighs us . . . she is standing this way!"

For a moment while they waited they spoke of Flatt, of how sad it was that they could not communicate to him in his unhearing madness that they were saved. But he was forgotten when someone proposed—and all the sailors agreed—that they break out more liquor to drink to their imminent release. It took all of Harrison's powers of persuasion to stop them; he argued that if they appeared in "any way disguised with liquor the ship might probably decline to take us on board, and [I] endeavored to convince them that their deliverance in a very great measure depended upon the regularity of this moment's behavior. My remonstrances had some effect and all but my mate, who had for a considerable time abandoned himself to the brutality of intoxication, very prudently postponed so untimely an instance of indulgence."

They watched the vessel approach with a feeling of excruciating suspense, "a most tumultuous agitation." In this hour the wind died, and the sea became calm. With two miles still separating her from the *Peggy*, the rescue ship was unable to come closer. A boat was hoisted out and was rowed vigorously toward the wreck. Their apprehension grew: so often thwarted and disappointed in these last months, they feared that even with help so close something would interfere and plunge them back into distress. Life and death seemed to sit on every stroke of the oars, "and as we still considered ourselves tottering on the very verge of eternity, the conflict between our wishes and our fears may be easily supposed by a reader of imagination."

When the boat finally reached them, her occupants were so astonished at the ghastly, inhuman appearance of the *Peggy*'s men that they rested upon their oars and demanded to know *what* they were looking at. After they had been convinced that the wretched castaways were indeed human, they scrambled aboard and urged them to hurry into the boat lest another gale strike before they could return to their vessel. The *Peggy*'s sailors hastened to comply, but their captain was so weak that he had to be lowered by ropes. They were about to push off when someone remembered the demented Flatt, still below deck and unaware of what had happened. "In the general hurry every man's attention was engaged by the thought of his own preservation and it was almost a matter of wonder that anybody remembered the absence of the mate."

Flatt was gone after and eventually led to the rail, holding in his hand a "can of joy with which he had been busy, having completely erased every idea of the preceding occurrences from his recollection." He appeared to be absolutely amazed to see strangers before him, but they managed to get him into the boat.

The passengers and crew had gathered on the deck of the rescue vessel, the *Susanna,* curious to see the castaways. A close look at their "hollow eyes, shriveled cheeks, long beards and squalid complections" appalled them. Even the captain, Thomas Evers, shook with horror as he assisted David Harrison to his own cabin. Before Harrison allowed himself to be led to luxury—indeed, as soon as he was brought on board—he dropped to his knees on the deck and, propping himself against a hen coop for support, prayed fervently with "sincerest gratitude to the great Author of all things for the abundance of his mercy, and in the fulness of my heart began also to express my sensibility to the captain for his readiness to assist the distressed."

★   ★   ★

Harrison had no appetite for four days and found when he tried to eat that he could not taste the food. By taking small amounts of broth and solids, he gradually began to improve, until one day

> having an occasion for a particular indulgence of nature, I thought I should have expired performing it. The pain it gave me was excruciating to the last degree and the parts were so contracted, having never once been employed for a space of thirty-six or thirty-seven days, that I almost began to despair restoring them to their necessary operations. I was, however, at last relieved by the discharge of a callous lump about

the size of a hen's egg, and enjoyed a tranquility of body, notwithstanding all my disorders, with which I was utterly unacquainted for some preceding weeks.

Soon he was able to eat well enough that he gorged himself on turkey and threw himself into a fever. It was an odd, dangerous triumph of sorts.

Even now, safely aboard the *Susanna* and under the care of a solicitous and generous captain, the former castaways were dogged by bad luck. A gale that had struck the ship earlier in her voyage had resulted in the loss of a large quantity of stores, including, noted the long-famished Harrison in a litany of mourning, "four hogs, four or five hogsheads of fresh water, forty or fifty head of fowl, and twenty or thirty geese and turkeys." With the added drain caused by the seven survivors now on board, Captain Evers was forced to institute rationing: two and a half pounds of bread per week along with a quart of water and eight ounces of salt provisions per day. A long series of storms battered the vessel and made her so leaky that the pumps had to be manned continually, and all on board hoped to encounter *another* ship that might provide them with help. To the *Peggy*'s men it must have seemed that the dreadful nightmare had begun again.

Yet it was not so. Eventually they sailed into Dartmouth and were able to go ashore.

> The next day my inconsiderate mate, Mr. Archibald Nicolson, who had so long wallowed, as I may say, in every mire of excess, having reduced himself by a continued intoxication to such a state that no proper sustenance would stay on his stomach, fell a martyr to his inebriety. Having a watch and some trinkets about him, which defrayed the expense of his funeral, he was decently interred.

It is here that the pious and stalwart Captain David Harrison ends the narrative of his travail. Most of his men were still weak, although he himself had recovered. In this respect there is a moral underpinning to the story, clear and strong enough to please any eighteenth-century gentleman: the officer who had steadfastly refused to descend to bestiality makes a complete and speedy recovery, while the villainous leader of the disobedient rabble dies of his own excesses after reaching safety.

One feature would seem to mar the symmetry of this conclusion. David Flatt, respected by Harrison and so loved by his comrades that they were reluctant to kill him, remained quite out of his mind.

Games of Chance
From *In the Heart of the Sea: The Tragedy of the Whaleship* Essex

BY NATHANIEL PHILBRICK

On August 12, 1819, the whaleship *Essex* slipped her moorings in Nantucket and set sail—into tragedy and history.

Over a year into her voyage, while cruising deep in the Pacific Ocean, the *Essex* was rammed and sunk by a bull sperm whale, an event which became the basis for Herman Melville's great novel, *Moby Dick*. The *Essex's* crew, led by Captain George Pollard and First Mate Owen Chase, made a desperate two-thousand mile journey in two open boats towards the coast of South America. As is demonstrated in this excerpt from Nathaniel Philbrick's bestselling *In the Heart of the Sea,* they were soon forced into the horrors of murder and cannibalism.

On February 6, the four men on Pollard's boat, having consumed "the last morsel" of Samuel Reed, began to "[look] at each other with horrid thoughts in our minds," according to one survivor, "but we held our tongues." Then the youngest of them, sixteen-year-old Charles Ramsdell, uttered the unspeakable. They should cast lots, he said, to see who would be killed so that the rest could live.

The drawing of lots in a survival situation had long been an accepted custom of the sea. The earliest recorded instance dates back to the first half of the seventeenth century, when seven Englishmen sailing from the Caribbean island of St. Kitts were driven out to sea in a storm. After seventeen days, one of the crew suggested that they cast lots. As it turned out, the lot fell to the man who had originally made the proposal, and after lots were cast again to see who should execute him, he was killed and eaten.

In 1765, several days after the crew of the disabled *Peggy* had eaten the remains of the black slave, lots were drawn to see who would be the next to serve as food. The lot fell to David Flatt, a foremastman and one of the most popular sailors in the crew. "The shock of the decision was great," wrote Captain Harrison, "and the preparations for execution dreadful." Flatt requested that he be given some time to prepare himself for death, and the crew agreed to postpone the execution until eleven the next morning. The dread of his death sentence proved too much for Flatt. By midnight he had become deaf; by morning he was delirious. Incredibly, a rescue ship was sighted at eight o'clock. But for David Flatt it was too late. Even after the *Peggy's* crew had been delivered to England, Harrison reported that "the unhappy Flatt still continued out of his senses."

Drawing lots was not a practice to which a Quaker whaleman could, in good conscience, agree. Friends not only have a testimony against killing people but also do not allow games of chance. Charles Ramsdell, the son of a cabinetmaker, was a Congregationalist. However, both Owen Coffin and Barzillai Ray were members of Nantucket's Friends Meeting. Although Pollard was not a Quaker, his grandparents had been, and his great-grandmother, Mehitable Pollard, had been a minister.

Faced with similarly dire circumstances, other sailors made different decisions. In 1811, the 139-ton brig *Polly*, on her way from Boston to the Caribbean, was dismasted in a storm, and the crew drifted on the waterlogged hull for 191 days. Although some of the men died from hunger and exposure, their bodies were never used for food; instead, they were used as bait. Attaching pieces of their dead shipmate's bodies to a trolling line, the survivors managed to catch enough sharks to sustain themselves until their rescue. If the *Essex* crew had adopted this strategy with the death of Matthew Joy, they might never have reached the extreme that confronted them now.

When first presented with young Ramsdell's proposal, Captain Pollard "would not listen to it," according to an account related by Nickerson, "saying to the others, 'No, but if I die first you are welcome to subsist on my remains.' " Then Owen Coffin, Pollard's first cousin, the eighteen-year-old son of his aunt, joined Ramsdell in requesting that they cast lots.

Pollard studied his three young companions. Starvation had ringed their sunken eyes with a dark, smudgelike pigmentation. There was little doubt that they were all close to death. It was also clear that all of them, including Barzillai Ray, the orphaned son of a noted island cooper, were in favor of Ramsdell's proposal. As he had two times before—after the knockdown in the Gulf Stream and the sinking of the *Essex*—Pollard acquiesced to the majority. He agreed to cast lots. If suffering had turned Chase into a compassionate yet forceful leader, Pollard's confidence had been eroded even further by events that reduced him to the most desperate extreme a man can ever know.

They cut up a scrap of paper and placed the pieces in a hat. The lot fell to Owen Coffin. "My lad, my lad!" Pollard cried out. "[I]f you don't like your lot, I'll shoot the first man that touches you." Then the captain offered to take the lot himself. "Who can doubt but that Pollard would rather have met the death a thousand times," Nickerson wrote. "None that knew him, will ever doubt."

But Coffin had already resigned himself to his fate. "I like it as well as any other," he said softly.

Lots were drawn again to see who would shoot the boy. It fell to Coffin's friend, Charles Ramsdell.

Even though the lottery had originally been his idea, Ramsdell now refused to follow it through. "For a long time," Nickerson wrote, "he declared that he could never do it, but finally had to submit." Before he died, Coffin spoke a parting message to his mother, which Pollard promised to deliver if he should make it back to Nantucket. Then Coffin asked for a few moments of silence. After reassuring the others that "the lots had been fairly drawn," he lay his down on the boat's gunwale. "He was soon dispatched," Pollard would later recall, "and nothing of him left."

In the Eagle's Shadow

[First Mate Owen] Chase and his men lay in the bottom of their boat in a cold drizzle. All they had to shield them from the rain was a piece of tattered, water-soaked canvas. "Even had it been dry," Nickerson wrote, "[it] would have been but a poor apology for covering."

On January 28, 1821, the breeze finally shifted into the west. But it brought them little comfort. "It had nearly become indifferent to us," Chase wrote, "from what quarter it blew." They now had too far to go and too few provisions to have any hope of reaching land. Their only chance was to be sighted by a ship. "[I]t was this narrow hope alone," Chase remembered, "that prevented me from lying down at once to die."

They had fourteen days of hardtack left, but that assumed they could live two more weeks on only an ounce and a half a day. "We were so feeble," Nickerson wrote, "that we could scarcely crawl about the boat upon our hands and knees." Chase realized that if he didn't increase their daily portion of bread, they all might be dead in as few as five days. It was time to abandon the strict rationing regime that had brought them this far and let the men eat "as pinching necessity demanded."

Success in a long-term survival situation requires that a person display an "active-passive" approach to the gradual and agonizing unfolding of events. "The key factor . . . [is] the realization that passivity is itself a deliberate and 'active' act," the survival psychologist John Leach writes. "There is strength in passivity." After more than two months of regimenting every aspect of his men's lives, Chase intuitively understood this—that it was now time to give "ourselves wholly up to the guidance and disposal of our Creator." They would eat as much bread as they needed to stave off death and see where the westerly wind took them.

By February 6 they were still alive, but just barely. "Our sufferings were now drawing to a close," the first mate wrote. "[A] terrible death appeared shortly to await us." The slight increase in food intake had brought a return to their hunger pangs, which were now "violent and outrageous." They found it difficult to talk and think clearly. Dreams of food and drink continued to torment them. "[O]ften did our fevered minds wander to the side of some richly supplied table," Nickerson remembered. His fantasies always ended the same way—with him "crying at the disappointment."

That night, rain squalls forced them to shorten sail. The off-islander Isaac Cole was on watch, and rather than awaken his companions, he attempted to lower the jib himself. But it proved too much for him. Chase and Nickerson awoke the next morning to find Cole despondent in the bilge of the boat. He declared that "all was dark in his mind, not a single ray of hope was left for him to dwell upon." Like Richard Peterson before him, he had given up, asserting that "it was folly and madness to be struggling against what appeared so palpably to be our fixed and settled destiny."

Even though he barely had the strength to articulate the words, Chase did his best to change Cole's mind. "I remonstrated with him as effectually as the weakness both of my body and understanding would allow of." Suddenly Cole sat up and crawled to the bow and hoisted the jib he had lowered, at such cost, the night before. He cried out that he would not give up and that he would live as long as any of them. "[T]his effort was," Chase wrote, "but the hectic fever of the moment." Cole soon returned to the bottom of the boat, where he lay despairing for the rest of the day and through the night. But Cole would not be permitted the dignity of a quiet and peaceful death.

On the morning of February 8, the seventy-ninth day since leaving the *Essex,* Cole began to rant incoherently, presenting to his frightened crew members "a most miserable spectacle of madness." Twitching spasmodically, he sat up and called for a napkin and water, then fell down to the bottom of the boat as if struck dead, only to pop up again like a possessed jack-in-the-box. By ten o'clock he could no longer speak. Chase and the others placed him on a board they had laid across the seats and covered him with a few pieces of clothing.

For the next six hours, Cole whimpered and moaned in pain, finally falling into "the most horrid and frightful convulsions" Chase had ever seen. In addition to dehydration and hypernatremia (an excess amount of salt), he may have been suffering from a lack of magnesium, a mineral deficiency that, when extreme, can cause bizarre and violent behavior. By four o'clock in the afternoon, Isaac Cole was dead.

It had been forty-three days since they'd left Henderson Island, seventy-eight days since they'd last seen the *Essex,* but no one suggested—at least that afternoon—that they use Cole's body for food. All night the corpse lay beside them, each man keeping his thoughts to himself.

When the crew of the *Peggy* shot and killed a black slave in 1765, one of the men refused to wait for the meat to be cooked. "[B]eing ravenously impatient for food," the sailor plunged his hand into the slave's eviscerated body and plucked out the liver and ate it raw. "The unhappy man paid dear for such an extravagant impatience," Captain Harrison wrote, "for in three days after he died raving mad." Instead of eating that sailor's body, the crew, "being fearful of sharing his fate," threw it overboard. No one dared to consume the flesh of a man who had died insane.

The next morning, February 9, Lawrence and Nickerson began making preparations for burying Cole's remains. Chase stopped them. All night he had wrestled with the question of what they should do. With only three days of hardtack left, he knew, it was quite possible that they might be reduced to casting lots. Better to eat a dead shipmate—even a tainted shipmate—than be forced to kill a man.

"I addressed them," Chase wrote, "on the painful subject of keeping the body for food." Lawrence and Nickerson raised no objections and, fearful that the meat had already begun to spoil, "[we] set to work as fast as we were able."

After separating the limbs from the body and removing the heart, they sewed up what remained of Cole's body "as decently" as they could, before they committed it to the sea. Then they began to eat. Even before lighting a fire, the men "eagerly devoured" the heart, then ate "sparingly of a few pieces of the flesh." They cut the rest of the meat into thin strips—some of which they roasted on the fire, while the others were laid out to dry in the sun.

Chase insisted that he had "no language to paint the anguish of our souls in this dreadful dilemma." Making it all the worse was the thought that any one of the remaining three men might be next. "We knew not then," the first mate wrote, "to whose lot it would fall next, either to die or be shot, and eaten like the poor wretch we had just dispatched."

The next morning they discovered that the strips of flesh had turned a rancid green. They immediately cooked the strips, which provided them with enough meat to last another six or seven days, allowing them to save what little bread they had left for what Chase called "the last moment of our trial."

In Captain Pollard's boat, on February 11, only five days after the execution of Owen Coffin, Barzillai Ray died. Ray, whose biblical first name means "made of iron, most firm and true," was nineteen years old. It was the seventh death George Pollard and Charles Ramsdell had witnessed in the month and a half since departing Henderson Island.

Psychologists studying the phenomenon of battle fatigue during World War II discovered that no soldiers—regardless of how strong their emotional makeup might be—were able to function if their unit experienced losses of 75 percent or more. Pollard and Ramsdell were suffering from a double burden; not only had they seen seven of nine men die (and even killed one of them), but they had been forced to eat their bodies. Like Pip, the black sailor in *Moby-Dick* who loses his mind after several hours of treading water on a boundless sea, Pollard and Ramsdell had been "carried down alive to the wondrous depths, where strange shapes of the unwarped primal world glided to and fro." Now they were alone, with only the corpse of Barzillai Ray and the bones of Coffin and Reed to sustain them.

Three days later, on February 14, the eighty-fifth day since leaving the wreck, Owen Chase, Benjamin Lawrence, and Thomas Nickerson ate the last of Isaac Cole. A week of living off human flesh, combined with their earlier decision to increase their daily ration of hardtack, had strengthened them to the point where they could once again manage the steering oar. But if they were stronger, they were also in a great deal of pain. As if the boils that covered their skin weren't enough, their arms and legs started to swell shockingly. Known as edema, this disfiguring accumulation of fluid is a common symptom of starvation.

Several days of westerly winds had brought them to within three hundred miles of the islands of Masafuera and Juan Fernandez. If they averaged sixty miles a day, they might reach safety in another five days. Unfortunately, they had only three days of hardtack left.

"Matters were now with us at their height," Chase wrote. "[A]ll hope was cast upon the breeze; and we tremblingly and fearfully awaited its progress, and the dreadful development of our destiny." Surrendering all prospects, the men were convinced that after two and a half months of suffering they were about to die nearly within sight of salvation.

That night Owen Chase lay down to sleep, "almost indifferent whether I should ever see the light again." He dreamed he saw a ship, just a few miles away, and even though he "strained every nerve to get to her," she sailed off into the distance, never to return. Chase awoke "almost overpowered with the frenzy I had caught in my slumbers, and stung with the cruelties of a diseased and disappointed imagination."

The next afternoon, Chase saw a thick cloud to the northeast—a sure sign of land. It must be the island of Masafuera—at least that was what Chase told Lawrence and Nickerson. In two days, he assured them, they would be on dry land. At first, his companions were reluctant to believe him. Gradually, however, after "repeated assurances of the favorable appearances of things" on the part of Chase, "their spirits acquired even a degree of elasticity that was truly astonishing." The wind remained favorable all night, and with their sails trimmed perfectly and a man tending the steering oar, their little boat made the best time of the voyage.

The next morning the cloud still loomed ahead. The end of their ordeal was apparently only days away. But for fifteen-year-old Thomas Nickerson, the strain of anticipation had become too much. After bailing out the boat, he lay down, drew the mildewed piece of canvas over him like a shroud, and told his fellow crew members that "he wished to die immediately."

"I saw that he had given up," Chase wrote, "and I attempted to speak a few words of comfort and encouragement to him." But all the arguments that had served the first mate so well failed to penetrate Nickerson's inner gloom. "A fixed look of settled and forsaken despondency came over his face," Chase wrote. "[H]e lay for some time silent, sullen, and sorrowful—and I felt at once . . . that the coldness of death was fast gathering upon him."

It was obvious to Chase that some form of dementia had seized the boy. Having watched Isaac Cole slip into a similar madness, Chase could not help but wonder if all of them were about to succumb to the temptations of despair. "[T]here was a sudden and unaccountable earnestness in his manner," he wrote, "that alarmed me, and made me fear that I myself might unexpectedly be overtaken by a like weakness, or dizziness of nature, that would bereave me at once of both reason and life." Whether or not it had been communicated to him through Cole's diseased flesh, Chase also felt the stirrings of a death wish as dark and palpable as the pillarlike cloud ahead.

At seven o'clock the next morning, February 18, Chase was sleeping in the bottom of the boat. Benjamin Lawrence was standing at the steering oar. Throughout the ordeal, the twenty-one-year-old boat-steerer had demonstrated remarkable fortitude. He was the one who, two months earlier, had volunteered to swim underneath the boat to repair a sprung plank. As Lawrence had watched Peterson, Cole, and now Nickerson lose their grip on life, he had clung, as best he could, to hope.

It was something his careworn family had become good at. His grandfather, George Lawrence, had married Judith Coffin, the daughter of a well-to-do merchant. For many years the Lawrences had been part of the island's Quaker elite, but by the time Benjamin came into the world, his grandfather had suffered several financial reversals. The proud old man decided to move to Alexandria, Virginia, where, he told an acquaintance, he could "descend into a humble sphere among strangers, rather than . . . remain in a place where every object reminded him of his lost prosperity."

When Benjamin was ten years old, his father died during a voyage to Alexandria, leaving his wife with seven children to support.

Safe in Lawrence's pocket was the piece of twine he had been working on ever since they'd left the wreck. It was now close to twelve inches long. He leaned into the steering oar and scanned the horizon. "There's a sail!" he cried.

Chase immediately scrambled to his feet. Just visible over the horizon was the speck of pale brown that Lawrence had taken for a sail. Chase stared for several suspenseful moments, gradually realizing that, yes, it was a sail—the topgallant of a ship, about seven miles away.

"I do not believe it is possible," Chase wrote, "to form a just conception of the pure, strong feelings, and the unmingled emotions of joy and gratitude, that took possession of my mind on this occasion."

Soon even Nickerson was up on his feet and gazing excitedly ahead.

Now the question was whether they could catch up to the much larger vessel. The ship was several miles to leeward, which was an advantage for the smaller vessel, and heading slightly north of their position, which meant that it might intercept their line of sail. Could their whaleboat reach that crossing point at approximately the same time the ship did? Chase could only pray that his nightmare of the missed rescue ship would not prove true. "I felt at the moment," Chase wrote, "a violent and unaccountable impulse to fly directly towards her."

For the next three hours they were in a desperate race. Their battered old whaleboat skimmed lightly over the waves at between four and six knots in the northwesterly breeze. Up ahead, the ship's sail plan continued to emerge from the distant horizon, revealing, with excruciating slowness, not only the topgallant sails but the topsails beneath and, finally, the mainsail and foresail. Yes, they assured themselves, they were catching up to the ship.

There was no lookout at the vessel's masthead, but eventually someone on deck saw them approaching to windward and behind. Chase and his men watched in tense fascination as the antlike figures bustled about the ship, shortening sail. Gradually the whaleboat closed the distance, and the hull of the merchantman rose up out of the sea, looming larger and larger ahead of them until Chase could read her quarterboard. She was the *Indian* from London.

Chase heard a shout and through glazed, reddened eyes saw a figure at the quarterdeck rail with a trumpet, a hailing device resembling a megaphone. It was an officer of the *Indian,* asking who they were. Chase summoned all his strength to make himself heard, but his dissiccated tongue stumbled over the words: "*Essex* . . . whaleship . . . Nantucket."

The narratives of shipwreck survivors are filled with accounts of captains refusing to take castaways aboard. In some instances the officers were reluctant to share their already low supply of provisions; in others they were fearful the survivors might be suffering from communicable diseases. But as soon as Chase explained that they were from a wreck, the *Indian's* captain immediately insisted that they come alongside.

When Chase, Lawrence, and Nickerson attempted to climb aboard, they discovered that they didn't have the strength. The three men stared up at the crew, their eyes wide and huge within the dark hollows of their skulls. Their raw, ulcerated skin hung from their skeletons like noxious rags. As he looked down from the quarterdeck, Captain William Crozier was moved to tears at what Chase called "the most deplorable and affecting picture of suffering and misery."

The English sailors lifted the men from their boat and carried them to the captain's cabin. Crozier ordered the cook to serve them their first taste of civilized food—tapioca pudding. Made from the root of the cassava plant, tapioca is a high-calorie, easy-to-digest food rich in the proteins and carbohydrates that their bodies craved.

Rescue came at latitude 33°45′ south, longitude 81°03′ west. It was the eighty-ninth day since Chase and his men had left the *Essex,* and at noon they came within sight of Masafuera. Chase had succeeded in navigating them across a 2,500-mile stretch of ocean with astonishing accuracy. Even though they had sometimes been so weak that they could not steer their boat, they had somehow managed to sail almost to within sight of their intended destination. In just a few days the *Indian* would be in the Chilean port of Valparaiso.

Trailing behind on a towline was the whaleboat that had served the Nantucketers so well. Captain Crozier hoped to sell the old boat in Valparaiso and establish a fund for the men's relief. But the next night the weather blew up to a gale, and the boat, empty of men for the first time in three months, was lost.

Three hundred miles to the south, Pollard and Ramsdell sailed on. For the next five days they pushed east, until by February 23, the ninety-fourth day since leaving the wreck, they were approaching the island of St. Mary's just off the Chilean coast. Over a year before, this had been the *Essex*'s first landfall after rounding Cape Horn. Pollard and Ramsdell were on the verge of completing an irregular circle with a diameter of more than three thousand miles.

It had been twelve days since the death of Barzillai Ray. They had long since eaten the last scrap of his flesh. The two famished men now cracked open the bones of their shipmates—beating them against the stone on the bottom of the boat and smashing them with the boat's hatchet—and ate the marrow, which contained the fat their bodies so desperately needed.

Pollard would later remember these as "days of horror and despair." Both of them were so weak that they could barely lift their hands. They were drifting in and out of consciousness. It is not uncommon for castaways who have been many days at sea and suffered both physically and emotionally to lapse into what has been called "a sort of collective confabulation," in which the survivors exist in a shared fantasy world. Delusions may include comforting scenes from home—perhaps, in the case of Pollard and Ramsdell, a sunny June day on the Nantucket Commons during the sheepshearing festival. Survivors may find themselves in conversation with deceased shipmates and family members as they lose all sense of time.

For Pollard and Ramsdell, it was the bones—gifts from the men they had known and loved—that became their obsession. They stuffed their pockets with finger bones; they sucked the sweet marrow from the splintered ribs and thighs. And they sailed on, the compass card wavering toward east.

Suddenly they heard a sound: men shouting and then silence as shadows fell across them and then the rustle of wind in sails and the creaking of spars and rigging. They looked up, and there were faces.

Of the *Dauphin*'s twenty-one-man crew, at least three—Dimon Peters, Asnonkeets, and Joseph Squibb—were Wampanoags from Cape Cod and Martha's Vineyard. As children they had been taught a legend about the discovery of Nantucket that told of how, long before the arrival of the Europeans, a huge eagle appeared over a village on Cape Cod. The eagle would swoop down out of the sky and carry off children in its talons, then disappear over the waters to the south. Finally the villagers asked a benevolent giant named Maushop to find out where the eagle was taking their children. Maushop set off to the south, wading through the water until he came to an island he had never seen before. After searching all over the island, he found the bones of the children piled high beneath a large tree.

On the morning of February 23, the crew of the *Dauphin* made a similar discovery. Looking down from a restless forest of spars and sails, they saw two men in a whaleboat filled with bones.

The men were not much more than skeletons themselves, and the story that would be passed from ship to ship in the months ahead was that they were "found sucking the bones of their dead mess mates, which they were loath to part with." The *Dauphin's* captain, Zimri Coffin, ordered his men to lower a boat and bring the two survivors aboard. Like Chase, Lawrence, and Nickerson before them, Pollard and Ramsdell were too weak to stand and had to be lifted up to the whaleship's deck. Both men were, in the words of a witness, "very low" when first brought aboard. But after being given some food, Pollard made an astonishing recovery.

At around five o'clock that evening, the *Dauphin* spoke the whaleship *Diana* from New York. The *Diana's* captain, Aaron Paddack, toward the end of a successful voyage, joined Captain Coffin for dinner. Also joining them was Captain George Pollard, Jr., formerly of the *Essex*.

Like many survivors, Pollard was animated by a fierce and desperate compulsion to tell his story. Just as the gaunt, wild-eyed Ancient Mariner of Coleridge's poem poured forth each harrowing detail to the Wedding Guest, so did Pollard tell them everything: how his ship had been attacked "in a most deliberate manner" by a large sperm whale; how they had headed south in the whaleboats; how his boat had been attacked once again, this time by "an unknown fish"; and how they had found an island where a "few fowl and fish was the only sustenance." He told them that three men still remained on the island. He told of how the rest of them had set out for Easter Island and how Matthew Joy had been the first to die. He told of how Chase's boat had become separated from them in the night and how, in rapid succession, four black men "became food for the remainder." Then he told how, after separating from the second mate's boat, he and his crew "were reduced to the deplorable necessity of casting lots." He told of how the lot fell to Owen Coffin, "who with composure and resignation submitted to his fate."

Lastly he told of the death of Barzillai Ray, and how Ray's corpse had kept both him and Ramsdell alive.

Later that night, once he had returned to the *Diana,* Captain Paddack wrote it all down, calling Pollard's account "the most distressing narrative that ever came to my knowledge." The question now became one of how the survivors would fare in the dark shadow of their story.

The Custom of the Sea
From *The Custom of the Sea*

BY NEIL HANSON

No listing of cannibalism and survival at sea can be complete without the story of the ill-fated yacht, *Mignonette*. In 1884, she set sail from Southhampton, England, bound for Sydney, Australia. As Neil Hanson narrates in his riveting *The Custom of the Sea,* the *Mignonette* was halfway through the 12,000 mile voyage when she was overturned and sunk by a freak forty-foot wave. Adrift with his three-man crew in a small lifeboat, Captain Tom Dudley made a decision that the weakest of his crew, a young cabin boy named Richard Parker, must be sacrificed to keep the others alive.

When they shared out the next ration of turnip, Tom held his piece in his mouth as long as he could, but most of the moisture had already evaporated from the tin and within a few minutes it felt as rough and dry as pumice. It was all he could do to chew and swallow it.

A lassitude had crept over them all. Their throats were so tight and sore that they barely spoke, staring into the green water, each alone with his thoughts. Towards dusk they ate the last of the first tin of turnips and shared the dribble of viscous, almost congealed fluid in the bottom of the tin. It was a relief when nightfall shrouded the others from Tom's sight.

Early the next morning, 9 July, Brooks saw a dark shape on the surface, just off their bow. For a moment terror gripped him, certain that the shark had returned to the attack. Then he recognized the shape of the creature and roused the others with a shout. 'A turtle! To the oars before it dives.'

The turtle was sleeping on the surface, no more than twenty yards off the port side of the boat. A few strokes of the oars brought them within range. Tom gripped the back of Stephens's shirt as he hung over the side of the boat, his fingers scrabbling for grip on the turtle's flippers as it struggled to break free.

Stephens lost his hold on the front flipper and threw himself further forward, his head dipping below the surface as he grabbed for it again. Then he straightened up, coughing and gasping, but clinging to the turtle. He dragged it over the side and dropped it on to the bottom boards, where it lay helpless on its back, its flippers waving.

Tom pulled out his knife. "We must drink the blood," he said. "It will do us more good than the meat."

He picked up the empty tin of turnips, then set it aside and reached for the chronometer case. Stephens held the turtle still as Tom slipped the case under its head and severed its neck with a single slash of his knife. Its struggles in its death throes sent blood pulsing into the metal bowl.

Craning his neck to watch Tom, Brooks had allowed the dinghy to drift beam-on to the waves. The next one broke over the gunwale, flooding the bottom of the boat and filling the chronometer case with sea-water. The men stared at it aghast.

Richard leaned forward. "It is only a little water, surely we can drink it still?"

Tom hesitated for a second, then threw it over the side. "It is contaminated with sea-water. It will send us mad."

Stephens stared at the red stain merging with the green water, then rounded on Brooks. "If you had minded your work, we, not the fishes, would have been drinking that."

Brooks clenched his fists and half rose to face him. "You mind your words or you'll be the one feeding the fishes."

Tom was again stooping over the turtle, catching the last few drops of blood as they dripped from its neck. He did not raise his eyes, but his voice cut through their shouts. "You'll both sit down. Fighting amongst ourselves will only hasten our end." He held out the case. "There's little enough. Each man must take only his fair share."

He handed it first to the boy, then passed it to Stephens and Brooks, and took the last and smallest share himself. There was barely a mouthful of the congealing blood remaining. It was warm, sweet and sickly and hard to force down but he felt a little strength returning almost as soon as he had swallowed it.

Richard baled out the dinghy, then Tom set down the chronometer case in the bottom of the boat and began to butcher the turtle. He severed the tough flippers and laid them in a row on one of the crossmembers, then tore the the turtle from its shell.

He removed the head and entrails and threw them over the side, but he dropped the heart and liver into the metal case and cut them in quarters. All four men fell on them ravenously, despite the fishy stench. Almost at once, Tom felt stronger.

He cut the turtle's flesh into strips and Stephens hung them around the boat to dry. There were only a few pounds of meat, but they were so overjoyed at their good fortune that, in the euphoria of the moment, they ate the rest of the second tin of turnips as well, savouring the sensation and the sweetness.

For over a week the gales continued. They were driven stern-first by a south-easterly gale—the trade winds that had failed them on the *Mignonette*—unable to turn and run before the wind for fear of being swamped. Even with the sea-anchor out, the bow of the dinghy constantly sheered off a few degrees either side of the wind. One man worked a steering oar at the stern, fighting to hold the dinghy head-on to each rising wave, but they broke constantly over the bows. At times they were a few seconds from foundering as the water level inside the boat rose to within inches of the gunwales. Everyone joined in frantic baling of the boat with anything that came to hand—the chronometer case, an empty tin or the wooden box that housed the sextant—until the water level began to drop again. Finally, on 13 July, the storm at last blew itself out, the seas slackened and they slumped into an exhausted sleep.

Each dawn Tom dragged himself up to search the horizon for a sail. Although he knew there was no land within hundreds of miles he could not stop himself from scanning the sky for the greenish tint of light reflected from the shallow water of a lagoon, or a telltale cloud formation—a patch of fixed cumulus in a clear sky or a thin line of the cloud—that indicated an island or a coastline nearby. There were no such signs on that day or on any of the succeeding days, only the endless march of the waves to the horizon.

At each passing squall or cloud they held out their oilskin capes to catch the rainwater. They put them on back to front, and held out their arms, as Stephens later said, "waiting with burning throats and stomachs, and praying to the Almighty for water until the squall had passed. If we caught a little, how thankful we were."

Many squalls seemed almost to mock them. On several occasions rain pocked the surface of the sea within sight of the dinghy, yet not a drop fell on them. The first of any rain that did fall had to be cast away, used only to clean the salt from their oilskins, and few squalls yielded more than a mouthful of drinkable water. Often even that would be spoiled by waves breaking over the boat before they could drink, but one storm gave them each about a pint.

As he drank it down, forcing himself to sip it and roll each mouthful around his mouth before swallowing it, Tom felt saliva in his mouth and the constriction of his throat ease for the first time in days.

It was to be the last rain for four days, however, and soon they were again suffering in the savage heat. They could talk for no more than a few seconds before their hoarse whispers turned into hacking coughs.

Tom cut off a bone button from his oilskins and placed it in his mouth, hoping it would ease his thirst like a pebble in the desert. It seemed to soften a little in his mouth and there was a faint taste on his tongue. As he sucked it over the next few hours the button grew smaller and eventually dissolved completely. He cut off another and another over the succeeding days, until they had all been used.

Every couple of hours they rinsed their mouths and gargled with sea-water. Late one burning afternoon, Tom thought he saw the boy swallowing a mouthful. "Lad, we are all driven mad with thirst, but you must not drink that."

The boy's sallow cheeks flushed. "Surely it will do no harm if we just drink a little of it."

"Regard it as the poison that will kill you."

The heat troubled them as much as their thirst. Their exposed flesh was burned an angry red, pocked with white blisters, and the rubbing of their salt-encrusted flannel shirts was agonizing to their skin.

To cool themselves, Stephens suggested soaking their flannel shirts, wringing them out and putting them on again. He and Brooks tried the experiment, but they soaked them again too close to dusk and shivered uncontrollably in their wet clothes during the night.

On the following days they all stripped naked and took turns to hang from the gunwale and dip themselves once or twice in the water. They did it one at a time, for only a few seconds, while the others remained in the boat on watch, for every time they bathed in this way, sharks would soon circle the boat, as if able to sense the naked bodies in the water.

The cool water on their skins refreshed them and even slaked their thirst a little, but as the days went by, they became too weak even to undress themselves. They could only ladle a little water over their heads and the effort required even for that task left them exhausted.

As Tom took his turn on watch, he looked with horror on the bodies of his crew. Their ribs and hip-bones were already showing through their wasting flesh. There were angry, ulcerating sores on their elbows, knees and feet, their lips were cracked and their tongues blackened and swollen.

They had continued to live on the turtleflesh for a week, even though some of the fat became putrid in the fierce heat. Tom cut out the worst parts and threw them overboard, but they devoured the rest and when the flesh was finished, they chewed the bones and leathery skin.

They ate the last rancid scraps of it on the evening of 17 July. When he had finished chewing on his piece, Tom looked at the others. "If no boat comes soon, we shall have to draw lots."

Richard darted him a nervous look, too scared to meet his eye. Neither of the others showed any surprise at the subject Tom had raised. There was a long silence. "We would be better to die together," Brooks said. After a moment, Stephens nodded.

"So let it be," Tom said, "but it is hard for four to die when perhaps one might save the rest."

"A boat will come," Brooks said.

"So it may, but if one does not, or if it passes us by . . ."

The boy gave him a frightened look. "Why would a ship pass us by?"

"If they see four mouths to feed," Brooks said, "they may not stop."

Richard turned towards Tom. "Surely no Christian men would leave us to die for want of a scrap of their bread and water."

Tom saw the plea in the boy's eyes, but knowing the truth of Brooks's words, he could only nod his head. "If the seas are high or the wind strong, they may fear wrecking themselves if they come to our aid."

Brooks interrupted him. "But we have all heard tales enough of ships that have sailed by a wreck though the water was as flat and calm as the Itchen on a summer's day. Some look away and pretend they have not heard, though the poor wretches plead, cry, rail and curse against them. Others, more brazen . . ." His voice trailed away as Richard buried his face in his hands and began to sob, a terrible dry, rasping sound. No one moved to console him, each man too wrapped in his own dark thoughts.

As the boy's hoarse sobs still echoed through the boat, Stephens rounded on Brooks. "What use was there in upsetting the boy with your foolish talk?"

"I spoke no more than the truth."

They began a senseless, bitter argument. Fists clenched, they glared at each other and might have fought had Tom not interposed himself and cursed them both to silence.

Brooks retreated to his sanctuary in the bow. He lay down and wormed his way under the scrap of canvas covering it, hiding his head like a child burrowing under his bedsheets, and spoke no more to anyone that day.

"We were now in our worst straits," Stephens later said. "We used to sit and look at each other gradually wasting away, hunger and thirst in each face. The nights were the worst time. We used to dread them very much; they seemed never to end. We were so weak and cramped that we could hardly move. If we did get any sleep our dreams would be of eating and drinking."

That night a rain squall passed over them and they caught some more water. Tom's hands were shaking so much that he spilled much of it as he tried to transfer some from his oilskin to the chronometer case, hoping to save it for a later moment.

There was no rain on the next day or the next, Sunday, 20 July, when Tom at last prevailed on them to give up their shirts. Stephens and the boy seemed past caring, lying listless in the bottom of the boat. Brooks began to argue again, then shrugged. "What does it matter? We're doomed anyway. We'll die of sunstroke or thirst, but die we shall." He took off his shirt and handed it to Tom.

Tom let Richard keep his shirt, but lashed the other three together, two above and one below, to form a triangular sail. They used an oar for a mast and split one of the boards for a yardarm. Tom hammered the back of his knife with the baler to open a crack in the wood, then forced it apart with the edge of the chronometer case until the board split along its length.

The shrouds and stays were fashioned out of the heart and outer strands of the boat's painter. With the makeshift sail rigged, the stern seats lashed up and a strong south-easterly blowing, they found the boat would run sternways before the wind, as long as there was not too much of a swell, and they made two or three knots.

Tom still had the burning determination within him to survive, but he could tell from the faces of the others that the faint hope of rescue to which they had clung was now extinguished.

The sting of salt on their skin added to the pain of their sunburn and together with the salt-water boils from which they were all suffering made even the slightest pressure unbearable. As they crawled about the cramped dinghy, taking their turns to steer and bail, it was impossible not to brush against each other, but the pain it caused was so agonizing that Stephens screamed aloud whenever he was touched.

When he asked to borrow Tom's knife and began scratching a further message in the lid of the sextant case, Tom knew that Stephens had given up his last hope of survival. Stephens scrawled his estimate of their position over the previous few days and then added:

> To whoever picks this up Sunday July 20th pm We Thomas Dudley, Edwin Stephens, Edmund Brooks and Richard Parker, the crew of the Yacht *Mignonette* which foundered on Saturday the 5th. of July, have been in our little dingy 15 days. We have neither food or water and are greatly reduced. We suppose our Latitude to be 25° South our Longitude 28° W May the Lord have mercy upon us Please forward this to Southampton.

That night the wind dropped and in the calmer conditions Richard took the night watch. Tom and Brooks were asleep but Stephens was only dozing when he heard an unfamiliar sound and opened his eyes. Richard was leaning over the side, scooping up sea-water in one of the empty tins. He drank some of it then looked round. He started as he saw the mate watching him.

Stephens put his finger to his lips, then worked his way back to the stern. He bent close to the boy's ear and whispered, "How does it taste, Dick?"

"Not so bad."

Stephens glanced behind him, then took the tin and swallowed a mouthful. He coughed and spluttered, then spat out the remainder. "It burns my throat like fire. It's madness, Dick, you should not do that again."

"Then what would you have me do—die of thirst instead?"

Stephens crawled back to his berth and huddled down in the bottom of the boat, but just before he closed his eyes, he again saw Richard lower the tin into the water.

Tom was woken by the sound of the boy retching and vomiting over the side. Brooks grabbed the steering oar and Richard fell back and lay on the bottom of the dinghy, gasping for breath.

Tom put his hand on the boy's forehead. It was burning hot. "What ails you, boy?"

"I—I drank sea-water."

"How much did you drink?"

"I don't know, perhaps three pints."

"Then you're worse than a fool," Brooks said.

Richard began to cry. No tears came from his matted eyes but his chest heaved with dry sobs. "I had to drink something."

Brooks hesitated, then put a hand on his shoulder. "Cheer up, Dicky, it will all come right."

He shook his head. "We shall all die."

They left him where he lay and over the next few hours his condition worsened. He began to suffer from violent diarrhoea and several times Tom and Brooks had to help him to squat over the gunwale as his body was shaken by spasms. Then he crawled back into the bottom of the boat and lay bent double from the pains in his stomach.

That night he became delirious, shouting and ranting, and he began slipping in and out of consciousness. Each time he woke, he said the same thing, "I want a ship to get on board."

The ship was all they ever heard him speak about. Whatever the frictions between them from time to time, the three others all shared an affection for the boy and did their best to lift his spirits, but he seemed barely to recognize them or hear their cracked voices. In one of his rare intervals of lucidity, he tried to drink some of his urine but was unable to do so, gagging and choking on it instead. He slumped down again.

There was a question in Tom's eyes as he glanced at the others, but neither man would meet his gaze. "Something must be done," he said.

Brooks looked up. "Let us not talk of that further. Another ship will come."

Tom shook his head and looked away. He pressed his fingers into the swollen flesh of his legs. The impressed marks turned white and remained visible for a long time after he released his grip. As he stared at them he felt something loose in his mouth. One of his teeth had dropped out. He spat it into his hand and threw it into the sea. He tested each of his other teeth with his fingers. All of them were loose in their sockets, barely held by his soft, pulpy gums.

Despite the positive face he took care to present to his crew, he was now beginning to despair. He took out the note he had begun writing to Philippa the morning after the shipwreck and scrawled a few more lines with the stub of his pencil.

9th picked up turtle. 21st July we have been here 17 days and have no food. We are all four living hoping to get passing ship if not dear we must soon die. Mr Thomson will put everything right if you go to him and I am sorry dear I ever started such a trip but I was doing it for our best. Thought so at the time. You know dear I should so much like to be spared you would find I should lead a Christian life for the remainder of my days. If ever this note reaches your hands dear you know the last of your Tom and loving husband. I am sorry things are gone against us thus far but hope to meet you and all our dear children in heaven. Do love them for my sake dear bless them and you all. I love you all dearly you know but it is God's will if I am to part from you but have hopes of being saved. We were about 1300 miles from Cape Town when the affair happened. So goodbye and God bless you all and may He provide for you all. Your loving husband, Tom Dudley.

There was no rain again that day. They lay sprawled in the boat without speaking, neither awake nor asleep, their minds drifting. Tom was astonished at the breadth and depth of his recall. Long-forgotten events, some great, some small, returned to him with crystal clarity. He heard the voices of childhood in his head and saw the village children scrambling over the fields, marshes and saltings. He saw Philippa at the piano in their first house in Oreston and heard every note of the songs she sang.

When he fell asleep, he was tortured by the same constant recurring dreams—soft rainfall speckling the surface of the Blackwater, morning mist hanging over Woodrolfe Creek, the cool shade of the trees in the sunlit meadows where he and Philippa used to walk, and the lemonade, cold from the cellar, that she would bring to him as he sat in the garden at Sutton and the children played in the grass around his feet.

Then he would jerk awake, dragged back to the present by his thirst and the pains in his body. To move was agony, but to remain still for long was an impossibility, as the rough boards dug into him and his salt-encrusted clothes chafed at his sores.

Even the effort of swallowing his urine tortured him. It was thick, yellow and stained with blood, and his throat seemed so dry and constricted that he could barely force it down without choking. It gave him no relief from his thirst.

By the following morning the men's mouths had become so parched and their tongues so swollen, they could hardly speak at all. Richard still lay in the bottom of the boat drifting between consciousness and oblivion.

Tom looked down at him, then glanced at the others. "Better for one to die than for all of us." Even to speak was torture, the words seeming to tear at his dry, cracked throat. "I am willing to take my chance with the rest, but we must draw lots."

"No. We shall see a ship tomorrow," Stephens said.

"And if we do not?"

No one replied.

The day passed without rain and when a shower did come just after midnight, it barely troubled their upturned mouths or dampened their capes.

Although he hardly slept at all, Tom's mind drifted constantly. Mirages began to appear to him. He saw lush islands and snow-capped mountains rising sheer from the sea, and a bank of haze lying on the water became the chalk cliffs of Kent. Sailing ships bore down on the dinghy and he was pulling himself upright, heart pounding with joy, when the vision faded again, leaving only the endless wastes of empty ocean.

Then he saw his father standing on the end of a jetty, beckoning to him. He felt drawn to the side of the dinghy and had to fight the urge to slip over the side into the water. He shook his head and shouted, "No, I cannot do it," in his cracked voice. The others barely stirred as he slumped down again.

Whenever he did lapse into unconsciousness, he dreamed of walking out of the dinghy across the sea to a beach or a waiting boat. Once he woke to find that his legs were already over the gunwale, his feet trailing in the water. The discovery barely shocked him; sometimes he saw himself slipping downwards as the green waters closed over him, and dreamed that he was already dead.

The next morning dawned hot and leaden once more. Tom leaned forward and laid his hand on the boy's forehead. It was still burning hot and his breathing was shallow and erratic. "Dick? Do you hear me, boy?" he said, his voice a cracked whisper.

There was no reply.

Tom say back on his haunches and looked at the others. "You both know what must be done."

"Better for us all to die than for that," Brooks said.

"Even when the death of one might save the lives of the rest? You are a bachelor, but Stephens and I are family men. It is not just our own lives, we have the fate of others to consider. Would you have us see our children cast into destitution, even the workhouse, when we have the means at hand to save ourselves and keep them from that fate?"

"I, too, have a—" Brooks began, then fell silent. "At least wait for him to die," he said. "Let us not have the boy's murder on our consciences."

"But if we wait for him to die, his blood will congeal in his veins. We must kill him if we are to drink the blood. And it must be done, it may save three lives."

Brooks again shook his head. He lay down in the bow and hid his head under the canvas.

Stephens did not speak, but Tom read a different message in his eyes.

That night Brooks had the watch from midnight. While he steered, Tom and Stephens sat in the bow, talking in whispers.

"What's to be done?" Tom said. "I believe the boy is dying. Brooks is a bachelor—or says he is—but you have a wife and five children, and I have a wife and three children. Human flesh has been eaten before."

Stephens hesitated. "See what daylight brings forth."

"But if sunrise brings no rain and no sign of a sail?"

Stephens stared out over the dark water, then muttered, "God forgive me," and nodded his assent.

Soon after dawn Tom and Stephens hauled themselves up in turn on the improvised rigging and searched the horizon for a sail. There was none in sight under the cloudless sky. Richard still lay in the bottom of the boat, with his head on the starboard side and his feet on the port side, his arm across his face. He was rapidly sinking into unconsciousness.

"We shall have to draw lots," Stephens said. "It is the custom of the sea."

Richard lay comatose in the bottom of the dinghy and gave no sign that he had heard Stephens's words. Brooks remained silent and Tom did not wait for a reply from him. He pulled out his knife and whittled four thin slivers of wood from the gunwale of the dinghy. He trimmed three to equal length and cut the other one a half-inch shorter.

"We'll have to draw Dick's lot for him," Stephens said.

The three men exchanged looks between themselves. Tom laid the pieces of wood across his palm, the ends protruding beyond his index finger. The shortest lot was on the right. Palm open, he showed them to Stephens and Brooks. Then, without changing their positions, he closed his hand over the bottom ends of the slivers and held them out.

Brooks licked his blackened lips and, as Stephens hesitated, he reached past him and took the left hand lot. Stephens took the next. Tom was about to complete the ritual by taking the next when he paused, looked the others in the eye and then threw the remaining slivers into the sea.

"Why go through this charade?" he said. "What is to be gained when one lies dying anyway? We all know what must be done. Let us be honest men about it, at least."

No further word was exchanged, but Stephens looked down at the boy and nodded. Both then turned towards Brooks. He hesitated, then bowed his head.

"Who is to do it?"

"I cannot," Brooks said.

Stephens shook his head. "Nor I."

"Then I shall have to," Tom said.

He stared at Brooks. "You had better go forward and have a rest. Stephens, take over the watch."

Stephens took the steering oar, while Brooks moved towards the bow and lay down, once more hiding his face under the canvas sheet.

Shading his eyes against the glare of the burning sun, Tom took hold of the shrouds and pulled himself up to search the horizon all around them for any trace of a ship. Nothing broke the glassy surface of the sea.

He remained motionless for a moment, offering a prayer for the boy's soul, and asking forgiveness of his Maker. Then he placed the chronometer case next to Richard's head, took out his knife and opened the blade. The sunlight glinted from the blue steel.

He glanced towards Stephens. "Hold the boy's legs if he struggles."

Richard had appeared to be unconscious but his eyes flickered open at the words. His pupils had lost almost all their pigment and were the colour of skimmed milk. Tom doubted whether he could even still see.

"What—me, sir?" he said.

Tom made no reply. He placed the knife against the boy's neck. Trying to close his mind to what he was about to do, he began reciting under his breath the instructions in *The Steward's Handbook* that he had been forced to learn years before on his first voyage as cook-steward. " 'Proceed immediately to bleed the beast. This is done by cutting up the gullet and severing the arteries and veins on each side of the neck, near to the head. The blood will now flow out quite freely.' "

He took a handful of the boy's hair in his left hand, holding his head still against the boards, then plunged the knife into his neck. He jerked the blade sideways, severing an artery and slicing into the windpipe, then dropped the knife and held the metal bowl against Richard's neck.

The boy did not even cry out, but as blood began to pump from the wound in a slow, palsied beat, his arms flailed and a terrible, wet sucking sound came from his torn windpipe. His white eyes stared sightlessly up at Tom.

He tried to shut his ears to the sound of the boy's death throes, but they echoed in his mind long after the noises had at last ceased and the twitching body lay still. Only a dribble of blood still flowed from the wound.

The blood he had collected in the chronometer case was thick and viscous and already beginning to congeal. They began to drink it in turn. Brooks scrambled from under his canvas cover. "Give me a drop of that," he said, and they shared it with him.

As soon as they had finished the blood, Tom and Stephens stripped the clothes from the boy's body. Tom then pushed the knife into the stomach just below the breastbone and forced it downwards, opening a deep slit in Richard's belly. Even strengthened a little by the blood, he was so weak and slow that the cut seemed to take minutes to complete.

He paused, his breath coming in hoarse gasps. " 'Now make a slit in the stomach and run the knife right up to the tail. Remove the fat from round the intestines and then pull out the intestines, paunch, and liver. Cut the gall bladder off the liver right away. Turn the kidney fat over and remove the kidneys. Now cut through the diaphragm, commonly called the skirt, which separates the organs within the chest from the intestines, and remove the lungs, heart, and thorax.' "

He reached into the still warm chest cavity and pulled out the heart and liver. He put them in the chronometer case and cut them up. The three men ate them ravenously, squabbling over the pieces like dogs.

When they had eaten the last scrap, Tom raised his gaze from the bloodstained bowl and stared at the others. Their faces were smeared with blood and their eyes were wild. He shuddered, knowing that his own visage was no different, but he could already feel strength flowing back into his body. " 'When this has all been done, get some warm water and wash out the carcass, and any blood that may be on it must be washed off.' "

He leaned over the gunwale and rinsed the blood from his face, then sent Brooks aft to steer the boat while Stephens helped him to butcher the body. Not wanting to see the dead boy's face in front of him as he worked, Tom first cut off the head and threw it overboard. His fingers slippery with blood, he worked as fast as he could, hacking off strips of flesh, which Stephens washed in the sea and laid across the crossbeams to dry.

At first Tom used the wooden cross-member as a butcher's block, but fearing that he might further damage the boat's thin planking as he hacked and sawed at the body with his knife, he did the heavier cutting—parting the joints and severing the tendons—against the brass crutches of the oars. It took three hours to complete the grisly task.

The larger bones, and Richard's feet, genitals and intestines, were also thrown overboard. They looked on in horror as, astern of the boat, sharks thrashed the water into a pink froth, fighting over the bloody fragments. One was bitten in the head by a larger shark as they fought over some part of the body. In an instant, every one of the pack of sharks circling the remains had turned on the wounded creature. It was ripped apart in little more than a minute.

Even when the blood and entrails had been consumed or dissipated by the waves, sharks continued to track the dinghy. A fin showed above the water from time to time and there was a grinding thud as one broke surface right alongside the dinghy, sending it crabbing sideways. Tom tried to drive it off by hitting it with an oar, but already weak and further exhausted by his struggle to butcher the carcass, he barely had the strength to raise it above his head.

Brooks took over, and though he did not manage to hit the shark, the noise of the oar banging on the water was enough to scare it off. From time to time they glimpsed the sharks astern of the dinghy, and even when unseen, all of them continued to fear their presence.

Part Three
Epic Tales of Cannibalism on Land

Bolters and Bushrangers
From *The Fatal Shore*

Australia in the eighteenth and nineteenth centuries was one vast and brutal
penal colony for the English and Irish convicts transported there, often for the
pettiest imaginable crimes. Escape was almost impossible, but that didn't keep the
toughened transportees from trying. The story of one escapee turned cannibal is
related in Robert Hughes's magnificent history of Australia, *The Fatal Shore*.

Ever since 1821, when Lieutenant-Governor Sorell had pitched
this dreaded prison settlement on the isolated west coast of Van
Dieman's Land, convicts had been trying to get away from it,
mostly on foot. In 1822 and 1823, one man in ten disappeared.
In 1824, the rate rose to nearly one in seven. They went inland, trying to
reach the settled and farmed districts to the east, and most of them died. In
the long list of Macquarie Harbor absconders for the first six years of settlement, only eight carry a brief remark like "Reported to have reached
the cultivated part of the island: this requires confirmation." The rest is a
gray official litany, punctuated by sparks of saturnine humor. Timothy
Crawley, Richard Morris, John Newton, June 2, 1824: "Seized the soldiers' boat, provicions, fire-arms &c., and supposed to have perished in
their way across the interior. The boat was afterwards found moored to a
Stump, and written upon her stern, with chalk, 'to be Sold.' " But the
usual requiem was "Supposed to have perished in the woods."

Only one man escaped from Macquarie Harbor twice. His
name was Alexander Pearce (1790–1824), a little pockmarked, blue-
eyed Irishman from County Monaghan who had been transported
for seven years at the Armagh Assizes in 1819, for stealing six pairs of
shoes. He had arrived in Van Diemen's Land in 1820, and as an as-

signed servant he gave continuous trouble to his masters by running away, stealing and getting drunk. He soon learned enough bush skills to "stay out" for three months at a stretch with some other absconders. Flogging did not impress him. Eventually, in 1822, he was sent to Macquarie Harbor for forging a two-pound money order and absconding from service. On September 20, 1822, Pearce seized an open boat from Kelly's Basin on Macquarie Harbor, where he had been working in a sawpit gang. Seven other convicts piled into the craft with him. Two of them had already tried to escape from Van Diemen's Land by stealing a schooner moored in the Derwent estuary: Matthew Travers, an Irishman under life sentence of transportation, and Robert Greenhill, a sailor from Middlesex. For that failed escape, they had been sent to Macquarie Harbor. The others were an ex-soldier, William Dalton (perjury in Gibraltar, fourteen years); a highway robber, Thomas Bodenham; William Kennelly, alias Bill Cornelius, transported for seven years and re-sentenced to Macquarie Harbor for an escape attempt; John Mather, a young Scottish baker, working a seven-year sentence and then sent to Macquarie Harbor for forging a £15 money order; and a man called "Little Brown," whose Christian name is unknown and who cannot, due to the commonness of his surname, be identified.

Flogged with the adrenaline of escape, the eight men rowed across the harbor, ran the boat ashore, smashed its bottom with a stolen axe, and set out on foot. At first they made good time through the dank maze of the shore forest, lugging their axes and their meager rations. They spent the night on the slopes of Mount Sorell, not daring to light a fire, and struck east the next morning toward the Derwent River, where they planned to steal a schooner, sail it downstream past Hobart and out into Storm Bay and so "proceed home," 14,000 miles to England. The first leg of their route lay across the Darwin Plateau, keeping to the north of the Gordon River.

Before them, although they did not know it, lay some of the worst country in Australia. Even today, bushwalkers rarely venture into the mountains between Macquarie Harbor and the inland plains: fold after fold, scarp on scarp, with giant trees growing to a hundred feet from clefts in the steep rock where, clambering along rotted limbs or floundering through the entangling ferns and creepers, one cannot possibly move in a straight line. The convicts struggled along in a gray, dripping twilight from dawn to dusk, with one man beating the scrub in front "to make the road." At night, like exhausted troglodytes, afraid of winds and shadows, they lit a fire in the cleft of a rock and huddled around it to sleep as best they could. Within a week, the weather turned to gales and sleet and their little store of tinder was soaked. Then they finished the last of their rations. Hungry, cold and failing, the band struggled for another two days through "a very rough country . . . in a very weak state for want of provisions."

But now the fugitives were straggling. "Little Brown . . . was the worst walker of any; he always fell behind, and then kept cooing [sic] so that we said we would leave him behind if he could not keep up better." No man felt able to gather all the wood for a fire. In the feeble hysteria of exhaustion, they began to squabble about who should do it; in the end, each convict scraped together enough twigs for himself and eight little fires were lit. Kennelly made what might or might not have been meant as a joke. "I am so weak," he said to Pearce and Greenhill, "that I could eat a piece of a man."

They thought about that all night, and "in the morning," Pearce's narrative goes on,

> there were four of us for a feast. Bob Greenhill was the first who introduced it, and said he had seen the like done before, and that it eat much like a little pork.

John Mather protested. It would be murder, he said; and useless, too, since they might not be able to choke the flesh down. Greenhill overrode him:

> "I will warrant you," said Greenhill, "I will well do it first myself and eat the first of it; but you must all lend a hand, so that you may all be equal in the crime." We then consulted who should fall. Greenhill said, "Dalton; as he volunteered to be a flogger, we will kill him."

In these flat declarative outlines, the scene might come from an Elizabethan revenge-tragedy: the conclave, the ritual to overcome the great taboo, the literary diction, the avenging choice of the flogger as victim. Indeed, it may be too pat; Dalton was never a flogger at Macquarie Harbor, and other "literary" touches in the narrative may come from the amanuensis to whom Pearce eventually dictated his story. But in any case, Dalton was killed. He fell asleep at about three in the morning, and Greenhill's axe

> struck him on the head, and he never spoke a word after . . . Matthew Travers with a knife also came and cut his throat, and bled him; we then dragged him to a distance, and cut off his clothes, and tore out his inside,

and cut off his head; then Matthew Travers and Greenhill put his heart and liver on the fire and eat it before it was right warm; they asked the rest would they have any, but they would not have any that night.

But the next morning, hunger won. They had been without food for four days. Dalton's flesh was carved and doled out into seven roughly equal portions, and the band got moving again.

Brown was walking slower and slower; he must have reflected as he limped along that he, the weakest, would be next. Kennelly, too, was afraid for his life. And so the two of them fell back, and silently disappeared in the forest mazes of the Engineer Range, hoping to get back to Macquarie Harbor. Realizing that their story "would hang us all," the others tried to catch them but failed. On October 12, Brown and Kennelly were found half-dead from exposure on the shore of Macquarie Harbor, still with pieces of human flesh in their pockets. Brown died in the prison hospital on October 15, and Kennelly four days later.

Now five convicts were left. They reached the Franklin River, swollen with rain, and spent two days trying to cross it; Pearce, Greenhill and Mather went across first and dragged the other two over with the help of a long pole. Mather was crippled with dysentery and the others "were scarcely able to move, for we were so cold and wet." But they struggled on across the Deception Range and then the Surveyor Range after that, and on October 15 they saw below them a fine open valley, probably the Loddon Plains. Here, in the long grass by a creek, thoughts of fresh food rose again. It was Bodenham's turn to die. As he slept, Greenhill split his skull. Ten years later, the first official explorer to reach the Loddon Plains, a surveyor, would find human bones in this valley.

Four men were left, and they kept marching. By about October 22, they had apparently reached the first line of the Western Tiers and before them lay "a very fine country," full of "many kangaroos and emus, and game of all kinds"; but they had no hunting weapons, and the frustration of starving while watching the mobs of shy gray marsupials bounding invulnerably past must have been overpowering. "We then said to ourselves," Pearce declared, "that we would all die together before anything should happen."

But Greenhill had no intention of dying together with anyone, and Mather was very apprehensive. He and Pearce "went to one side, and Mather said, Pearce, let us go on by ourselves; you see what kind of a cove Greenhill is; he would kill his father before he would fast one day." But on that open button-grass moor, which may have been the King William Plains, they could not have lost Greenhill. Since he carried the only axe they had left, he could not be killed; and none of the famished men could hobble faster than the rest. Thus bound together, they went on; and around the last week in October (from here, the chronology of Pearce's accounts grows hazier), they stopped by a little creek and lit a fire to boil the last of Bodenham, "which scarcely kept the Faculties in Motion."

Mather could not eat his share. He had gathered some fern roots, which he boiled and wolfed down, but

> he found it would not rest on his stomach (no wonder) for such a Mess It could not be expected would ever digest in any Mortal whatever, which occasioned him to vomit to ease his Stomach & while in the act of discharging it from his Chest, Greenhill still showing his spontaneous habit of bloodshed seized the Axe & crept behind him gave him a blow on the head.

It did not kill Mather. He jumped up and grappled with Greenhill, wresting the axe from him. Pearce and Travers managed, for a time, to calm the two men down. But Mather was doomed, and that night the four men made camp around a fire "in a very pensive and melancholy mood." Greenhill and Travers, bosom friends, were determined to eat Mather next; Pearce, without telling Mather, was secretly on their side. He walked a little way from the fire and looked back: "I saw Travers and Greenhill collaring him." The team was at work again, and Pearce made no effort to save poor John Mather, who now made ready to die a Christian death, very far from England.

> They told him they would give him half an hour to pray for himself, which was agreed to; he then gave the Prayer-book to me, and laid down his head, and Greenhill took the axe and killed him. We then stopped two days in this place.

The three men kept heading east, but Travers was sinking. He had been bitten on the foot by a snake and could no longer walk. Terrified that his two companions would eat him, he begged them to leave him to die and go on with what remained of Mather, which might be rations enough to carry them to a settlement. Greenhill refused to abandon him. He and Pearce stayed with the delirious Travers for five days, tending him. Travers lapsed in and out of his fever, "in great agitation for fear that they would dispose of him. . . . [T]he unfortunate Man all this time had but little or no sleep."

They half-dragged, half-carried Travers for several days more. But it was no use:

> [Greenhill and Pearce] began to Comment on the impossibility of ever being able to keep *Traviss* up with them for their strength was so nearly exhausted it was impossible for them to think of making any Settlement unless they left him. . . . It would be folly for them to leave him, for his flesh would answer as well for Subsistence as the others.

Travers awoke and, through his haze of pain, heard them talking.

> In the greatest agony [he] requested them in the most affecting manner not to delay themselves any longer, for it was morally impossible for him to attempt Travelling any more & therefore it would be useless for them to attempt to take him with them. . . . The Remonstrances of *Traviss* strengthened the designs of his companions.

They killed Travers with the axe. The victim "only stretched himself in his agony, and then expired."

Now they were two. But for the kangaroos, the terrain through which Pearce and Greenhill were now walking was not unlike England: undulating fields of grass sprinkled with little copses, a mild and fruitful landscape ringed with hills, all golden in the early summer light.

> Greenhill began to fret, and said he would never get to any port with his life. I kept up my spirits all along, and thought we must shortly come to some inhabited parts of the country, from the very great length we had travelled.

But there could be no doubt that one would sooner or later eat the other. Greenhill had the axe, and the two men walked at a fixed distance apart. When Pearce stopped, so did Greenhill. When one squatted, so did the other. There was no question of sleep. "I watched Greenhill for two nights, for I thought he eyed me more than usual." One imagines them: a small fire of eucalyptus branches in the immense cave of the southern night, beneath the drift and icy prickle of unfamiliar stars; the secret bush noises beyond the outer ring of firelight—rustle of grass, flutter and croaking of nocturnal birds—all sharpened and magnified by fear, with the two men fixedly watching one another across the fire. One night Pearce became convinced of Greenhill's "bad disposition as to me." He waited, and near dawn his adversary fell asleep. "I run up, and took the axe from under his head, and struck him with it, and killed him. I then took part of his arm and thigh, and went on for several days."

Pearce was now utterly alone. "I then took a piece of a leather belt," he notes laconically, "and was going to hang myself; but I took another notion not to do it." He walked on a little further and blundered into his first stroke of good luck since Macquarie Harbor: a deserted aboriginal campsite. The blacks had seen him coming and had fled, leaving pieces of game scattered around their still-lit cooking fires.

Pearce settled down and gorged himself on the first nonhuman meat he had tasted in nearly seven weeks. It gave him strength to keep going for several days until, from a hilltop, he glimpsed the landmark that signalled his arrival in the farmed country of the Derwent Valley: Table Mountain, a hill just south of Lake Crescent. Below him lay the Ouse, a large tributary stream of the Derwent.

Two days later, following the river down, Pearce came on a flock of sheep. He managed to grab and dismember a lamb. As he was devouring its raw flesh, a convict shepherd emerged from the bush "and said he would shoot me if I did not stop immediately."

The shepherd's name was McGuire, and he soon realized that he knew the blood-boltered little goblin he had at gunpoint. Before his banishment to Macquarie Harbor, Pearce had worked on a sheep run nearby. McGuire "carried the remains of the lamb, and took me with him into his hut, and made meat ready for me, where I stopped for three days, and he gave me all attendance." He would not turn a fellow Irishman in to the authorities, and for several weeks more Pearce hid in the huts of McGuire and other Irish convict shepherds. Then he fell in with a pair of bushrangers, Davis and Churton, who armed him; and they skulked about in the bush together for two more months. But his new companions had a £10 reward on their heads, and convict solidarity—never a dependable bond—could not hold up forever against that. On January 11, 1823, near the town of Jericho, the three of them were arrested by soldiers of the 48th Regiment acting on the word of informers and were brought down to Hobart in chains.

Churton and Davis were tried and hanged, an automatic punishment for bushrangers. While in jail, Pearce confessed the whole story of his escape—cannibalism and all—to the acting magistrate, the Reverend Robert Knopwood. It was transcribed and sealed, and not a word of it was believed. The authorities assumed—in the manner of the Cretan paradox—that since all convicts were liars, this one could only be covering for his "mates," who must still be alive and at large. This grotesque tall story could only be the invention of a felon's debased mind. There were no living witnesses to that nightmare trek from Macquarie Harbor to the Derwent, and no *corpus delicti*. And so Pearce was not executed; instead, they sent him back to Macquarie Harbor, where he arrived in February 1823.

He became, of course, a celebrity among the convicts. He was living proof that a man could get out of Macquarie Harbor, and only he kept the secret of how to do it. One newly arrived convict, a young laborer named Thomas Cox, kept begging to come along the next time. Finally, Pearce gave in to Cox's whispered entreaties; but he would not try the eastern route again. Instead, he decided to try and go north to Port Dalrymple—once again, through totally unexplored territory, but perhaps not as bad as the Western Tiers. On November 16, 1823, the two men absconded.

They did not get far. On November 21, a lookout on Sarah Island saw a plume of smoke rising from a distant beach. The fire was also seen by a convict transport, the *Waterloo,* as it made sail for Hell's Gates. The ship lowered a boat, and the shore guard dispatched a launch. Before dark, the exhausted Pearce was back in the settlement where he told the commandant that he had killed Cox two days before and had been eating him since. By way of proof, he produced a piece of human flesh weighing about half a pound. Next morning he led a search party to the bank of a stream, where Cox's body lay "in a dreadfully mangled state," according to one official report,

> being cut right through the middle, the head off, the privates torn off, all the flesh off the calves of the legs, back of the thighs and loins, also off the thick part of the arms, which the inhuman wretch declared was the most delicious food.

Probably Pearce killed Cox in rage, not gluttony; his own account rings true, despite its apparent gratuitousness:

> We travelled on several days without food, except the tops of trees and shrubs, until we came upon King's River. I asked Cox if he could swim; he replied he could not; I remarked that had I been aware of it he should not have been my companion. . . . [T]he arrangement for crossing the river created words, and I killed Cox with the axe. . . . I swam the river with the intention of keeping the coast around [to] Port Dalrymple; my heart failed me, and I resolved to return.

The authorities did the only thing they could. Pearce was shipped straight down to Hobart on the *Waterloo,* tried and hanged. When he was dead, a local artist, Thomas Bock, drew his likeness. The court had ordered that, as its ultimate brand of infamy, Pearce should be "disjointed" after death—delivered to the anatomizing surgeons. This was done, and Mr. Crockett, the head doctor in the Hobart Colonial Hospital, made a souvenir of the cannibal's head. He skinned it and scraped the flesh away, plucked out the eyes and the brain, and boiled the skull clean. Thirty years later, the relic was given to an American phrenologist, Dr. Samuel Morton, who was busy assembling his collection of skulls and shrunken heads, more than a thousand specimens, known as "The American Golgotha." It went into a glass cabinet in the Academy of Natural Sciences in Philadelphia, where it may still be seen, a yellowed label pasted across the blackened ivory bone, recording its small role in the taxonomy of an extinct scientific fad.

Cannibalism
From *Ice Blink: The Tragic Fate of Sir John Franklin's Lost Polar Expedition*

BY SCOTT COOKMAN

Many consider it to be the greatest disaster in the history of exploration. Led by Arctic explorer John Franklin, 128 hand-picked men—the best and the brightest of the British empire—sailed from Greenland in July of 1845 in search of the legendary Northwest Passage. Not one man returned. Many of the bodies of these men were found frozen over a century later, perfectly preserved. Modern evidence points to botulism from imperfectly canned food as the killer which decimated the expedition. Using informed speculation and forensic science, Scott Cookman, in his engrossing *Ice Blink,* tells the story of the cannibalism which was the group's last resort as they attempted to flee the frozen northern wastes.

(they were) carrying a number of skulls . . . there were more than four . . . also bones from legs and arms that appeared to have been sawed off.
—Captain Francis M'Clintock,
reporting Inuit eyewitness accounts

At what is today Booth Point, with the men starving, weak, sick, and unable to drag the boats another yard, Crozier was forced to halt altogether. It was not mere exhaustion that stopped him in his tracks, but the crushing discovery of the last thing he expected to find. Beyond the point, the shore of King William Land, which had all along been leading southeast toward Back's River, suddenly bent back to the northeast as far as he could see. It was not part of the North American mainland at all, but an island; the ice-choked water now blocking the way south wasn't an inlet or a bay, but a narrow strait. It was still frozen, to be sure, but when the ice went out, it would open into an east-west road some 6 to 20 miles wide. He was looking—finally, incomprehensibly—at the fabled Northwest Passage. They had, in spite of everything, found it, found what men had been seeking for 300 years: the gateway across the top of the world.

He may have called for three cheers, but the men—doll-eyed and cadaverous—were beyond cheering, beyond caring. If he still carried his sextant, chronometer, and compass, he almost certainly fixed the position and inked it in his log. But his bitterness and despair may have been too great. All that had been risked, suffered, and endured was repaid with ashes. The news of their discovery would not survive if they didn't and it was of no earthly good to them now. At that point, he would have gladly traded the Passage for a cask of ship's biscuit.

As evidenced from more stone tent circles, the party encamped for some time, perhaps deliberating what to do next. The men left alive (dozens may have perished on the grueling march south) were barely alive and clearly incapable of going another step. They could certainly no longer drag the boats. They were paper-thin skeletons, moving painfully on scurvy-swollen legs and gangrenous, frostbitten feet, blinded by snow glare, tortured by thirst, shivering with cold, and, above all, tormented with hunger. Those with any strength left may have feebly foraged the shoreline or brought in some saxifrage, and the officers, with what little powder and shot remained, may have managed to shoot some seabirds; all of this would have been thrown into a kettle, heated over whatever could be found to make a fire, and doled out, in painstakingly equal measure, to each man. But it was not nearly enough to begin to feed ravenous men; indeed some men were so weak, they probably could not eat at all. They lay down in the snow and the mud, crying with hunger; the rest attempted to do their tasks, but something went out of them, too. By turns, they knelt, sat, or laid down and nothing Crozier did could move them.

One of these men, apparently a seaman suffering the last stages of starvation, scurvy, and exposure, soon died. His corpse, however, wasn't buried; it was left where it lay. One can only imagine Crozier at his ebb, his ragged greatcoat flapping in the wind, dying men collapsed all around him, the icy Passage mocking him. His eyes, like those of the men, may have gone blank with hopelessness. It had been his driving leadership, after all, that had carried them to a place from which it now seemed they could never escape. The survivors, who at every step of the awful march looked to him to sustain them, could not have helped but notice that Crozier too had reached his end. Something rather like an eclipse swept over them all. This is quite likely the moment when Crozier proposed the unthinkable. He may have asked the surviving surgeons point-blank: without food, how long could they live? The answer would have been obvious: without something to eat, sooner or later, they would all die like the seaman lying before them, like so many others they had left behind.

Faced with certain death, Crozier was forced to make a horrible and repugnant decision, the only one left him. It was certainly Crozier who made it: he was the ranking officer and among the few officers the native Inuit later reported seeing alive. He apparently chose life. He may have put it to an officers' vote or perhaps a vote of the whole party, but at most this would have merely been a ratification. The decision had to have been Crozier's. The dead man, who had served so long and faithfully, could serve his shipmates again. With provisions exhausted, and still far from the river and with the crews broken beyond all forbearance, Crozier decided to cannibalize the dead.

Discoveries made by Beattie and Geiger in 1981 first revealed it. In one Booth Point tent site, they uncovered shell buttons, of the type worn by sailors, and broken clay pipestems that could only have come from Crozier's party. Scattered outside the stone tent circle were thirty-one human bone fragments, which forensic examination confirmed were the remains of a single individual: male, Caucasian, aged twenty to twenty-five at the time of death. The bones showed pitting and scaling consistent with scurvy, but they also showed parallel knife marks consistent with butchering. Near the entrance of the tent site were skull fragments, again of the same individual. Fracture lines indicated the skull had been forcibly broken. The face, both jaws, and all the teeth were missing. Evidence the body had been intentionally dismembered was further supported by the selective parts of the skeleton found. Besides the face, most of the skeleton was missing, including twenty-four ribs, breastbone, all twenty-four vertebrae of the back, the hips, collarbones, and shoulder blades.

More than likely, one of the surviving surgeons was deputed to butcher the corpse. Assistant Surgeon Harry Goodsir of the *Erebus* had trained as an anatomist, so was particularly qualified. Moreover, his surgical kit contained the tailor-made tools. A surgeon could have made quick work of this and, however repulsive it may have been to him, it was likely a comfort to the crew. The task would be done "proper," by a medical man, an officer and gentleman. The corpse was likely carried into one of the tents, out of sight of the rest and, attended by one or two men, the surgeon commenced.

From his medicine chest, Goodsir would have probably first selected a capital saw—a long, full-bladed saw, like a carpenter's. With this, he removed the head, sawed off the arms at the shoulder, and sawed through the pelvic bone to remove both legs. Switching to a metacarpal saw—a straight-bladed saw, about the size of a butcher knife—he divided the arms at the elbows and the legs at the knees and likely cut off the hands and feet. With catlins—long, thin, extremely sharp scalpels resembling filleting knives—he removed the meatiest portions first: buttocks, thighs, and the backs of the shins from the legs; deltoids, biceps, and triceps from the upper arms. Cut in thin strips, these were probably dropped immediately into a kettle set to boil over whatever barrel staves or planking the survivors could scavenge. The flesh from the trunk of the body—pectorals, shoulder blades, back, and sides—was next carved off and possibly laid in the sun to dry. In hours, they would brown into a stiff, uncured jerky unrecognizable as a man. Using tenaculum—slender, sharp-pointed instruments for holding—the sternum was cracked and the ribs removed one by one.

No part of the body, at this stage, was wasted. The heart, liver, and kidneys, all major organs, were probably extracted entire. More than likely the cooks, Diggle and Wall, chopped these up into tidbits with an axe and dropped them into the stew. As Goodsir knew, the intestines and the stomach, if well washed, were valuable food and the bone marrow especially. He would have used a Hey's saw—a long-handled, double-edged serrated saw—to open the abdominal sac. The guts were set aside, like the head, hands, and feet, for later. Then he may have used forceps to crack the long bones, and a raspator—a curved scraping tool, like a woodcarver's gouge—to remove the chunky, red marrow. The marrow was dumped straightaway into the kettle.

The dead man had been rendered from a human being into food. Goodsir probably retreated at once from the tent where this dismemberment had taken place and paced, ashamedly, back and forth in the snow. But before long, he began to smell the cook's fire and the indescribably wonderful aroma of fresh meat.

Undoubtedly that wasn't the end of it. There is overwhelming proof that the Franklin survivors practiced cannibalism on a far wider scale than that evidenced at Booth Point. In 1992, archeologist Margaret Bertulli and anthropologist Anne Keenleyside made a particularly gruesome find in Erebus Bay (on the west shore of King William Island). The discovery of over 200 artifacts—wood fragments and nails from a ship's boat, buttons, glass, clay pipes, traces of leather shoes and cloth, wire gauze from snow goggles and percussion caps—clearly marked the site as one inhabited by Franklin survivors. More ominous was the recovery of almost 400 human bones, representing the remains of at least eight and as many as eleven individuals. All of them were estimated to be under the age of fifty at the time of death (consistent with the ages of the expedition's crew). A quarter of these bones, scanned under an electron microscope, showed cut marks characteristic of knives. What's more, the cut marks were "consistent with intentional disarticulation," indicating that the dead had been dismembered and the flesh meticulously carved away.

Located quite close to the "Boat Place" found by Lt. Hobson in 1859, this was probably another party laboring to return to the deserted ships. But at this point, they apparently stopped, desperate for food. Lacking a surgeon, they set about butchering the dead bodies with sailor's knives, as best as they knew how. The cut marks showed they had acquired experience. They cut through the joints and proceeded—quite systematically—to carve every ounce off the remains in a pattern Bertulli and Keenleyside concluded was "consistent with defleshing or removal of muscle tissue." Whether this propelled them any nearer to their goal is unknown. For a time however, it kept them alive.

In life-or-death situations, cannibalization is by no means uncommon. The living invariably choose life and the dead are, after all, dead—beyond all suffering and offering the sole remaining hope of life. It is never entered into lightly. Although practiced in the utmost extremity by the Inuit, Chippewyan, and other native American nations of the Arctic and sub-Arctic, it is considered the greatest taboo. But the more extreme the circumstances, the more extreme the choices. Most usually it begins with the survivors eating the dead; only later does it progress to survivors eating each other.

The experience of the infamous Donner Party, trapped by record snowfall in the Sierra Nevada in 1846–1847, at almost the same time Crozier's party was trapped on King William Island, is typical. So long as any food remained, it was divided equally. "The families shared with one another as long as they had anything to share," remembered a survivor. "Each one's portion was very small. The hides [of the last cattle] were boiled and the bones burned brown and eaten. We tried to eat a decayed buffalo robe, but it was too tough and there was no nourishment in it. Some of the few mice that came into camp were caught and eaten."

When every morsel of food was gone, real starvation set in. With the snow over six feet deep and the ground below hard-frozen, the Donner Party, like Crozier's, was unable to bury its dead. Their remains, according to an eyewitness, were "wasted by famine or evaporated by the dry atmosphere [and] presented the appearance of mummies." These mummified corpses, however, promised the only hope of salvation. The remains were butchered and eaten. Rescuers found "bodies entire, with the exception that the abdomens had been cut open and the entrails extracted. . . . Strewn about the cabins were dislocated and broken skulls, in some instances sawed asunder with care, for the purpose of extracting the brains . . . human skeletons, in short, in every variety of mutilation." Of the eighty-nine members of the Donner Party, only forty-nine— eating the dead—survived.

Arctic expeditions were particularly subject to cannibalism. Sir John Franklin's 1819 expedition down the Coppermine River was only the first. In 1881–1884, American Lt. Adolphous Greely's polar expedition, marooned three years in a makeshift hut far above the Arctic Circle, suffered the same horror. One of its members, Private Henry, was discovered eating its dead. Greely was revulsed and made short work of the matter. He penned a terse order: "Private Henry will be shot today, all care being taken to prevent his injuring anyone, as his physical strength is greater than any two men. Decide the matter of death by two balls and one blank cartridge. This order is imperative and absolutely necessary for any chance of life." Henry was summarily shot. But his execution didn't end the matter. When rescuers finally found Greely and seven survivors—the sole survivors among twenty-six men—they also found corpses from which the flesh had been stripped away and eaten. To hide the fact, the commander of the relief expedition suggested to the Navy Department that the remains of the dead be sealed in metal coffins.

The somber feast at Booth Point evidently went on for several days. After the meatiest portions of the body were consumed, the men likely slept sound. The flesh and marrow stew, though each got only a cup, rejuvenated them. For a time they would have felt invigorated. When they awoke, each man got an equal portion of the flesh that had been laid in the sun to dry. But there were still too many mouths to feed and great care and industry was taken to extract every scrap of nutriment from the corpse.

Dr. Goodsir likely hacked the jaws from the skull and removed the protein-rich brains. These, along with the stomach and intestines saved from the day before, went into the cook's kettle. The bones he had scraped of marrow earlier went into the pot as well, to boil out every particle of blood and fat. Sea water answered for salt and some seaweed thickened every man's cupful: it was enough for another hot meal, another night's sleep. The twenty-four ribs, breastbone, marrow-rich vertebrae, pelvis, collarbone, and shoulder blades were carefully stowed in the boats to eat later.

The effect of this meat must have been miraculous. The men were able to haul the boats once more and Crozier took them south across the ice of 23-mile-wide Simpson Strait. About this time, the survivors were startled to see people: the first other human beings they had laid eyes on in nearly three years. It must have caused a wild celebration: surely these were the rescuers sent down from Great Slave Lake to find them. They were saved.

But as the parties approached one another, Crozier could see they weren't Europeans, but fur-clad, tattooed Esquimaux (Inuit)—men, women, and children out on the ice in the strait, hunting seals. For their part, the Inuit were just as shocked to encounter *kabloonans* (white men), coming from out of nowhere, dragging strange, monstrous contraptions over the ice. The encounter was surreal—and short.

Charles Francis Hall, the American who later searched for Franklin survivors, interviewed some of these Inuit nearly twenty years afterward. "Several native families," he reported, "provided an officer thought to be Crozier and a group of his men with seal meat. The Inuit then left, ignoring pleas for further aid." At the time, this was accepted as proof the native Americans abandoned Crozier and his pleading, begging men. In fact, that they shared what little seal meat they had was noble; that they stole away at the first opportunity is understandable.

Imagine yourself on a family camping trip when, suddenly, a gang of fifty hairy, incoherent Hell's Angels appear out of nowhere. They're plainly starving, heavily armed with guns, knives, and hatchets—and openly carrying human body parts. The Inuit, thinking they might be next on the menu, were clearly terrified. They gave what seal meat they had and got away as fast and as far as they could.

The fat-rich seal meat, eaten raw, was like ambrosia to Crozier's men. It stilled, for a time, the bitter disappointment of the Inuit's departure and enabled them to drag the boats farther across the strait. But when they reached the mainland—at a place now called Starvation Cove—they were again starving, entirely broken, and unable to go on. At this bleak place, another seaman, whose remains were found by Schwatka in 1879, died and was eaten. Temporarily, starvation and scurvy were staved off. The mouth of Back's River, their goal, was only another 62 miles, but no more of the survivors died so conveniently to feed the rest.

The men left alive were, by this time, no strangers to the taste and life in human flesh. The strong may have looked at the weak, those who could no longer haul, not as shipmates but as food. At that point another, far more gruesome, decision confronted them.

The *taking* of human life for food, rather than just feeding on the dead, is the ultimate desperation. This is quite rare, but Crozier's men were apparently soon forced to adopt the practice. It's even more repulsive and psychologically damaging than cannibalizing the dead. One of the few clearly documented cases of this involved the wreck of the brig *Essex,* stove and sunk by an 85-foot sperm whale on Nov. 20, 1820. The ship went down in the most remote part of the Pacific Ocean.

Her twenty-man crew, most of whom were off hunting whales at the time, returned to find her sinking. In three whaleboats, they managed to get off all hands: seven in Captain Pollard's boat, six in the boat of First Mate Owen Chase, and seven in the boat of Second Mate Matthew Joy. Desperately, they retrieved some tools, one pistol, two compasses, two quadrants, and two books on navigation. The only provisions they could save were two casks of ship's biscuit, a half-dozen casks of water, and two live turtles they had taken on in the Galapagos Islands for fresh meat. What happened to them next—in all likelihood—happened to Crozier's survivors at Starvation Cove.

Steering for South America, each man was at first issued one ship's biscuit and a half-pint of water a day. In short order, they killed the turtles, drank the blood, and warmed the meat after a fashion over a fire built in the shells. When this was gone some flying fish, unfortunate to land in the boats, were devoured raw. Next, the barnacles were scraped off the bottoms of the boats and eaten. By sheer luck they struck Henderson Island, a minute dot of land in the mid-Pacific, and for four days scrounged crabs, clubbed nesting gulls and sucked down their eggs, and refilled their water casks from a tiny spring. But there was not enough food or water to sustain twenty men. A vote was taken: three men elected to remain; seventeen took to the boats again on December 27, 1820.

On January 12, 1821, Third Mate Hendrick's boat disappeared in a storm and was never seen again. On January 28, another storm separated the last two boats. Alone on the ocean, Captain Pollard sailed eastward. The only food was one and a half ounces of ship's biscuit per man a day and what rainwater they could catch in their sail. This kept them alive for nine weeks until both bread and water were gone. Four men remained barely alive: Pollard, his nephew Owen Coffin (a cabin boy), and two seamen—Charles Ramsdell and a free black man named Barzillai Ray. They were still over 1,600 miles from the nearest landfall. As captain, Pollard faced a horrible, inescapable decision: if any were to live, one had to die to feed the rest.

They drew lots. To Pollard's horror, his own nephew, young Owen Coffin, drew the short straw. They drew lots again to determine who would do the killing. Mortified, able-bodied seaman Ramsdell drew the short straw. There was nothing to stop the thing; they all understood the necessity and the love and regard for one another that made it a necessity. Coffin laid his head on the gunwale. Pollard gave his pistol to Ramsdell and turned away. He shot Coffin in the back of the head. The rest of the body was hauled into the boat. The still-hot blood was drunk, the quivering flesh sliced from the skeleton and eaten raw. The bones were later broken open, the marrow picked out and every fragment sucked clean. Coffin's corpse sustained them almost two weeks until Barzillai Ray died. Pollard and Ramsdell fed off his remains until February 23, 1821, when they were rescued by the whaler *Dauphin*.

The execution of his nephew, the cannibalization of Coffin's and Ray's corpses, haunted Pollard the rest of his days. He went to sea only one more time, was shipwrecked once more, and was never again trusted with command of a ship. He ended his life as a town watchman in Nantucket. Scorned and shunned, he hid biscuit and salt pork in the rafters of his house until he died.

Crozier now faced the same horror, but on a far larger scale. He still had as many as thirty or more men to feed and, other than what could be scavenged from the sterile shores around Starvation Cove (lichens mostly, perhaps some whelkfish), there was no food. The boats could not be moved. The men were too weak to hunt and, beyond gulls, there was nothing they knew how to hunt. It was September, the first snow began to fall, and they were still not yet to the river. If they were ever to make the 850-mile journey to Great Slave Lake, they had to begin at once, before the river began to freeze.

For a time, Crozier probably waited grimly. He had grown used to death. The dead were done with suffering at least. He was numb; the tears didn't come anymore; the twist in his stomach constricted no further; he felt everything less and less. He probably welcomed it; it was the mind and body shutting off, preparing him for what was to come. A few of the weakest might yet die in their sleep to feed the rest. Just a few more dead, a few more meals, would fuel the survivors long enough to drag the boats to the river. Once there, they could at last float the boats and, with a favorable wind, commence the journey south. On the river, they would surely find fish and likely game along its banks and, God willing, the Hudson's Bay Company coming downriver.

But the men that remained alive were survivors. Exposure and starvation dimmed their eyesight and devoured their bodies, but they hung on somehow, and soon Crozier could wait no longer. Some, not just one or two, would have to die to save the rest. None would survive otherwise. He could not ask any man to volunteer; that would be too much to ask of men who had already given everything. They would leave it in God's hands.

Courage was the only thing the expedition had left in abundance. Lots were likely drawn, every officer and man taking his chance. In the disastrous retreat of the British army from Kabul during the Afghan War of 1842, lots were drawn to determine who would remain behind with the sick and wounded, tantamount to a death sentence. On the shore of Starvation Cove, these were plucked one at a time by trembling, emaciated fingers. Who or how many may have sacrificed themselves is unknown. It could have been Francis Dunn, twenty-eight, the caulker's mate from *Erebus* or David Leys, forty, an able-bodied seaman aboard *Terror* or Sergeant David Bryant, thirty-five, head of the marine contingent on *Erebus*. By the same selfless token, it may have been Third Lieutenant George Hodgson of the *Terror* (whose custom-made sextant was found among the gear earlier abandoned at Victory Point) or John Cowie, thirty-five, a stoker from the *Erebus* or twenty-one-year-old Thomas Evans, a midshipman from the *Terror.* How they were dispatched is, of course, unknown. Powder and shot would have been too precious to waste. Knives may have been employed instead. Their bodies were consigned to any of the surgeons who remained alive, or to their shipmates, who quickly rendered them into life for the survivors.

This food carried them to Montreal Island, near the mouth of Back's River. Searchers later discovered two iron barrel hoops, some other corroded pieces of metal, and the remains of one of Goldner's preserved meat cans (long before emptied of food and likely carried as a cookpot). Beyond that point, no more artifacts, skeletons, or boats were ever found. Most probably, those that were left finally floated their boats and ascended the river. It was their only chance. Ice, cold, and death had still not stopped them. Ironically, as long as they had each other for food, they went upriver.

Weakened and delirious, it's unlikely they got far. Some may have fallen victim to the river's treacherous rapids and drowned. Winter may have overtaken the rest. The very last survivors—coming out of the north, from the land of the Inuit, who had warred with the Chippewyans for centuries—may have been killed. More likely, in that rocky, treeless wilderness, they finally laid down and died. They could do no more. No men could.

Years later—as Rae, Hobson, M'Clintock, Hall, and Schwatka searched the area—it was rumored that Crozier had survived. He was said to have lived for a time among the Chippewyans, nomadic hunters of the far north. If true, it would make sense. Crozier had been a nomad in the north his entire life and, perhaps at last, had found a place where he was accepted for what he was; not for who he was born or where he came from. It was the place that Barrow, in first undertaking the expedition, had tried to make—an aristocracy of character, refined by adversity, sustained by courage and humanity, and undiluted by anything else.

The Forlorn Hope
From *Deceived: The Story of the Donner Party*

BY PETER R. LIMBURG

The trials of the Donner Party, trapped high in the Sierra Nevada mountains during the brutal winter of 1846-47, have entered into the legend and folklore of American history. Peter Limburg's narrative, *Deceived: The Story of the Donner Party*, brings it back freshly to life. The following excerpt depicts the horrendous suffering of a group of escapees who flee the main Donner party, seeking help. They call themselves, with evident irony, "The Forlorn Hope."

Dec. 6, The morning fine and clear—Stanton and Graves manufacturing snowshoes for another mountain scrabble. . . . Dec. 16, Fair and pleasant, froze hard last night—the company started on snowshoes to cross the mountains, wind S.E.
            —Diary of Patrick Breen, printed anonymously in
                The California Star, May 22, 1847

The escape party—they dubbed themselves "the Forlorn Hope"—strapped on their snowshoes and left the morning of December 16. Their determination was increased by the death of Baylis Williams, the Reeds' handyman, the day before. There were seventeen in the party, twelve men and five women, mostly young adults. Eddy and Stanton were the leaders; with them were Sutter's two Indian trail guides, Luis and Salvador. Uncle Billy Graves, still vigorous at fifty-seven, led a detachment from his family: Sarah and Jay Fosdick and the beautiful Mary. From the Murphy clan there were William and Sarah Foster, twelve-year-old Lemuel and eleven-year-old Billy, and the recently widowed Harriet Pike. Amanda McCutchen joined them; she was anxious to join her husband down in the settlements. She left her year-old baby behind, probably in the care of Aunt Betsy Graves. She was not the only young mother to leave a child behind at the Mountain Camp. Sarah Foster left one and Harriet Pike left two. It was a heartrending choice to make. But it was impossible to carry small children over the difficult terrain, deep in snow, and at the cabins the little ones would at least be warm and sheltered.

The remainder of the party were Dutch Charley Burger, Antoine the herder, and Patrick Dolan. Lewis Keseberg could not go because his foot had not yet healed, and Patrick Breen, another still-vigorous man, was ailing with "the gravel," an old term for kidney and bladder stones.

Historians have done a great deal of moralizing about the decision of the men and women of the Forlorn Hope. Were they selfishly taking a gamble on saving their own lives while leaving their families behind? Or were they being noble in risking their lives to bring help for the others? Probably both selfish and altruistic motives were at work here—but in fact the real choice was between dying of exhaustion on the trail or dying of starvation at the cabins.

The Forlorn Hope took little enough in the way of provisions. In their packs, each member had a small ration of tough, dried beef—enough to give them a two-finger-wide strip three times a day for five or six days. This amounted to about one ounce per meal. They also had a little coffee and sugar, but no salt—that essential had run out by the time they reached the lake. The men had a little tobacco, considered a manly necessity. Each person had a single blanket or quilt to keep warm with, but no extra clothing. The tents were now serving as cabin roofs and could not be spared—the snowshoers would have to sleep out in the open after a day's exhausting slogging through the snow.

They took with them a single hatchet to chop firewood, a few pistols for defense, a little powder and shot, and Foster's hunting rifle in case they should sight any game. The rifle was a heavy burden for the half-starved men and women, but they could manage by taking turns carrying it. That was all—not an ounce of unnecessary weight.

It was a poignant moment when the Forlorn Hope said farewell to their families, knowing they might never see them again. They had reason to worry, for those they left behind were already painfully thin. Patrick Dolan, who had no family to provide for, generously requested that Mrs. Reed and her children should have a share of the beef he owned. Eddy felt like crying at the sight of his wife's hollow cheeks, sunken eyes, and wasted figure. But stress numbed him, and the tears did not come.

The morning of the departure offered favorable travel conditions. The snow was dry and feathery, which meant it would not cling to the snowshoes, and the weather was fair and cold, so that the snow would not thaw into a wet, clinging mass. The party planned to follow the established emigrant trail, if only they could find it beneath the snow. The route ran along the ridgelines of the mountains as much as possible, since the going for the wagons was easiest there. But there were many steep descents and climbs between one ridge and the next.

After crossing the pass, the trail led through a pleasant mountain meadow called Summit Valley, about two miles long, following the headwaters of the south fork of the Yuba River, which rises near the pass. Then the river (at this point a shallow stream only a few yards wide) dropped into a canyonlike valley, while the trail held to the valley rim for several miles before slanting steeply down to the valley floor and rejoining the Yuba. Then there were a few miles of level going along the Yuba Bottoms, until the trail climbed over a divide to the watershed of the American River. The trail then dipped down into a small hollow called Dry Valley and went through a notch in the mountains that formed the valley's north side, called Emigrant Gap. On the far side of Emigrant Gap the slope was so steep that wagons had to be let down by ropes that were snubbed around trees to provide friction. At the bottom of this hazardous slope, about twelve miles from the Yuba Bottoms, lay the lovely, parklike Bear Valley, where the precipitous canyon of the Bear River widened out.

Bear Valley was far from the end of the trail, however. At the foot of the valley the road entered another canyon carved by the Bear River, but soon climbed up to a dividing ridge. Bear Canyon lay on the right; another canyon, called Steep Hollow, lay on the left. The road followed the ridge top because the slopes on either side were too steep for a wagon to remain upright, and in places the ridge top itself was so narrow that the wagon tracks straddled it.

About ten miles beyond Bear Valley was a spot called Mule Springs, a favored campground of the emigrants and their tired teams. About another ten miles farther on, the ridge ended precipitously where Steep Hollow ran into Bear Canyon. This was another spot where wagons had to be lowered with ropes, while oxen and horses slipped and stumbled down the slopes as best they could. But this cliff marked the end of the high mountains and canyons. The road now led down over foothills that grew gentler and gentler, until it entered the plains of the great central valley that Hastings had described in such alluring terms. From there it was about thirty-seven miles to the first settlement, Johnson's Ranch. Sutter's Fort lay another forty miles beyond Johnson's ranch.

The distance from the lake to Bear Valley was about thirty miles, and Stanton had ridden it in a day that fall. The whole distance from the lake to the end of the foothills was about fifty miles. Hastings's wagons had made it in seven days. However, they had done it on mostly snow-free ground and with people in good condition—a far cry from a malnourished and poorly clad band of desperate souls struggling through deep snow.

The snowshoe party calculated that they had enough food to see them to Bear Valley, about halfway across the mountains. There, with luck, they might find deer to shoot or even locate a cache of food left by a family trying to lighten its wagonload.

The Forlorn Hope started off in single file, the leaders breaking a trail for the others. Even with the snowshoes they sank halfway to their knees in the soft, powdery snow at each step. There were not enough snowshoes to go around, so Burger and the two Murphy boys brought up the rear, stepping carefully in the snowshoe tracks. However, the snow was not packed hard enough to bear their weight, and they kept breaking through and floundering.

Billy Murphy gave out and had to turn back; he got back to the cabins that evening. Burger also dropped out, but no one noticed his absence for some time. Then they simply assumed that he had turned back to the cabins and did not bother to search for him. (He did get back safely, but long after Billy Murphy.) Lemuel Murphy struggled on gamely in the grown-ups' snowshoe tracks until the party reached some packsaddles from Sutter's mules that had been jettisoned by the trail. Graves and Stanton ripped these apart and fashioned a pair of snowshoes for Lem out of their components.

That first day the Forlorn Hope made only four miles, camping a little way above the head of the lake. From their campsite they could see the smoke of the cabins, a discouraging reminder of how little progress they had made. The next day, however, they crossed the pass. As they climbed, Mary Graves, at the rear of the column, looked up at her heavily muffled companions and thought that they looked like a picture of

Norwegian trappers among the icebergs that she had seen in a book long ago.

The party paused at the top of the pass for a last look at their loved ones. Although by now they loathed the snow and the mountains, they could not help admiring the magnificent view. Someone said jokingly that they must be about as close to heaven as they could get.

They made camp that afternoon a short distance west of the pass, being too tired to go farther. They judged they had traveled about six miles that day. The snow at the campsite was twelve feet deep, but the Forlorn Hope had learned one thing since their first fiasco: how to keep a fire going in deep snow.

The trick was to cut two green saplings and lay them parallel on top of the snow, a few feet apart. Over these one laid crosspieces of green wood to make a platform. The fire was built on top of this. As long as someone kept the fire going all night, the travelers would stay warm even without tents and with only one blanket apiece.

The following day, December 18, they had a downhill slope to help them. This was well, for they were beginning to weaken after two days' arduous climbing with only a few tiny strips of lean, saltless beef to sustain them. It was an excellent reducing regimen, but losing flesh was the last thing the Forlorn Hope needed. Another trouble now struck them: The glare of the sun on the snow of Summit Valley caused Stanton to go snowblind. He had to stop, but was able to continue when the sun got low, and caught up with his comrades about an hour after they had made camp. That day they made about five miles.

For the next few days the Forlorn Hope kept on along the highlands, making a few miles each day. They were favored with clear, pleasant weather most of the time, and they used the sun as a guide. Stanton, however, kept going snowblind, dropping behind, and coming in each evening after sunset. Since he was the only one who really knew the trail, his misfortune affected the whole group.

By now the hard-pressed little band of refugees were not only horribly emaciated, but in bad mental shape as well. They began to hallucinate as they dragged themselves through the snow. Fine, big farmhouses, fields full of crops, and lovely gardens appeared before their eyes. When they camped at night they heard familiar farm sounds where there was nothing to make them: dogs barking, roosters crowing, cowbells tinkling, and the voices of men talking. When they slept, they dreamed of food—huge banquets of their favorite dishes prepared just the way they liked best. Yet, as their vitality drained away, they gradually lost their sense of hunger and wanted above all to sleep.

One morning—it was December 21—Eddy searched through his little pack to see if there was anything he could discard to lighten his load. At the bottom he found a half pound of bear meat with a note from his wife attached. The note told him to save the meat for the last extremity, as it might save his life. It was signed "Your own dear Eleanor." The loyal Eleanor had hoarded the meat from her own share of the grizzly bear for just such an emergency. Eddy made this self-sacrificing gift from his wife last a long time.

That morning, Stanton did not start out with his comrades but stayed by the campfire, calmly smoking his pipe. Don't worry, he told the others; he would catch up with them later. The Forlorn Hope started off, guided rather uncertainly by the Indians, who had been over the trail only once, and then when the ground was free of snow. Moreover, the Indians had been going in the other direction. So it was not surprising that the party gradually veered in the wrong direction, away from Bear Valley. (This would cost them many painful days and miles, but they didn't discover how badly lost they were for more than a week.) That night they used up the last of the beef they had brought with them from the Mountain Camp and waited for Stanton to come in to the warmth and light of the campfire. He did not come.

The next day they had traveled only about a mile when the snow began to fall. They halted and made camp, and waited again for Stanton. It was a foodless day for all—Eddy would surely not have dared nibble on his secret hoard of bear meat in front of his starving companions. They waited and waited, but Stanton still did not come staggering through the snow. At nightfall they gave him up for dead. A gentleman to the last, little Charley Stanton had sacrificed his own life rather than endanger his companions by holding them back.

The following day, December 23, they climbed the barren, rocky dome of Cisco Butte, the highest peak in the vicinity, and tried to take their bearings. Now that Stanton was no longer there to guide them, they had to plot their own route. The easiest way appeared to be toward the south, where the mountains looked less menacing than those to the north and west. Unfortunately, this led them away from Bear Valley—but they had no way of knowing this.

A foot of snow fell that night, but the painful journey continued the next morning, December 24, the day before Christmas. The party limped two or three miles before the wind shifted to the southwest, and a heavy snow began to fall. By now the members of the Forlorn Hope had become experts at forecasting snow. A wind from the south or southwest brought snow (on moisture-laden winds from the ocean), while an east or northeast wind (from the dry interior) meant clear weather.

The fourteen remaining members of the Forlorn Hope sat down among the falling flakes and took counsel. All the men except Eddy wanted to give up and return to the Mountain Camp, reasoning they had not tasted food for two days and had been on starvation rations for a week before that. It was a suicidally foolish idea, since, in their weakened condition, they could not possibly have made it back. Eddy and the women stood firm, however. They vowed they would go through with their mission or perish. Strangely, the women bore the physical and mental stress far better than the men, a phenomenon that would happen again and again before their trials were over.

Finally Patrick Dolan, the once-carefree bachelor, voiced the thought that must have crossed everyone's mind: One must die to save the rest. Dolan proposed that they draw lots to determine who should be killed so the rest might eat. (At this point the starving emigrants back at the Mountain Camp and Alder Creek had not yet begun to eat their dead.) Eddy seconded the motion, but Foster did not want to take the risk of being the one who made the sacrifice, and he opposed it.

Eddy then proposed that two men each take a revolver and shoot it out until one or both were killed. This sporting proposition was also turned down. Finally Eddy, by now the de facto leader, suggested that they simply travel on until someone died, letting nature solve the problem. After some querulous argument the others finally agreed, and they staggered on through the storm for another two or three miles.

Disasters now fell on them almost as thickly as the snowflakes. The snow and wind made it almost impossible to get a fire started. But at last the flame caught, and the bone-chilled emigrants piled on fuel to make a big, cheering bonfire. If they had nothing to eat, they could at least be warm. But one of them did not enjoy it for long. Antoine, the Mexican cattle herder, lay in an exhausted slumber by the blaze. The others could hear that he breathed with difficulty, for his breath rattled gruesomely in this throat. In his sleep, he flung out an arm, and his hand landed in the fire. Eddy saw it happen, but was too exhausted to help the sleeping young man. Unable to rouse himself, he thought that the pain would surely wake Antoine soon enough, and he would pull his hand out of the fire by himself. Antoine slumbered on, breathing heavily and unnaturally. His hand doubled up and began to roast in the fire. This was more than Eddy could bear, and he pulled the unconscious herder's hand and arm away from danger. Antoine soon flung out his arm again, and Eddy realized that it was no use to help him. Antoine died without showing a sign of pain as his hand burned to a crisp.

Shortly after this, a terrible storm of wind, snow, and hail swept down upon them. At the same time, the fire began to eat its way down into the snow from its own intense heat. The dismayed emigrants watched helplessly as it sank slowly down, blazing logs, platform, and all. Then the supply of firewood ran out. One of the men took the party's lone hatchet and went to cut more. As he chopped away, the head flew off the hatchet and was lost in the depths of the snow, impossible to find in the dark and the howling storm even if they had had the strength to dig for it.

Still the fire kept burning, shielded from the storm by its self-made well in the snow. By midnight it had sunk to ground level, eight feet below the surface of the snow, and the emigrants crouched miserably around it with their feet in the ice-cold meltwater.

It was obvious even to the starvation-dulled minds of the emigrants that the fire would soon sputter out in the melted snow if something were not done. A few who were a little more alive than the rest stood the half-burned foundation logs on end and built the fire up again on top. At this point one of the Indians stood up to get closer to the warmth. Clumsy with cold and weariness, he lurched against the fire platform. Down went the rickety structure, and the flames hissed out in the icy pool of water in which the men and women stood. It looked as if everyone was doomed to perish from the cold. Despair set in, and everyone began to pray to God for a merciful death—everyone but Eddy and one or two of the women.

The resourceful Eddy finally persuaded his companions to try a trick he had heard about from someone on the trail, before the Donner Party made its fatal turn onto the Hastings cutoff. It was a mountain man's way of surviving a blizzard. One way or another, he prodded them out of the pit and made them spread blankets on the surface of the snow. The people sat on the blankets in a tight circle with their feet in the center, while Eddy dragged himself around the circle and spread other blankets over them. Last of all, he slipped into the circle himself. The blankets, with the snow that fell on top of them, formed a snug, insulating tent that held in their body heat and kept them warm.

It was a simple enough procedure, but some of the emigrants were so apathetic that they didn't want to move. It took an hour or more before Eddy had coaxed and bullied everyone into position beneath the blankets. Uncle Billy Graves had been weakening visibly since early in the evening. Now Eddy told him he was dying. Uncle Billy replied feebly that he didn't care; he soon sank into death. But before he died, he urged his daughters to eat his body so that they might live.

Christmas morning brought no holiday cheer to the wretched snowshoe party. The storm still raged outside their tent of blankets. Then Patrick Dolan became delirious and began to babble senselessly, in vague and disjointed phrases. He cried out to Eddy that he, Dolan, was the only one in the group who could be counted on. The deranged man then pulled off his boots and most of his clothes and shouted to Eddy to follow him down to the settlements. They would get there in just a few hours, cried Dolan.

With a great deal of difficulty the others managed to overpower him and bring him back under the blankets. He thrashed about for a while, but they held him down. After a while, his energy exhausted, Dolan became quiet and submissive, like an obedient child, as one of the survivors later commented. As he drifted into death, his companions thought he looked as if he were enjoying a calm and pleasant sleep. Thus died jolly Patrick Dolan, the children's favorite.

In the evening, with the storm still raging, Lemuel Murphy became delirious and started talking uncontrollably about food. In fact, none of the party had eaten for four days, for so far neither men nor women had been able to eat the flesh of any of the three corpses they had on hand.

The next morning—December 26—Eddy tried to start a fire beneath the blanket tent with the aid of gunpowder. His cold, weak hands were clumsy; there was a flareback; and the powderhorn exploded, burning Eddy's face and hands severely. Amanda McCutchen and Sarah Foster, who were sitting nearby, were also burned, though not seriously.

That afternoon the storm finally blew over. Eddy, despite his injuries, immediately climbed out from under the blankets and found a huge, dead pine tree standing nearby. He commandeered some shreds from the cotton lining of Harriet Pike's cloak and dried them in the sun. Using these as tinder, he lit them with sparks from flint and steel and coaxed them into a precarious flame. He fed the tiny flame with bits of dead twigs until it grew; before long he managed to set fire to the dead pine's dry, resin-laden trunk.

The emigrants lay down around the burning tree to enjoy the warmth. The flames roared up the massive trunk in a most gratifying fashion, but then big, burning limbs began to fall in their midst. The people of the Forlorn Hope were now so weak and uncaring that they didn't even try to dodge the flaming menaces. But fortunately none of the falling limbs struck anyone.

It is hard to tell just what happened during the next few days, for the survivors' memories were understandably confused, and the early historians of the Donner Party, unable to straighten out the sequence of events, were equally confused. But at some point the remaining emigrants realized that they had to eat something or die. Up to then, their horror of cannibalism had held them back from eating the flesh of their dead comrades. And they had lost their appetites, a characteristic of the later stages of starvation. But still they wanted to live.

Someone again brought up the dreaded subject of eating human flesh, and this time they did not reject it. They cut strips of flesh from Patrick Dolan's arms and legs, which was fitting, because he had been the first to propose cannibalism and moreover was not related to any of the survivors.

They roasted the lean, stringy meat over the campfire and ate it, turning their faces away from each other. Overcome by guilt and grief, Eddy and the two Indians did not share in the loathsome meal.

Suffering and Safety

I could state several most horrid circumstances connected with this affair: such as one of the women being obliged to eat part of the body of her father and her brother, another saw her husband's heart cooked &c; which would be more suitable for a hangmans [sic] journal than the columns of a family newspaper.

—From an anonymous letter printed in The California Star, *February 13, 1847*

Sarah Murphy Foster and Harriet Murphy Pike tried to feed a little of Dolan's flesh to their young brother, Lemuel Murphy, but he was beyond help. The boy grew steadily weaker and died in the early morning

hours, with his head in his oldest sister's lap. The living members of the
Forlorn Hope were not so far from death themselves. As Thornton described them, they were mere walking skeletons. The skin on their faces
was drawn tight over the bones, like a mummy's, and from their ghastly
countenances their eyes glared out fierce and wild.

By this time most of them had resigned themselves to dying.
When Eddy, hiding his own fears, tried to cheer them up, they responded with sighs, tears, and moans. But the meal of human flesh, repellent as it was, had given them new strength. The women regained a
bit of spirit, although the men remained sunk in despondency.

The depleted band of survivors stayed on at the scene of their
tragedies four days after Christmas, resting and drying the meager flesh
of their dead relatives and friends for rations on the trail. Although the
first taboo—against eating human flesh—had been broken, no one
touched the flesh of his or her own kin. But Sarah Murphy Foster was
almost prostrated when she saw one of her companions roasting the
heart of her younger brother over a campfire.

On December 30 the Forlorn Hope left the Camp of Death, as
they had christened the dreadful spot. It was a wonder that they were
able to travel at all, for their feet had swollen so badly that the skin burst.
They wrapped their injured feet in rags and pieces of blanket (for the
dead no longer needed their blankets to keep them warm) to cushion
them, but the pain was still so excruciating that they made little progress.

The Indian Luis, who spoke a little broken English, now confessed to Eddy that he and Salvador were lost. This was not their own
country, and without familiar landmarks to guide them they were as
helpless as the white strangers they were guiding. Still the expedition
kept on going mechanically, bushwhacking their way westward. Their
only alternative was to die where they were.

That night it was Eddy who gave out. He had long since used up
the half pound of bear meat that his wife had so carefully hidden in his
knapsack, and he was faint and weak from starvation. His companions
looked at him and told him he was dying—he'd better have something
to eat. At first he pooh-poohed the idea, but then he recognized that he
had the same symptoms of lassitude and weakness that he'd seen in those
who had died. To save his life, and bring help to his wife and children, he
reluctantly took his first cannibal meal. The others willingly shared their
rations of human flesh with him (he had evidently taken none himself)
because they knew that without his leadership they would not make it.

As Eddy ate, the thought crossed his mind that he was committing a horrifying act. But he actually felt no loathing or disgust. As Thornton later wrote, "The hard hand of necessity was on him, and he was compelled to eat or die."

The night passed as quietly as could be expected for people who had just gone through such soul-wrenching experiences. Eddy, once more able to attempt to raise the group's morale, assured them that everyone would get through to safety. They did not believe him, but they recovered enough to curse Lansford W. Hastings bitterly, and to vow vengeance on him for having lured them onto his cutoff.

All the last day of 1846 they traveled along a high, sharp-crested ridge. Although they had no idea of where they were, they had actually blundered back on the trail, for this was the ridge that divided Steep Hollow from the canyon of the Bear River. It was the most terrifying journey they had yet made. They crossed ravines on frail bridges of snow; now and then they could look down through a hole in the snow and see the icy torrent far below. The men and women of the Forlorn Hope had their hearts in their throats as they inched apprehensively over the snow bridges, teetering on their clumsy snowshoes. But their luck held. No one lost his or her balance, and the snow held firm under their weight.

After an eternity of negotiating these terrors, they reached a high spot along the spine of the ridge and paused for a view. In the distance, off to the west, they could see a vast, green plain that seemed to spread out forever—the Sacramento Valley, their goal. But their joy was damped by the sight of the mountains and canyons that still lay across their path. As Mary Graves later remembered, each time they reached the summit of a mountain, another mountain, even higher, lay ahead.

Late that afternoon they reached the end of the ridge. Before them lay a slope that plunged precipitously to a canyon bottom two thousand feet or more below. (This was, in fact, one of the spots where the wagons had to be gingerly let down with ropes.) The exhausted men and women could see that the canyon on the left (Steep Hollow) made a bend below them and joined the canyon (Bear River) on their right. Unable to go farther, they made camp.

New Year's Day 1847 brought the Forlorn Hope no more cheer than Christmas had. The only difference was that there were no storms, and no one had died. The entire day was spent negotiating the formidable canyon. Going down was not too difficult—on the gentler slopes the people squatted down on their showshoes and slid to the bottom, where they usually fetched up in a snowdrift. Then, hampered by their packs and snowshoes, they laboriously worked themselves free and went on. It would have been comical if the situation had not been so grave.

The fierce cold of the mountains had done them one favor: It had frozen the headwaters of the Bear River so that the stream was low. They were able to cross it without any difficulty severe enough to be remembered. But the climb up the far slope more than made up for this lucky break. For the first fifty feet, the slope was so steep that the hunger-weakened men and women had to cling to bushes and cracks in the rock to avoid sliding back to the bottom. Then the slope became a little less vertical, enough so that snow could cling and trees grow. They dug their snowshoes into the snow and stairstepped up. They moved very slowly, for each step was an effort, and blood from their damaged feet marked the trail. It was evening before they reached the top, and Fosdick barely made it. That night they ate the last of the human flesh they had brought with them.

They were now on a broad plateau with fairly level ground. Although they were foodless, they had a compensation. The snow was so firm that they could walk on it without their snowshoes, a great relief. But their feet could not heal while walking through the snow, and this day they were worse than ever. Fosdick's weakness held the whole group back, and one of the Indians was in even worse condition: His frostbitten toes began to drop off at the first joint.

But on January 3 there were encouraging signs. The snow remained firm, and it looked as if they were at last coming down from the mountain heights, for there were oaks among the conifers. When they camped that night the snow was only three feet deep, an occasion for rejoicing. Figuring that they no longer needed their snowshoes, whose rawhide strings had begun to rot, they toasted the strings over the campfire and dined on them. Eddy also toasted and ate a worn-out pair of moccasins. At least their stomachs had something to work on, even if the leather held no nourishment.

The next day, again, they had nothing to eat, and Fosdick was so weak that they made only two miles. But that night they camped for the first time on bare ground, in a grove of oak trees!

Foster now proposed that the whites kill and eat the Indians. To most white Westerners, an Indian was not quite human, and an enemy at that, so no one was shocked by the suggestion. Except for Eddy. To him, these two dark-skinned youths were fellow human beings and moreover faithful companions. To kill them would be a shabby reward for their having brought food over the Sierras to the whole Donner Party, perhaps saving their lives.

One can imagine the responses he got when he reproached his companions: The Indians were just savages! The Indians had gotten them lost! It was those Indians' fault that they had turned back beyond the pass on their first attempt, just because of Sutter's mules! And so on.

Unable to change his fellow travelers' minds, Eddy secretly warned Luis. Luis looked stunned for a moment, then concealed his emotions as a respectable man of his tribe was brought up to do. He whispered briefly to Salvador, and the two Indian *vaqueros* silently disappeared.

The Forlorn Hope still had its lone rifle and meager supply of munitions, faithfully dragged through snow and mountains and canyons. Eddy decided to take the gun and go hunting. It was a no-lose gamble. If he had luck, he would save the lives of his seven remaining companions. If he failed, they would be no worse off. But when he dropped a hint of his plan to the women, they wept and carried on and begged him to remain, pleading that their lives depended on his staying with them.

But Eddy's mind was made up. The next morning he took the gun, only to be assailed by a reproachful, weeping chorus of women. Harriet Pike threw her arms around his neck and implored him not to go, and the others joined in, fearing he might never come back. But Mary Graves decided to go with Eddy. She was the only one still strong enough to keep up with him.

Eddy was not acting on a deranged whim. An experienced hunter, he thought that the fact that they were now on snow-free ground meant there might be animals around. After he and Mary had trudged about two miles, his keen eyes caught sight of a place where a deer had lain down for the night. Eddy burst into tears of happiness—his first since he had left the Mountain Camp. He turned around and saw Mary also weeping like a child. Although neither was in the least bit religious, both of them fell on their knees and prayed in gratitude. (Some recent commentators believe that Thornton made up this whole passage because he thought that this was how Eddy and Mary Graves *ought* to have behaved. I cannot say.)

Now emotionally relieved, they went on and soon saw a large buck about eighty-five yards away. Eddy raised his gun, but found to his dismay that he was too weak to aim it. Try as he might to hold it still, the gun wavered uncontrollably. He changed his grip and tried again. Again he failed. He heard Mary sobbing behind him. Alarmed and afraid that she would frighten the deer off, Eddy whispered to her to be quiet. "Oh, I am afraid you will not kill it!" she exclaimed, and then fell silent.

For the third time Eddy lifted his rifle to his shoulder. He raised the muzzle above the deer and lowered it slowly. As soon as the deer was in the sights, he pulled the trigger. The rifle cracked; the deer leaped three feet into the air and then stood still. Mary lost her self-control and wept, "O merciful God, you have missed it!"

Eddy told her that he knew his aim was on the deer at the instant he fired. Also, he explained, the deer had dropped its tail between its legs, a sign that it was wounded. At this, the deer recovered its wits and ran off. Eddy and Mary limped after it as fast as they could, sliding down a thirty-foot drop-off cushioned by a snowbank at the bottom. The deer ran about two hundred yards and fell. It was still alive when Eddy reached it, seized it by the antlers, and cut its throat with his penknife. Before he had finished, Mary was at his side, and the two famished humans drank the deer's blood as it gushed out.

They rested a bit and then found the strength to roll the deer's carcass to a spot where they could make a fire. Their faces were covered with blood, but they didn't care. They were going to eat.

They ate part of the deer's liver and some other internal organs for supper, then enjoyed a good night's sleep without dreams of food. During the night Eddy fired his gun several times to alert his comrades. Up on the plateau, Fosdick had heard the first crack of all, and knew what it meant. To his wife he exclaimed feebly, "There! Eddy has killed a deer! Now, if only I can get to him, I shall live!"

Fosdick's hopes were in vain. During the night he died. He and Sarah Graves had been married less than a year. Sarah, heartbroken, wrapped his body in their one remaining blanket and lay down on the bare ground to die herself. Somehow she survived the subfreezing cold of the night and revived with morning. To her horror she saw two of her traveling companions (the early chroniclers discreetly suppressed their names, but they were probably William and Sarah Foster) approaching her campsite. They were sure that both she and her husband had died during the cold night, and were coming up to help themselves to their flesh as well as their jewelry, watches, and money. Embarrassed at finding Sarah Fosdick still alive, they turned back to their own campsite and there met Eddy, who had come up from the valley with roasted venison for all hands.

As Eddy dried the remaining deer meat by the fire, Mrs. Fosdick and the two Fosters returned to Jay Fosdick's body. Sarah Fosdick gave her dead husband a last kiss. Then, in spite of her entreaties, the Fosters cut out her newly dead husband's heart and liver before her eyes and also took his arms and legs, the meatiest parts of the body.

The poor young widow, only twenty-two, made a little bundle of her valuables and went back to the campsites with the two people who had just callously butchered her husband. Uncaring, they impaled Fosdick's heart on a stick and began to roast it as she looked on. Sarah Fosdick could bear no more, and retreated to Eddy's campsite, which was a little way off.

During the next couple of days the handful that remained of the Forlorn Hope struck the north branch of the American River and crossed it. They had to climb another steep canyon wall by clinging to the bushes and small trees that grew in crevices. Their bleeding feet soaked their wretched wrappings of blanket scraps. But the weather, at least, was good, and everyone sat down peacefully to eat the last of the venison. Eddy made a little speech, mourning their lost companions. He tactfully avoided mentioning that they had been eaten by the survivors.

After supper, Foster took Eddy aside. Ever since the Forlorn Hope had left the Mountain Camp, Foster had been strangely apathetic and unhelpful, incapable of making a decision on his own and totally dependent on Eddy. Suddenly taking the initiative, he wanted Eddy to help him kill Amanda McCutchen, on the excuse that she was a nuisance and could not keep up.

Eddy, shocked and revolted, told Foster that she had a husband and children. Besides, she was one of their comrades, she was helpless, and she depended on them for protection. Foster kept whimpering objections, until Eddy finally told him sternly that Mrs. McCutchen was not going to die for his sake.

Foster's hunger-crazed mind turned to the sisters Sarah Fosdick and Mary Graves. Neither of them had a child, he slyly pointed out, and Sarah Fosdick no longer had a husband. After hearing this heartless proposal, Eddy warned the two women in the presence of the whole company.

Foster became angry and boasted that he didn't care what Eddy said; he could handle Eddy. Eddy, losing patience, challenged Foster to settle their differences on the spot. He grabbed a large stick, whacked it on a log to test its soundness, and threw it to Foster, telling him to defend himself. He seized a knife that had belonged to the late Jay Fosdick and went for Foster as fast as his weakness would permit. Eddy was almost within striking distance when the women, three of whom Foster had just proposed to kill and eat, seized him, dragged him to the ground, and took the knife away. Luckily, Foster stood dazed, missing this opportunity to kill Eddy.

Eddy, recovering, warned Foster once more that he would kill him if he ever again showed the slightest inclination to take the life of any member of the party. If anyone were to die, he said, it would be either Foster or himself. And they would settle the question of who was to die by fighting, since Foster had never been willing to take his chances by drawing lots, the only fair way, said Eddy, of selecting a victim.

On January 8 they left the Camp of Strife, as they named the place, and after about two miles found the bloody tracks of Sutter's Indians. Foster, sunk into a deranged bestiality, vowed that he would track down the Indians and kill them. Another couple of miles farther on, they found the two Indian *vaqueros,* collapsed on the ground and dying. It was no wonder, for they had been without food for a week and without fire for four days.

Eddy wanted to let the poor Indians die in peace—surely they could not last for more than a few hours—but Foster would not wait. Eddy felt there was no point in trying to stop him, since the Indians would soon be dead anyway, but he walked away so as not to witness the evil deed.

Foster, savoring his triumph, hobbled over to Luis, callously told him what he was about to do, and shot him through the head. He killed Salvador a moment later. Then, perhaps helped by the women, he cut the Indians' flesh from their bones and dried it.

That night Eddy ate only dried grass, refusing the flesh of the slain Indian youths. And from that night on only Foster's wife and his sister-in-law, Harriet Pike, camped with the slayer. The others slept a safe distance away, and one of them always stayed awake to keep an eye on their former friend, no longer trustworthy.

By now they saw numerous deer, but Eddy was so weak that he could no longer aim the gun. When he walked, he staggered like a drunk, and when he came to a fallen log only a foot high, he lacked the strength to step over it. Instead, he had to stoop down, put both hands on the log, and roll himself over it. All the survivors were now so enfeebled that they had to sit down and rest every quarter mile. The slightest obstacle caused them to stumble and fall. When the women fell, they wept like babies, got up, and tottered on again. There is no record of how the men behaved.

They had to cross rough terrain. Eddy still lived on grass, refusing to touch the flesh of his slain Indian companions. A cold rain began to fall on the wretched wanderers and did not stop. At last, on January 12, they reached an Indian village in the foothills. Dreadful experiences with the Spaniards had taught these Indians to fear and mistrust the white man. Yet when they saw these miserable wraiths, skeleton-thin and wrapped in rags, they burst into tears of pity.

After their first outburst of emotion, the Indians hurried to bring the survivors their own staple food of acorn bread. The starving whites did not get much nourishment from this unaccustomed food, and Eddy got sick and had to go back to eating grass.

The next day the chief of the village sent runners ahead to the next village, telling them to take care of the emigrants and have food ready for them. An escort from the village accompanied them, with an Indian on either side of each emigrant to support them and help them along. In this way they were passed along from village to village toward the white settlements.

On January 17 they reached a village where the chief had managed to collect a large handful of pine nuts. He gave them to Eddy, who ate them and felt miraculously restored. With new energy he led his comrades on. But the others gave out after a mile and collapsed on the ground, ready to die. The Indians, greatly distressed, were unable to help them.

Eddy thought again of his wife and children starving up in the snows of the Sierras and resolved to get through or die in the attempt. The elderly chief detailed one of his men to guide Eddy to the nearest white settlement, but after about five miles Eddy's new strength began to run out. Luckily, another Indian happened by, and Eddy prevailed on him to join them in return for some tobacco. After another five miles Eddy's strength failed completely, but the Indians half-carried him along, his bleeding feet dragging on the ground.

About half an hour before sunset they arrived at the home of a settler named M. D. Ritchie, who had arrived late in the fall of 1846 and built a shack on Johnson's ranch to spend the winter in. Come spring, he would go out and claim his own spread. Several other emigrants lived in winter quarters nearby.

Ritchie's young daughter, Harriet, heard a noise outside the shack and went to the door. There she saw the two Indians supporting a hideous bundle between them. The bundle spoke in English and asked for bread. Harriet burst into tears and led Eddy into the house. They instantly put him to bed, fed him, and heard his story. For four days he remained in bed, too exhausted even to turn over. He had traveled eighteen miles on foot that day, and he had been thirty-one days on the trail from the cabins by the lake.

Harriet Ritchie ran immediately to the neighbors with the news of the starving refugees who had escaped from the snow. The housewives collected all the bread they could spare. To this they added sugar, tea, and coffee—what was left of the limited supplies that they had brought over the mountains last fall. Beef from California's huge herds of half-wild cattle went into the food packets as well. Husbands and bachelors, not to miss out on the excitement, leaped on their horses and dashed importantly back and forth between the cabins bearing messages and collecting food.

Four men took backpacks loaded with as much food as they could carry and set off on foot, guided by the Indians (they did not want to risk their horses by riding at night). They reached the remaining members of the Forlorn Hope about midnight. One man stayed up all night cooking for them. Eddy had warned the rescue party not to give the survivors too much to eat, but they wept and begged for food so pathetically that the men gave them all they asked for, until all the food was gone. The result of this gorging on starved stomachs was that they all got sick.

In the morning came more men carrying food, this time on horseback. They had no trouble following the trail—for the past six miles it was marked by the blood from Eddy's feet. The rescuers could hardly believe that a starving man could cover such a distance. Indeed, they would not have believed it at all if they had not just traveled the same route and seen his tracks themselves.

That night the five women and Foster were brought to the settlement. The Forlorn Hope had reached a haven in California at last. But only seven had lived to reach it out of fifteen who began the deadly journey from the far side of the mountains.

Alive

From *Alive: The Story of the Andes Survivors*

BY PIERS PAUL READ

In October of 1972, an airplane carrying the members of a Uruguayan rugby team, plus family and friends, disappeared while flying through the towering Andes. A search turned up nothing and the group was presumed lost. The extraordinary story of how sixteen courageous and highly religious people managed to survive is captured forever in Piers Paul Read's 1974 classic, Alive.

T hey awoke on the morning of Sunday, October 22, to face their tenth day on the mountain. First to leave the plane were Marcelo Pérez and Roy Harley. Roy had found a transistor radio between two seats and by using a modest knowledge of electronics, acquired when helping a friend construct a hi-fi system, he had been able to make it work. It was difficult to receive signals in the deep cleft between the huge mountains, so Roy made an aerial with strands of wire from the plane's electric circuits. While he turned the dial, Marcelo held the aerial and moved it around. They picked up scraps of broadcasts from Chile but no news of the rescue effort. All that came over the radio waves were the strident voices of Chilean politicians embroiled in the strike by the middle classes against the socialist government of President Allende.

Few of the other boys came out into the snow. Starvation was taking its effect. They were becoming weaker and more listless. When they stood up they felt faint and found it difficult to keep their balance. They felt cold, even when the sun rose to warm them, and their skin started to grow wrinkled like that of old men.

Their food supplies were running out. The daily ration of a scrap of chocolate, a capful of wine, and a teaspoonful of jam or canned fish—

131

eaten slowly to make it last—was more torture than sustenance for these healthy, athletic boys; yet the strong shared it with the weak, the healthy with the injured. It was clear to them all that they could not survive much longer. It was not so much that they were consumed with ravenous hunger as that they felt themselves grow weaker each day, and no knowledge of medicine or nutrition was required to predict how it would end.

Their minds turned to other sources of food. It seemed impossible that there should be nothing whatsoever growing in the Andes, for even the meanest form of plant life might provide some nutrition. In the immediate vicinity of the plane there was only snow. The nearest soil was a hundred feet beneath them. The only ground exposed to sun and air was barren mountain rock on which they found nothing but brittle lichens. They scraped some of it off and mixed it into a paste with melted snow, but the taste was bitter and disgusting, and as food it was worthless. Except for lichens there was nothing. Some thought of the cushions, but even these were not stuffed with straw. Nylon and foam rubber would not help them.

For some days several of the boys had realized that if they were to survive they would have to eat the bodies of those who had died in the crash. It was a ghastly prospect. The corpses lay around the plane in the snow, preserved by the intense cold in the state in which they had died. While the thought of cutting flesh from those who had been their friends was deeply repugnant to them all, a lucid appreciation of their predicament led them to consider it.

Gradually the discussion spread as these boys cautiously mentioned it to their friends or to those they thought would be sympathetic. Finally, Canessa brought it out into the open. He argued forcefully that they were not going to be rescued; that they would have to escape themselves, but that nothing could be done without food; and that the only food was human flesh. He used his knowledge of medicine to describe, in his penetrating, high-pitched voice, how their bodies were using up their reserves. "Every time you move," he said, "you use up part of your own body. Soon we shall be so weak that we won't have the strength even to cut the meat that is lying there before our eyes."

Canessa did not argue just from expediency. He insisted that they had a moral duty to stay alive by any means at their disposal, and because Canessa was earnest about his religious belief, great weight was given to what he said by the more pious among the survivors.

"It is meat," he said. "That's all it is. The souls have left their bodies and are in heaven with God. All that is left here are the carcasses, which are no more human beings than the dead flesh of the cattle we eat at home."

Others joined the discussion. "Didn't you see," said Fito Strauch, "how much energy we needed just to climb a few hundred feet up the mountain? Think how much more we'll need to climb to the top and then down the other side. It can't be done on a sip of wine and a scrap of chocolate."

The truth of what he said was incontestable.

A meeting was called inside the Fairchild, and for the first time all twenty-seven survivors discussed the issue which faced them—whether or not they should eat the bodies of the dead to survive. Canessa, Zerbino, Fernández, and Fito Strauch repeated the arguments they had used before. If they did not they would die. It was their moral obligation to live, for their own sake and for the sake of their families. God wanted them to live, and He had given them the means to do so in the dead bodies of their friends. If God had not wished them to live, they would have been killed in the accident; it would be wrong now to reject this gift of life because they were too squeamish.

"But what have we done," asked Marcelo, "that God now asks us to eat the bodies of our dead friends?"

There was a moment's hesitation. Then Zerbino turned to his captain and said, "But what do you think *they* would have thought?"

Marcelo did not answer.

"I know," Zerbino went on, "that if my dead body could help you to stay alive, then I'd certainly want you to use it. In fact, if I do die, and you don't eat me, then I'll come back from wherever I am and give you a good kick in the ass."

This argument allayed many doubts, for however reluctant each boy might be to eat the flesh of a friend, all of them agreed with Zerbino. There and then they made a pact that if any more of them were to die, their bodies were to be used as food.

Marcelo still shrank from a decision. He and his diminishing party of optimists held onto the hope of rescue, but few of the others any longer shared their faith. Indeed, a few of the younger boys went over to the pessimists—or the realists, as they considered themselves—with some resentment against Marcelo Pérez and Pancho Delgado. They felt they had been deceived. The rescue they had been promised had not come.

The latter were not without support, however. Coche Inciarte and Numa Turcatti, both strong, tough boys with an inner gentleness, told their companions that while they did not think it would be wrong, they knew that they themselves could not do it. Liliana Methol agreed with them. Her manner was calm as always but, like the others, she grappled with the emotions the issue aroused. Her instinct to survive was strong, her longing for her children was acute, but the thought of eating human flesh horrified her. She did not think it wrong; she could distinguish between sin and physical revulsion, and a social taboo was not a law of God. "But," she said, "as long as there is a chance of rescue, as long as there is *something* left to eat, even if it is only a morsel of chocolate, then I can't do it."

Javier Methol agreed with his wife but would not deter others from doing what they felt must be done. No one suggested that God might want them to choose to die. They all believed that virtue lay in survival and that eating their dead friends would in no way endanger their souls, but it was one thing to decide and another to act.

Their discussions had continued most of the day, and by midafternoon they knew that they must act now or not at all, yet they sat inside the plane in total silence. At last a group of four—Canessa, Maspons, Zerbino, and Fito Strauch—rose and went out into the snow. Few followed them. No one wished to know who was going to cut the meat or from which body it was to be taken.

Most of the bodies were covered by snow, but the buttocks of one protruded a few yards from the plane. With no exchange of words, Canessa knelt, bared the skin, and cut into the flesh with a piece of broken glass. It was frozen hard and difficult to cut, but he persisted until he had cut away twenty slivers the size of matchsticks. He then stood up, went back to the plane, and placed them on the roof.

Inside there was silence. The boys cowered in the Fairchild. Canessa told them that the meat was there on the roof, drying in the sun, and that those who wished to do so should come out and eat it. No one came, and again Canessa took it upon himself to prove his resolution. He prayed to God to help him do what he knew to be right and then took a piece of meat in his hand. He hesitated. Even with his mind so firmly made up, the horror of the act paralyzed him. His hand would neither rise to his mouth nor fall to his side while the revulsion which possessed him struggled with his stubborn will. The will prevailed. The hand rose and pushed the meat into his mouth. He swallowed it.

He felt triumphant. His conscience had overcome a primitive, irrational taboo. He was going to survive.

Later that evening, small groups of boys came out of the plane to follow his example. Zerbino took a strip and swallowed it as Canessa had done, but it stuck in his throat. He scooped a handful of snow into his mouth and managed to wash it down. Fito Strauch followed his example, then Maspons and Vizintín and others.

Meanwhile Gustavo Nicolich, the tall, curly-haired boy, only twenty years old, who had done so much to keep up the morale of his young friends, wrote to his *novia* in Montevideo.

Most dear Rosina:
I am writing to you from inside the plane (our *petit hotel* for the moment). It is sunset and has started to be rather cold and windy which it usually does at this hour of the evening. Today the weather was wonderful—a beautiful sun and very hot. It reminded me of the days on the beach with you—the big difference being that then we would be going to have lunch at your place at midday whereas now I'm stuck outside the plane without any food at all.

Today, on top of everything else, it was rather depressing and a lot of the others began to get discouraged (today is the tenth day we have been here), but luckily this gloom did not spread to me because I get incredible strength just by thinking that I'm going to see you again. Another of the things leading to the general depression is that in a while the food will run out: we have only got two cans of seafood (small), one bottle of white wine, and a little cherry brandy left, which for twenty-six men (well, there are also boys who want to be men) is nothing.

One thing which will seem incredible to you—it seems unbelievable to me—is that today we started to cut up the dead in order to eat them. There is nothing else to do. I prayed to God from the bottom of my heart that this day would never come, but it has and we have to face it with courage and faith. Faith, because I came to the conclusion that the bodies are there because God put them there and, since the only thing that matters is the soul, I don't have to feel great remorse; and if the day came and I could save someone with my body, I would gladly do it.

I don't know how you, Mama, Papa, or the children can be feeling; you don't know how sad it makes me to think that you are suffering,

and I constantly ask God to reassure you and give us courage because
that is the only way of getting out of this. I think that soon there will
be a happy ending for everyone.
You'll get a shock when you see me. I am dirty, with a beard, and a little thinner, and with a big gash on my head, another one on my chest
which has healed now, and one very small cut which I got today
working in the cabin of the plane, besides various small cuts in the legs
and on the shoulder; but in spite of it all, I'm all right.

Those who first peered through the portholes of the plane the next
morning could see that the sky was overcast but that a little sun shone
through the clouds onto the snow. Some darted cautious looks toward
Canessa, Zerbino, Maspons, Vizintín, and the Strauch cousins. It was not
that they thought that God would have struck them down, but they
knew from their *estancias* that one should never eat a steer that dies from
natural causes, and they wondered if it might not be just as unhealthy to
do the same with a man.

The ones who had eaten the meat were quite well. None of them
had eaten very much and in fact they felt as enfeebled as the others. As
always, Marcelo Pérez was the first to raise himself from the cushions.

"Come on," he said to Roy Harley. "We must set up the radio."

"It's so cold," said Roy. "Can't you get someone else?"

"No," said Marcelo. "It's your job. Come on."

Reluctantly Roy took his shoes down from the hat rack and put
them on over his two pairs of socks. He squeezed himself out of the line
of dozing figures and climbed over those nearest the entrance to follow
Marcelo out of the plane. One or two others followed him out.

Marcelo had already taken hold of the aerial and was waiting
while Roy picked up the radio, switched it on, and began to turn the
dial. He turned it to a station in Chile which the day before had
broadcast nothing but political propaganda; now, however, as he held
the radio to his ear, he heard the last words of a news bulletin. "The
SAR has requested all commercial and military aircraft overflying the
cordillera to check for any sign of the wreckage of the Fairchild number five-seventy-one. This follows the cancellation of the search by
the SAR for the Uruguayan aircraft because of negative results."

The newscaster moved on to a different topic. Roy took the
radio away from his ear. He looked up at Marcelo and told him what he
had heard. Marcelo dropped the aerial, covered his face with his hands,
and wept with despair. The others who had clustered around Roy, upon

hearing the news, began to sob and pray, all except Parrado, who looked calmly up at the mountains which rose to the west.

Gustavo Nicolich came out of the plane and, seeing their faces, knew what they had heard.

"What shall we tell the others?" he asked.

"We mustn't tell them," said Marcelo. "At least let them go on hoping."

"No," said Nicolich. "We must tell them. They must know the worst."

"I can't, I can't," said Marcelo, still sobbing into his hands.

"I'll tell them," said Nicolich, and he turned back toward the entrance to the plane.

He climbed through the hole in the wall of suitcases and rugby shirts, crouched at the mouth of the dim tunnel, and looked at the mournful faces which were turned toward him.

"Hey, boys," he shouted, "there's some good news! We just heard it on the radio. They've called off the search."

Inside the crowded cabin there was silence. As the hopelessness of their predicament enveloped them, they wept.

"Why the hell is that good news?" Páez shouted angrily at Nicolich.

"Because it means," he said, "that we're going to get out of here on our own."

The courage of this one boy prevented a flood of total despair, but some of the optimists who had counted on rescue were unable to rally. The pessimists, several of them as unhopeful about escape as they had been about rescue, were not shocked; it was what they had expected. But the news broke Marcelo. His role as their leader became empty and automatic, and the life went out of his eyes. Delgado, too, was changed by the news. His eloquent and cheerful optimism evaporated into the thin air of the cordillera. He seemed to have no faith that they would get out by their own efforts and quietly withdrew into the background. Of the old optimists, only Liliana Methol still offered hope and consolation. "Don't worry," she said. "We'll get out of here, all right. They'll find us when the snow melts." Then, as if remembering how little food remained besides the bodies of the dead, she added, "Or we'll walk to the west."

To escape: that was the obsession of the new optimists. It was disconcerting that the valley in which they were trapped ran east, and that to the west there was a solid wall of towering mountains, but this did not deter Parrado. No sooner had he learned of the cancellation of the search than he announced his intention of setting off—on his own, if necessary—to the west. It was only with great difficulty that the others restrained him. Ten days before he had been given up for dead. If anyone was going to climb the mountains, there were others in a much better physical condition to do so. "We must think this out calmly," said Marcelo, "and act together. It's the only way we'll survive."

There was still sufficient respect for Marcelo and enough team discipline in Parrado to accept what the others decided. He was not alone, however, in his insistence that, before they got any weaker, another expedition should set out, either to climb the mountain and see what was on the other side or to find the tail.

It was agreed that a group of the fittest among them should set off at once, and a little more than an hour after they had heard the news on the radio, Zerbino, Turcatti, and Maspons set off up the mountain, watched by their friends.

Canessa and Fito Strauch returned to the corpse they had opened the day before and cut more meat off the bone. The strips they had put on the roof of the plane had now all been eaten. Not only were they easier to swallow when dried in the outside air, but the knowledge that they were not going to be rescued had persuaded many of those who had hesitated the day before. For the first time, Parrado ate human flesh. So, too, did Daniel Fernández, though not without the greatest effort of will to overcome his revulsion. One by one, they forced themselves to take and swallow the flesh of their friends. To some, it was merely an unpleasant necessity; to others, it was a conflict of conscience with reason.

Some could not do it: Liliana and Javier Methol, Coche Inciarte, Pancho Delgado. Marcelo Pérez, having made up his mind that he would take this step, used what authority he still possessed to persuade others to do so, but nothing he said had the effect of a short statement from Pedro Algorta. He was one of the two boys who had been dressed more scruffily at the airport than the others, as if to show that he despised their bourgeois values. In the crash, he had been hit on the head and suffered total amnesia about what had happened the day before. Algorta watched Canessa and Fito Strauch cutting the meat but said nothing until it came to the moment when he was offered a slice of flesh. He took it and swallowed it and then said, "It's like Holy Communion. When Christ died he gave his body to us so that we could have spiritual life. My friend has given us his body so that we can have physical life."

It was with this thought that Coche Inciarte and Pancho Delgado first swallowed their share, and Marcelo grasped it as a concept which would persuade others to follow his example and survive. One by one they did so until only Liliana and Javier Methol remained.

Now that it was established that they were to live off the dead, a group of stronger boys was organized to cover the corpses with snow, while those who were weaker or injured sat on the seats, holding the aluminum water makers toward the sun, catching the drops of water in empty wine bottles. Others tidied the cabin. Canessa, when he had cut enough meat for their immediate needs, made a tour of inspection of the wounded. He was moderately content with what he saw. Almost all the superficial wounds were continuing to heal, and none showed signs of infection. The swelling around broken bones also was subsiding; Alvaro Mangino and Pancho Delgado, for example, both managed, despite considerable pain, to hobble around outside the plane. Arturo Nogueira was worse off; if he went outside the plane he had to crawl, pulling himself forward with his arms. The state of Rafael Echavarren's leg was growing serious; it showed the first indications of gangrene.

Enrique Platero, the boy who had had the tube of steel removed from his stomach, told Canessa that he was feeling perfectly well but that a piece of his insides still protruded from the wound. The doctor carefully unwound the rugby shirt which Platero continued to use as a bandage and confirmed the patient's observation; the wound was healing well but something stuck out from the skin. Part of this projection had gone dry, and Canessa suggested to Platero that if he cut off the dead matter the rest might be more easily pushed back under the skin.

"But what is it sticking out?" asked Platero.

Canessa shrugged his shoulders. "I don't know," he said. "It's probably part of the lining of the stomach, but if it's the intestine and I cut it open, you've had it. You'll get peritonitis."

Platero did not hesitate. "Do what you have to do," he said, and lay back on the door.

Canessa prepared to operate. As scalpel he had a choice between a piece of broken glass or a razor blade. His sterilizer was the subzero air all around them. He disinfected the area of the wound with eau de cologne and then carefully cut away a small slice of the dead skin with the glass. Platero did not feel it, but the protruding gristle still would not go back under the skin. With even greater caution Canessa now cut yet closer to the living tissue, dreading all the time that he might cut into the intestine, but again he seemed to have done no harm and this time, with a prod from the surgeon's finger, the gut retired into Platero's stomach where it belonged.

"Do you want me to stitch you up?" Canessa asked his patient. "I should warn you that we don't have any surgical thread."

"Don't worry," said Platero, rising on his elbows and looking down at his stomach. "This is fine. Just tie it up again and I'll be on my way."

Canessa retied the rugby shirt as tightly as he could, and Platero swung his legs off the door and got to his feet. "Now I'm ready to go on an expedition," he said, "and when we get back to Montevideo I'll take you on as my doctor. I couldn't possibly hope for a better one."

Outside the plane, following the example of Gustavo Nicolich, Carlitos Páez was writing to his father, his mother, and his sisters. He also wrote to his grandmother:

> You can have no idea how much I have thought about you because I love you, I adore you, because you have already received so many blows in your life, because I don't know how you are going to stand this one. You, Buba, taught me many things but the most important one was faith in God. That has increased so much now that you cannot conceive of it. . . . I want you to know that you are the kindest grandmother in the world and I shall remember you each moment I am alive.

Zerbino, Turcatti, and Maspons followed the track of the plane up the mountain. Every twenty or twenty-five steps the three were forced to rest, waiting for their hearts to beat normally again. The mountain seemed almost vertical, and they had to clutch at the snow with their bare hands. They had left in such a hurry that they had not thought of how they should equip themselves for the climb. They wore only sneakers or moccasins and shirts, sweaters, and light jackets, with thin trousers covering their legs. All three were strong, for they were players who had been in training, but they had barely eaten for the past eleven days.

The air that afternoon was not so cold. As they climbed, the sun shone on their backs and kept them warm. It was their feet, sodden with freezing snow, which suffered most. In the middle of the afternoon they reached a rock, and Zerbino saw that the snow around it was melting. He threw himself down and sucked at drops of water suspended from the disintegrating crystals. There was also another form of lichen, which he put into his mouth, but it had the taste of soil. They continued to climb but by seven o'clock in the evening found that they were only halfway to the peak. The sun had gone behind the mountain and only a short span of daylight remained. They sat down to discuss what they should do. All agreed that it would get much colder and if they stayed on the mountain the three of them might well die of exposure. On the other hand, if they simply slid back down, the whole climb was for nothing. To get to the top or find the tail with the batteries was the only chance of survival for all twenty-seven. They made up their minds to remain on the mountain for the night and look for an outcrop of rocks which would provide some shelter.

A little farther up they found a small hillock where the snow had been blown away to reveal the rocks underneath. They piled up loose stones to form a windbreak and, as dark was almost upon them, lay down to sleep. With the dark, as always, came the cold, and for all the protection their light clothes afforded them against the subzero wind, they might as well have been naked. There was no question of sleep. They were compelled to hit one another with their fists and feet to keep their circulation going, begging one another to be hit in the face until their mouths were frozen and no words would come from them. Not one of the three thought he would survive the night. When the sun eventually rose in the east, each one was amazed to see it, and as it climbed in the sky it brought a little warmth back to their chilled bodies. Their clothes were soaked through, so they stood and took off their trousers, shirts, and socks and wrung them out. Then the sun went behind a cloud so they dressed again in their wet clothes and set off up the mountain.

Every now and then they stopped to rest and glance back toward the wreck of the Fairchild. By now it was a tiny dot in the snow, indistinguishable from any of the thousand outcrops of rock unless one knew exactly where to look. The red S which some of the boys had painted on the roof was invisible, and it was clear to the three why they had not been rescued: the plane simply could not be seen from the air. Nor was this all that depressed them. The higher they climbed, the more snow-covered mountains came into view. There was nothing to suggest that they were at the edge of the Andes, but they could only see to the north and the east. The mountain they were climbing still blocked their view to the south and west, and they seemed little nearer its summit. Every time they thought they had reached it, they would find that they were only at the top of a ridge; the mountain itself still towered above them.

At last, at the top of one of these ridges, their efforts were rewarded. They noticed that the rocks of an exposed outcrop had been broken, and then they saw scattered all around them the twisted pieces of metal that had once been part of the wingspan. A little farther up the mountain, where the ground fell into a small plateau, they saw a seat face down in the snow. With some difficulty they pulled it upright and found, still strapped to it, the body of one of their friends. His face was black, and it occurred to them that he might have been burned from the fuel escaping from the engine of the plane.

With great care Zerbino took from the body a wallet and identity card and, from around the neck, a chain and holy medals. He did the same when they came across the bodies of the three other Old Christians and the two members of the crew who had fallen out the back of the plane.

The three now made a count of those who were there and those who were below, and the tally came to forty-four. One body was missing. Then they remembered the floundering figure of Valeta, who had disappeared in the snow beneath them on that first afternoon. The count was now correct: six bodies at the top of the mountain, eleven down below, Valeta, twenty-four alive in the Fairchild, and the three of them there. All were accounted for.

They were still not at the summit, but there was no sign of the tail section or any other wreckage above them. They started back down the mountain, again following the track made by the fuselage, and on another shelf on the steep decline they found one of the plane's engines. The view from where they stood was majestic, and the bright sunlight reflecting off the snow made them squint as they observed the daunting panorama around them. They all had sunglasses, but Zerbino's were broken at the bridge, and as he climbed the mountain they had slipped forward so that he found it easier to peer over them. He did the same as they started to slide down again, using cushions they had taken from the seats at the top as makeshift sleds. They zigzagged, stopping at each piece of metal or debris to see if they could find anything useful. They discovered part of the plane's heating system, the lavatory, and fragments of the tail, but not the tail itself. Coming to a point where the track of the fuselage followed too steep a course, they crossed to the side of the mountain. By this time, Zerbino was so blinded by the snow that he could hardly see. He had to grope his way along, guided at times by the others. "I think," said Maspons, as they approached the plane once again, "that we shouldn't tell the others how hopeless it seems."

"No," said Turcatti. "There's no point in depressing them." Then he said, "By the way, what's happened to your shoe?"

Maspons looked down at his foot and saw that his shoe had come off while he was walking. His feet had become so numb with cold that he had not noticed.

The twenty-four other survivors were delighted to see the three return, but they were bitterly disappointed that they had not found the tail and appalled at their physical condition. All three hobbled on frozen feet and looked dreadful after their night out on the mountainside, and Zerbino was practically blind. They were immediately taken into the fuselage on cushions and brought large pieces of meat, which they gobbled down. Next Canessa treated their eyes, all of which were watering, with some drops called Colirio which he had found in a suitcase and thought might do them good. The drops stung but reassured them that something was being done for their condition. Then Zerbino bandaged his eyes with a rugby shirt, keeping it on for the next two days. When he removed his bandage he could still see only light and shadow, and he kept the rugby shirt as a kind of veil, shielding his eyes from the sun. He ate under the veil, and his blindness made him intolerably aggressive and irritable.

Their feet had also suffered. They were red and swollen with the cold, and their friends massaged them gently. It escaped no one's notice, however, that this expedition of a single day had almost killed three of the strongest among them, and morale once again declined.

On one of the days which followed, the sun disappeared behind clouds, rendering the water-making devices useless, so the boys had to return to the old method of putting the snow in bottles and shaking them. Then it occurred to Roy Harley and Carlitos Páez to make a fire with some empty Coca-Cola crates they had found in the luggage compartment of the plane. They held the aluminum sheets over the fire, and water was soon dripping into the bottles. In a short time they had enough.

The embers of the fire were still hot; it seemed sensible to try cooking a piece of meat on the hot foil. They did not leave it on for long, but the slight browning of the flesh gave it an immeasurably better flavor—softer than beef but with much the same taste.

The aroma soon brought other boys around the fire, and Coche Inciarte, who had continued to feel the greatest repugnance for the raw flesh, found it quite palatable when cooked. Roy Harley, Numa Turcatti, and Eduardo Strauch also found it easier to overcome their revulsion when the meat was roasted and they could eat it as though it were beef.

Canessa and the Strauch cousins were against the idea of cooking the meat, and since they had gained some authority over the group, their views could not be ignored. "Don't you realize," said Canessa, knowledgeable and assertive as ever, "that proteins begin to die off at temperatures above forty degrees centigrade? If you want to get the most benefit from the meat, you must eat it raw."

"And when you cook it," said Fernández, looking down on the small steaks spitting on the aluminum foil, "the meat shrinks in size. A lot of its food value goes up in smoke or just melts away."

These arguments did not convince Harley or Inciarte, who could hardly derive nutrition from raw meat if they could not bring themselves to eat it, but in any case the limit to cooking was set by the extreme shortage of fuel—there were only three crates—and the high winds which so often made it impossible to light a fire out in the snow.

In the next few days, after Eduardo Strauch became very weak and emaciated, he finally overcame his revulsion to raw meat—forced to by his two cousins. Harley, Inciarte, and Turcatti never did, yet they were committed to survival and managed to consume enough to keep alive. The only ones who still had not eaten human flesh were the two eldest among them, Liliana and Javier Methol, and as the days passed and the twenty-five young men grew stronger on their new diet, the married couple, living on what remained of the wine, chocolate, and jam, grew thinner and more feeble.

The boys watched their growing debility with alarm. Marcelo begged them over and over again to overcome their reluctance and eat the meat. He used every argument, above all those words of Pedro Algorta. "Think of it as Communion. Think of it as the body and blood of Christ, because this is food that God has given us because He wants us to live."

Liliana listened to what he said, but time and again she gently shook her head. "There's nothing wrong with you doing it, Marcelo, but I can't, I just can't." For a time Javier followed her example. He still suffered from the altitude and was cared for by Liliana almost as though he were her child. The days passed slowly and there were moments when they found themselves alone; then they would talk together of their home in Montevideo, wondering what their children were doing at that hour, anxious that little Marie Noel, who was three, might be crying for her mother, or that their ten-year-old daughter, María Laura, might be skipping her homework.

Javier tried to reassure his wife that her parents would have moved into their house and would be looking after the children. They talked about Liliana's mother and father, and Liliana asked whether it would be possible when they returned to have her parents come and live in their house in Carrasco. She looked a little nervously at her husband when she suggested it, knowing that not every husband likes the idea of his parents-in-law living under the same roof, but Javier simply smiled and said, "Of course. Why didn't we think of that before?"

They discussed how they might build an annex onto the house so that Liliana's parents could be more or less independent. Liliana worried that they might not be able to afford it or that an extra wing might spoil the garden, but on every point Javier reassured her. Their conversation, however, weakened his resolution not to eat human meat, and so when Marcelo next offered him a piece of flesh, Javier took it and thrust it down his throat.

There remained only Liliana. Weak though she was, with life ebbing from her body, her mood remained serene. She wrote a short note to her children, saying how dear they were to her. She remained close to her husband, helping him because he was weaker, sometimes even a little irritable with him because the altitude sickness made his movements clumsy and slow, but with death so near, their partnership did not falter. Their life was one, on the mountain as it had been in Montevideo, and in these desperate conditions the bond between them held fast. Even sorrow was a part of the bond, and when they talked together of the four children they might never see again, tears not only of sadness but of joy fell down their cheeks, for what they missed now showed them what they had had.

One evening just before the sun had set, and when the twenty-seven survivors were preparing to take shelter from the cold in the fuselage of the plane, Liliana turned to Javier and told him that when they returned she would like to have another baby. She felt that if she was alive it was because God wanted her to do so.

Javier was delighted. He loved his children and had always wanted to have more, yet when he looked at his wife he could see through the tears in his eyes the poignance of her suggestion. After more then ten days without food the reserves had been drawn from her body. The bones protruded from her cheeks and her eyes were sunk into their sockets; only her smile was the same as before. He said to her, "Liliana, we must face up to it. None of this will happen if we don't survive."

She nodded. "I know."

"God wants us to survive."

"Yes. He wants us to survive."

"And there's only one way."

"Yes. There's only one way."

Slowly, because of their weakness, Javier and Liliana returned to the group of boys as they lined up to climb into the Fairchild.

"I've changed my mind," Liliana said to Marcelo. "I will eat the meat."

Marcelo went to the roof of the plane and brought down a small portion of human flesh which had been drying in the sun. Liliana took a piece and forced it down into her stomach.

★ ★ ★

They ate nothing that day, and that night, as they huddled together to try and sleep, they all followed Carlitos in the rosary. The next day, October 31, was his nineteenth birthday. The present he would most have wanted, after a cream cake or a raspberry milkshake, was a break in the weather, but when he climbed up the tunnel to the open window the next morning, he saw that it was snowing just as heavily. He returned and predicted to the others, "We'll get three days of bad weather and then three of sunshine."

The bitter cold combined with their wet clothes to deplete their strength. They had eaten nothing for two days and now felt enormously hungry. The bodies of those who had been killed in the crash remained buried in the snow outside the plane, so the cousins uncovered one of those who had been smothered in the avalanche and cut meat off the body right before everyone's eyes. The meat before had either been cooked or at least dried in the sun; now there was no alternative but to eat it wet and raw as it came off the bone, and since they were so hungry, many ate larger pieces, which they had to chew and taste. It was dreadful for all of them; indeed, for some it was impossible to eat gobbets of flesh cut from the body of a friend who two days before had been living beside them. Roberto Canessa and Fito Strauch argued with them; Fito even forced Eduardo to eat the meat. "You must eat it. Otherwise you will die, and we need you alive." But no arguments or exhortations could overcome the physical revulsion in Eduardo Strauch, Inciarte, and Turcatti, and as a result their physical condition deteriorated.

The first of November was All Saints' Day and Pancho Delgado's birthday. As Carlitos had predicted it had stopped snowing, and six of the boys climbed out onto the roof to warm themselves in the sun. Canessa and Zerbino dug the snow off the windows to let more light into the plane, and Fito and Eduardo Strauch and Daniel Fernández melted snow for drinking water, while Carlitos smoked a cigarette and thought about his family, for it was also his father's and sister's birthday. He felt certain now that he would see them again. If God had saved him in both the accident and the avalanche, it could only be to reunite him with his family. The nearness of God in the still landscape set a seal on his conviction.

When the sun went behind a cloud it became cold again, and the six climbed back into the Fairchild. All they could do now was wait.

In the days which followed, the weather remained clear. There were no heavy falls of snow, and the stronger and more energetic among the nineteen survivors were able to dig a second tunnel out through the back of the plane. Using shovels made from pieces of metal or plastic broken off the body of the plane, they hacked at the hard snow, recovering objects which had been lost in the avalanche. Páez, for example, found his rugby boots.

Once a tunnel had been made, they were able to set about removing from the cabin both the snow and the bodies buried beneath it. The snow was like rock and their tools were inadequate. The corpses, frozen into the last gestures of self-defense, some with their arms raised to protect their faces like the victims of Vesuvius at Pompeii, were difficult to move. Some of the boys could not bring themselves to touch the dead, especially the bodies of their close friends, so they would tie one of the long nylon luggage straps around the shoulders of the corpse and drag it out.

Those buried inside near the entrance were left there, encased in the wall of ice which protected the living from a further avalanche. They provided a reserve supply of food, in case a second avalanche or heavy blizzard should cover and conceal the bodies they had just taken out, for those who had died in the crash were now completely lost under the snow. For the same reason, when the survivors came in at night, they would leave a limb or a portion of a torso on the "porch," in case the weather the next day made it impossible for them to go out.

It took eight days for the plane to be made more or less habitable, but a wall of snow remained at either end and the space they had to live in was more restricted than before—even allowing for the fewer numbers. Many looked back with mild regret to the halcyon days before the avalanche: "We thought we were badly off then, but what luxury and comfort compared to this!" There was only one advantage to ensue from the avalanche: the extra clothes which could be taken from the dead bodies. Feeling that God would help them if they helped themselves, the survivors not only set about the tasks which would make their immediate life more bearable but planned and prepared for their ultimate escape.

Before the avalanche it had been decided that a party of the fittest among them should set off for Chile. At first there had been a division of opinion between those who thought a larger group would stand a better chance and those who felt that it would be wise to concentrate their resources on a group of only three or four. As it became clear during the weeks following the crash, and especially during the stormy days after the avalanche, that the conditions encountered on any expedition would be severe, the reasoning of the second group prevailed. Four or five would be chosen as expeditionaries. They would be given larger rations of meat and the best places to sleep and be excused from the daily labor of cutting meat and clearing snow, so that when summer finally settled in and the snow began to melt toward the end of November they would be strong, healthy, and fit for their walk to Chile.

The first factor to be considered in choosing these expeditionaries was their physical condition. Some who had been unharmed in the accident had suffered since. Zerbino's eyes had not fully recovered from his climb up the mountain. Inciarte had painful boils on his leg. Sabella and Fernández were well enough but, not being players, they were less fit than those in the first fifteen of the Old Christians. Eduardo Strauch, strong at the outset, had been weakened by the revulsion he felt for eating human flesh immediately after the avalanche. The choice narrowed to Parrado, Canessa, Harley, Páez, Turcatti, Vizintín, and Fito Strauch. Some of them were more enthusiastic candidates than others. Parrado was so determined to escape that, had he not been chosen, he would have gone on his own. Turcatti too was emphatic that he should be one of the expeditionaries; he had two previous expeditions to prove his physical and mental stamina, and the younger boys had great faith that if he went the expedition would succeed.

Canessa had more imagination than some of the others and foresaw the danger and hardship which would be involved, but he felt that because of his exceptional strength and acknowledged inventiveness it was his duty to go. In the same way Fito Strauch volunteered, more from a sense of obligation than a real desire to leave the relative safety of the Fairchild, but nature intervened to settle his case, for eight days after the avalanche he developed severe hemorrhoids which effectively excluded him. His two cousins were delighted that he was to stay.

The remaining three, Páez, Harley, and Vizintín, all wanted to be expeditionaries but, though they were considered fit enough, some doubts were felt as to their maturity and strength of mind. And so it was decided that these three should go on a trial expedition which would last a day. Already, since the avalanche, there had been some minor sorties from the immediate surroundings of the plane. Francois and Inciarte had climbed three hundred feet up the mountain, resting after every ten steps to smoke a cigarette. Turcatti had gone up to the wing with Algorta, climbing with less energy and more effort than he had shown before, for he too had been weakened by his distaste for raw meat.

Páez, Harley, and Vizintín set out at eleven o'clock in the morning seven days after the avalanche to prove themselves. Their plan was to walk down across the valley to the large mountain on the other side. It seemed to be an attainable objective for a one-day expedition.

They wore two sweaters each, two pairs of trousers, and rugby boots. The surface of the snow was frozen so they walked easily down the valley, zigzagging where the descent was too steep to follow a direct path. They carried nothing with them to hamper their progress. After walking like this for an hour and a half they came upon the rear door of the plane and, scattered beyond it, some of the contents of the galley: two empty aluminum containers for storing coffee and Coca-Cola, a trash can, and a jar of instant coffee, empty but for a residue of powder left at the bottom. The three immediately put snow into the jar, melted it as best they could, and drank the coffee-flavored water. They then emptied out the rubish bin and to their delight found some broken pieces of candy, which they scrupulously divided into thirds and sucked, sitting on the snow. They were, for those few moments, in ecstasy. Though searching further, all they could find was a cylinder of gas, a broken thermos, and some maté. They put the maté in the thermos and took it with them as they continued on their way.

After walking down and across the valley for another two hours they began to realize that distances are deceptive in the snow and they were little nearer to the mountain opposite than when they started. Their progress had also become more difficult because the midday sun had melted the surface of the snow, and they now fell into it up to their knees. At three o'clock they decided to return to the plane, but as they retraced their tracks they quickly discovered how much more difficult it was to walk up the mountain than it had been to come down. Ominously, the sky had clouded over and a few flakes of snow began to fall and swirl around them in the wind.

They reached the coffee jar and refreshed themselves again with coffee-flavored water. Roy and Carlitos picked up the two containers from the galley, realizing that they would be useful for making water back at the plane, but found them too heavy and discarded them. Vizintín, however, held on to the large trash can and used it as a kind of staff to push himself up the mountain.

The climb became exceptionally difficult. They still sank to their knees in the snow, the slopes were steeper, the flurries turned to heavy snow, and all three were tired. Roy and Carlitos were close to panic. In the confused dimensions of the snow-covered landscape, they had lost all sense of how near or far they were from the plane. There were undulations in the side of the mountain, and as they reached the summit of each one they expected to see the Fairchild, but it was never there; and with each disappointment, their spirits fell. Roy began to cry, and Carlitos finally collapsed in the snow. "I can't go on," he said. "I can't, I can't. Leave me. You go on. Leave me here to die."

"Come on, Carlitos," said Roy through his tears. "For God's sake, come on! Think of your family . . . your mother . . . your father. . . ."

"I can't, I can't move. . . ."

"Get up, you sissy," said Vizintín. "We'll all freeze if we stay here."

"All right, I'm a sissy. A coward. I admit it. You go on."

But they would not leave, and they bombarded Carlitos with a mixture of exhortation and abuse that eventually brought him to his feet again. They climbed a bit farther, to the crest of another hill, and still the plane was not in sight.

"How much farther is it?" asked Carlitos. "How much farther?"

A little later he again collapsed in the snow.

"You go on," he said, "I'll follow you in a minute."

But again Vizintín and Harley would not abandon him, and once again they insulted him and pleaded with him until he got to his feet and walked on through the blinding snow.

They got back to the plane after the sun had set. The other boys had gone in and were waiting for them anxiously. When the three tumbled down the tunnel into the Fairchild, utterly exhausted, Carlitos and Roy in tears, it was apparent to all that the test had been severe and that some had failed.

"It was impossible," said Carlitos. "It was impossible and I collapsed, wanted to die, and cried like a baby."

Roy shivered, wept, and said nothing.

Vizintín's small, close-set eyes were quite dry. "It was tough," he said, "but possible."

Thus Vizintín became the fourth expeditionary. Carlitos withdrew his candidacy after his experience on the trial expedition, and Roy was told by Parrado that he could not be an expeditionary because he cried too much, whereupon Roy burst into tears. He was disappointed, however, only because he thought Fito was going. He had known Fito since they were children and felt safe by his side. When Fito developed hemorrhoids and withdrew, Roy was quite happy to be among those who were to stay behind.

Once the four expeditionaries had been chosen, they became a warrior class whose special obligations entitled them to special privileges. They were allowed anything which might improve their condition in body or mind. They ate more meat than the others and chose which pieces they preferred. They slept where, how, and for as long as they liked. They were no longer expected to share the everyday work of cutting meat and cleaning the plane, though Parrado and, to a lesser extent, Canessa continued to do so. And just as their bodies were coddled, so were their minds. Prayers were said at night for their health and well-being, and all conversation in their hearing was of an optimistic nature. If Methol thought that the plane was in the middle of the Andes, he would make sure not to say so to an expeditionary. If ever their position was discussed with them, Chile was only a mile or two away on the other side of the mountain.

It was inevitable, perhaps, that the four should to some extent take advantage of their favored position and that this should provoke resentment. Sabella had to sacrifice his second pair of trousers to Canessa;

Francois had only one pair of socks while Vizintín had six. Pieces of fat which had been carefully scavenged from the snow by some hungry boy would be requisitioned by Canessa, saying, "I need it to build up my strength, and if I don't build up my strength you'll never get out of here." Parrado took no advantage of his position, however; nor did Turcatti. Both worked as hard as they had done before and showed the same calm, affection, and optimism.

The expeditionaries were not the leaders of the group but a caste apart, separated from the others by their privileges and preoccupations. They might have evolved into an oligarchy had not their powers been checked by the triumvirate of the Strauch cousins. Of all the subgroups of friends and relatives that had existed before the avalanche, theirs was the only one to survive intact. The gang of younger boys had lost Nicolich and Storm; Canessa had lost Maspons; Nogueira had lost Platero; Methol had lost his wife. Gone too was Marcelo, the leader they had inherited from the outside world.

The closeness of the relationship between Fito Strauch, Eduardo Strauch, and Daniel Fernández gave them an immediate advantage over all the others in withstanding not the physical but the mental suffering caused by their isolation in the mountains. They also possessed those qualities of realism and practicality which were of much more use in their brutal predicament than the eloquence of Pancho Delgado or the gentle nature of Coche Inciarte. The reputation which they had gained, especially Fito, in the first week for facing up to unpalatable facts and making unpleasant decisions had won the respect of those whose lives had thereby been saved. Fito, who was the youngest of the three, was the most respected, not just for his judicious opinions but for the way in which he had supervised the rescue of those trapped in the avalanche at the moment of greatest hysteria. His realism, together with his strong faith in their ultimate salvation, led many of the boys to pin their hopes on him, and Carlitos and Roy suggested that he be made leader in place of Marcelo. But Fito refused this crown they offered him. There was no need to institutionalize the influence of the Strauch cousins.

Of all the work that had to be done, cutting meat off the bodies of their dead friends was the most difficult and unpleasant, and this was done by Fito, Eduardo, and Daniel Fernández. It was a ghastly task which even those as tough as Parrado or Vizintín could not bring themselves to perform. The corpses had first to be dug out of the snow, then thawed in the sun. The cold preserved them just as they had been at the moment of death. If the eyes remained open, they would close them, for it was hard to cut into a friend under his glassy gaze, however sure they were that the soul had long since departed.

The Strauches and Fernández, often helped by Zerbino, would cut large pieces of meat from the body; these would then be passed to another team, which would divide the chunks into smaller pieces with razor blades. This work was not so unpopular, for once the meat was separated from the bodies it was easier to forget what it was.

The meat was strictly rationed, and this again was done by the two Strauches and Daniel Fernández. The basic ration which was given out at midday was a small handful, perhaps half a pound, but it was agreed that those who worked could have more, because they used up energy through their exertions, and that the expeditionaries could have almost as much as they liked. One corpse was always finished before another was started.

They had, from necessity, come to eat almost every part of the body. Canessa knew that the liver contained the reserve of vitamins; for that reason he ate it himself and encouraged others to do so until it was set aside for the expeditionaries. Having overcome their revulsion against eating the liver, it was easier to move on to the heart, kidneys, and intestines. It was less extraordinary for them to do this than it might have been for a European or a North American, because it was common in Uruguay to eat the intestines and the lymphatic glands of a steer at an *asado*. The sheets of fat which had been cut from the body were dried in the sun until a crust formed, and then they were eaten by everyone. It was a source of energy and, though not as popular as the meat, was outside the rationing, as were the odd pieces of earlier carcasses which had been left around in the snow and could be scavenged by anyone. This helped fill the stomachs of those who were hungry, for it was only the expeditionaries who ever ate their fill of meat. The others felt a continuous craving for more, yet realized how important it was that what they had should be rationed. Only the lungs, the skin, the head, and the genitals of the corpses were thrown aside.

These were the rules, but there arose outside the rules an unofficial system of pilfering tolerated by the Strauches. This was why the task of cutting up the larger pieces was so popular; every now and then a sliver could be popped into one's mouth. Everyone who worked at cutting up the meat did it, even Fernández and the Strauches, and no one said anything so long as it did not go too far. One piece in the mouth for every ten cut up for the others was more or less normal. Mangino sometimes brought the proportion down to one for every five or six and Páez to one for three, but they would not hide what they did and desisted when the others shouted at them.

This system, like a good constitution, was fair in theory and flexible enough to allow for the weakness of human nature, but the burden fell on those who either could not or would not work. Echavarren and Nogueira were trapped in the plane by their broken, swollen, septic, and gangrenous legs, and only occasionally could they drag themselves down from their hammock and crawl out to defecate or to melt snow for drinking water. There was no question of their cutting up meat or scavenging in the snow. Delgado, too, had a broken leg, and Inciarte's leg was septic. Methol was still hampered by altitude sickness. Bobby Francois and Roy Harley were also crippled to some extent, not in their limbs but in their will; they could have worked but the shock of the crash or, in Roy's case, the shock of the avalanche followed by the abortive trial expedition seemed to have destroyed all sense of purpose. They simply sat in the sun.

The workers felt little compassion for those they thought of as parasites. In such extreme conditions lethargy seemed criminal. Vizintín thought that those who did not work should be given nothing to eat until they did. The others realized they had to keep their companions alive but saw no reason to do much more. They were harsh, too, in their assessment of the malingerers' condition. Some thought that Nogueira's legs were not broken and that he only imagined the pain he felt. They also thought that Delgado exaggerated the pain of his fractured femur. Mangino, after all, had broken his leg too, yet he managed to work at cutting up meat. They had little respect for Methol's altitude sickness or Francois's frozen feet. The result was that the only supplement to the ration for the "parasites" were the cells of their own bodies.

Some of the boys continued to find it difficult to eat raw human flesh. While the others extended the limit of what they could stomach to the liver, heart, kidneys, and intestines of the dead, Inciarte, Harley, and Turcatti still balked at the red meat of the muscles. The only occasions on which they found it easy to eat was when the meat was cooked; and every morning Inciarte would look across to Páez, who was in charge of this department, and ask, "Carlitos, are we cooking today?"

Carlitos would reply, "I don't know; it depends on the wind," for they could only light a fire if the weather was fair. But there were other factors involved. The supply of wood was limited; when they had used up all the Coca-Cola crates, there were only thin strips of wood which made up part of the wall of the plane. There was also Canessa's argument that proteins died at a high temperature and Fernández's that frying the meat made it shrink so that there was less to be eaten. Thus, cooking was allowed once or twice a week as the weather permitted, and on those occasions the less fastidious would hold back so that the others could eat more.

Part Four
Cannibalism in War: "A Ghastly Harvest"

American Indian Cannibalism
From *The Wild Frontier: Atrocities During the American-Indian War*

BY WILLIAM W. OSBORN

Probably the thing that terrified early white settlers the most, writes William
Osborn in *The Wild Frontier,* was not the threat of torture or enslavement, or
even death—but Indian cannibalism.

Indian Cannibalism occurred over a long period of time, indeed,
longer than the war itself. [. . .]
   The first report of cannibalism in the New World occurs in a
1493 letter from Christopher Columbus. He indicated that he had
found no monsters, nor had he had a report of any "except in an
island 'Carib,' . . . which is inhabited by a people who are regarded in all
the islands as very fierce and who eat human flesh." The word *cannibal*
comes from the Carib Indians.
   Some Indians in the Caribbean prized human flesh. The Caribs
and Tupians "relished human flesh and ate it in preference to other
food." They were tribes who made war to get victims and ate the heart
and other parts of the body in the belief they would get the courage or
other qualities of the victim. Others found it repellent.
   Cannibalism was not confined, however, to the Carib island. It
was described in detail by Amerigo Vespucci, who made important voy-
ages to the New World and whose writing was published around 1504.
He related that the Indians of Brazil

> cruelly kill one another, and those whom they bring home captive
> from war they preserve, not to spare their lives, but that they may be
> slain for food; for they eat one another, the victors the vanquished,

and among other kinds of meat human flesh is a common article of diet with them. Nay be the more assured of this fact because the father has already been seen to eat children and wife, and I knew a man whom I also spoke to who was reputed to have eaten more than three hundred human bodies. And I likewise remained twenty-seven days in a certain city where I saw salted human flesh suspended from beams between the houses, just as with us it is the custom to hang bacon and pork. I say further: they themselves wonder why we do not eat our enemies and do not use as food their flesh which they say is most savory.

Indian cannibalism in English literature first appeared in a translation of a Dutch pamphlet published about 1511. In describing Indian life it reported Indians "ete also on[e] another[.] The man eteth his wyfe[,] his chylderene as we also have seen and they hange also the bodyes or persons fleeshe in the smoke as men do with swynes fleshe."

Richard Slotkin, among others, stated that almost all the Indian tribes practiced ritual cannibalism. Harold E. Driver said cannibalism (as well as torture and human sacrifice) occurred in all tribes from the Iroquois in the northeast to the Gulf tribes in the southeast:

The pattern of warfare in a particular region is partly determined by the contacts with peoples on the outside and by the ideas and values derived from these contacts. For example, the torture of prisoners, or their sacrifice to the supernatural, and cannibalism, occur in a continuous area from the Iroquoians in the Northeast to the Gulf tribes in the Southeast, thence south through Northeast Mexico to Meso-America and the Caribbean.

Christy Turner II believes that the skeletal remains of at least 286 Hopi (radiocarbon-dated to about 1580) indicate that they had been cannibalized by other Hopi. He also believes that 12 percent of 870 Anasazi skeletons he examined indicate cannibalization, an additional 69 people.

The Iroquois would force their male captives to run the gauntlet, accept some of those who made it into the tribe, perhaps give those who did not to the widows of warriors, and "still other captives might be cooked and eaten so that their strength could be absorbed by the Iroquois warriors."

Pierre Esprit Radisson was captured by Mohawk while duck hunting in Quebec. He was adopted into the tribe. He went on a hunting trip with three Mohawk warriors and a Huron captive. The Huron captive proposed that they kill their captors and escape, which they did. But other Mohawks caught up with them fourteen days later. "The Huron was killed and his heart eaten by the Mohawks."

Alan Axelrod wrote that "cannibalism was widespread and was reported among Indians well into the nineteenth century."

Cannibalism was not confined to Indians. In 1607, after widespread starvation, some settlers ate corpses and at least one ate his wife. Other settlers considered it. In 1703, William Clap wrote a letter recounting how he had been taken prisoner by the French and forcibly marched to Canada. The party was in such dire straits that the two French guards considered killing and eating him. Clap prayed in their presence, and one of the Frenchmen, who seemed to have tears in his eyes, told him to get up and they would try one day longer.

After Barbara Leininger was captured in 1755, she was put with a captive Englishwoman, who later tried to escape. The Indians scalped her, laid burning splinters on her body, and cut off her ears and fingers. A French officer "took compassion on her, and put her out of her misery." An English soldier named John had escaped from prison at Lancaster and joined the French. He cut a piece of flesh from the Englishwoman's body and ate it. She was then chopped in two and her body devoured by the dogs.

Anne Jamison wrote that she and her children were in a large party fleeing Indian attacks by floating down the Mississippi on a raft. They ran out of food. The only surviving adult male in her party proposed consuming a child chosen by lot. Jamison dissuaded him.

There were reports of Indian cannibalism in New England. Puritans said that Indians gnawed flesh from settler bones after tying their captives to trees. Around 1625, the Mohegan sachem Wonkus ate part of the body of the Narranganset sachem Miantonomo, then commented, "It is the sweetest meat I ever ate." In 1676 Nathaniel Saltonstall told about an incident in New England where the Indian executioner flung one end of a rope over a post and hoisted the victim up like a dog "and with his Knife made a Hole in his Breast to his Heart, and sucked out his Heart-Blood." The Algonquins as well as the Iroquois were cannibals.

In 1724 the Creeks offered to mediate a war between the Seneca and the Cherokee. The Seneca replied that they could not afford to make peace because "we have no people to war against nor yet no meal to eat but the Cherokees." A French half-breed, Charles Langlade, led Ojibway, Potawatomis, and Ottawas against the Miami capital, Pickaw-illany (near Piqua, Ohio) in 1752. One trader and thirteen Miami warriors were killed. Three other traders and Miami chief Memeskia were captured. "Chief Memeskia was killed and ritually devoured by his assailants."

In 1754, the *Boston Evening Post* reported that

> the Enemies had 2 kill'd and as many wounded in the Engagement, which being over, the Indians cut open Capt. Donahew's Breast, and suck'd his Blood and hacked and mangled his Body in a most inhuman and barbarous Manner, and then eat a great part of this Flesh. They also suck'd the Blood and mangled the Bodies of the other Slain.

After Fort William Henry fell in 1757, Paul Roubaus, missionary to the Abnaki Indians, ordered them not to participate in ritual cannibalism as the Ottawas had done before.

Governor Clinton reported before 1814 that the Indians "utterly destroyed their enemies by eating their bodies, not because they had an appetite for such fare but in order to excite themselves to greater fury." French officer Louis Antoine de Bougainville, comte de Bougainville, wrote to his mother that "her child shudders at the horrors which we will be forced to witness" in combat employing this most "ferocious of all people, and cannibals by trade," his Indian allies. He wrote to his brother that the Indians had been "drawn from 500 leagues by the smell of fresh human flesh and the chance to teach their young men how one carves up a human being destined for the pot."

While John Tanner was a captive of the Indians between 1789 and 1817, he encountered medicine man Aiskawbawis. Tanner admitted he never thought well of Aiskawbawis, who claimed to talk with the Great Spirit, beat his drum incessantly at night, driving all the game away, and had "once eaten his own wife because of hunger." The Indians wanted to kill him for this, but didn't.

Some of the tribes on the northwestern coast were cannibals. They had secret societies. Alvin M. Josephy told about them:

One of the best known was the Kwakiutl Cannibal Society, whose initiates were possessed by the Cannibal Spirit at the North End of the World. Working up to a frenzy, the dancers bit flesh from the arms of those watching them, and then ate of the body of a specially killed slave or of an animal masked to resemble a human.

In the 1860s, three Indian tribes attacked the Tonkawa Indians, who were hated for their adherence to Texas and accused of practicing cannibalism. The Comanche fought the Tonkawas in 1874 and lost. The Comanche hated them because they served the army as scouts against other Indians and because they were, or had been, cannibals.

The Tonkawas practiced cannibalism for food, not ritual. A Tonkawa band, together with settlers in Texas, chased some Comanche horse thieves. Three Tonkawas killed a Comanche rear guard, then rode to a neighboring farm. Noah Smithwick was invited to their feast and remembered what happened:

> Having fleeced off the flesh of the dead Comanche, they borrowed a big wash kettle . . . into which they put the Comanche meat, together with a lot of corn and potatoes—the most revolting mess my eyes ever rested on. When the stew was sufficiently cooked and cooled to allow of its being ladled out with the hands, the whole tribe gathered round, dipping it up with their hands and eating it as greedily as hogs. Having gorged themselves on this delectable feast, they lay down and slept till night, when the entertainment was concluded with the scalp dance.

The Lipans in Texas practiced cannibalism. Texas Ranger Robert Hall was invited to dinner after a Lipan skirmish with the Comanche. " 'They offered me a choice slice of Comanche,' he remarked, 'but I politely informed them that I had just eaten a rattlesnake and was too full to eat any more.' "

The fact that some Indians were cannibals was a serious impediment to a satisfactory relationship between Indians and settlers. Bernard W. Sheehan put it like this:

> No fantasy-ridden portrayal of savage violence cut more deeply into the Indian's reserve of humanity than the charge of cannibalism. Some commentators denied the accusation; others made palliating distinctions over the circumstances in which Indians would eat human flesh.

James Adair protested that they consumed only the heart of the enemy in order to inspire them with his courage, and at the same time, he denied that Indians were cannibals. An occasional account took pleasure in a blood anecdote. John Long quoted the story of a Jesuit missionary who described an Indian woman feeding her children when her husband arrived with an English prisoner: "She immediately cut off his arm, and gave her children the streaming blood to drink," asserting at the priest's protestation that she wanted her children to be warriors "and therefore fed them with the food of men." A sergeant named Jordan wrote to his wife from the Northwest in 1812 and told of an incident that occurred immediately following his capture by "four damned yellow Indians." One of the natives agreed to spare his life because Jordan had once given him tobacco at Fort Wayne. But the savage went to the body of Captain Wells who lay nearby, "cut off his head and stuck it on a pole, while another took out his heart and divided it among the chiefs, and they ate it up raw." The fact could not be disputed, Indians had eaten human flesh and thus had offended against the moral basis of human existence. No amount of explanation could quite cover the crime, nor would any fanciful description replace the accusation.

Judge Webb and Japanese Cannibalism
From *Hidden Horrors: Japanese War Crimes in World War II*

It was a secret known to Allied authorities but closely guarded, lest the public find out: during the course of the savage South Pacific fighting in World War II, the starving Japanese devoured Allied prisoners and combat dead. Yuki Tanaka's *Hidden Horrors: Japanese War Crimes in World War II*, is one of the first books to deal directly with cannibalism as a war crime.

The Tokyo Tribunal and Cannibalism

On December 6, 1946, H.V. Evatt, Australia's minister for foreign affairs, sent a telegram to Judge William F. Webb, who was then in Tokyo for the International Military Tribunal for the Far East. The telegram asked Webb to advise Evatt as to whether Australia should adopt the recent British decision regarding the B and C Class trials. Britain wanted to bring to these trials only those suspects who were charged with crimes punishable by either death or more than seven years' imprisonment. It was a matter of some importance for the Australian government to come to a decision on this matter. If the British and Australian governments adopted different policies for bringing suspected war criminals to trial, there would be the potential for a major political problem. The Australian government at this time was concentrating on the prosecution of major war crimes and was not actively prosecuting war crimes punishable by less than twelve months' imprisonment. Evatt wanted Webb to give his opinion as to whether Australia should also cease to prosecute "intermediate" war crimes for which prison sentences ranged between one and seven years.

Webb cabled his opinion to Evatt on December 10, 1946: "Your 388. Consider test of probable sentence unsatisfactory. Suggest all deliberate act or omissions causing, or likely to cause, death or grievous bodily harm. Also, *cannibalism* and torturing." [Emphasis added.] It is clear from this cable that Webb was of the opinion that all those accused of war crimes in the B and C Class involving murder, grievous bodily harm, cannibalism, or torture should be taken to trial and that there should be no compromise. However, there is no evidence to suggest that Webb had actually brought the issue of cannibalism to the attention of the A Class tribunal, of which he was president.

During the war, as the chairman of the War Crimes Committee, Webb had viewed substantial numbers of documents and reports prepared by the Australian Army on the issue of cannibalism. In some cases he had personally interrogated witnesses to such crimes. Australia was the only member of the Allied nations to recognize cannibalism and mutilation of the dead as specific war crimes, and this was probably because of the detailed investigations and reports gathered by Webb in the three reports on Japanese war crimes trials over which he had presided in the years 1944 to 1946. Nevertheless, it appears that Webb had no intention of revealing his knowledge of such crimes while participating in the A Class tribunals. Theoretically it was not possible for Webb, as a judge at these tribunals, to select which war crimes would come to trial. However, in practice Webb maintained close contact with the Australian prosecutors and was a close friend of the chief Australian prosecutor, A.J. Mansfield. It seems highly unlikely that they would not have discussed the issue of cannibalism at some stage of the proceedings. Australia brought the most representative cases of murder, grievous bodily harm, and torture to the A Class tribunal but not those of cannibalism. Why did Webb neglect to have this issue brought to the attention of the tribunal? Before this question is answered, it is necessary to analyze the actual occurrences of cannibalism committed by Japanese forces.

Evidence of Japanese Cannibalism

There is a certain amount of Japanese writing suggesting that Japanese forces committed acts of cannibalism in the Philippines and New Guinea during the Asia–Pacific War. A typical example is found in the novel *Fires on the Plane* by Ōoka Shōhei. The 1987 Japanese documentary film *Yuki Yuki te Shingun* (Onward Holy Army) contains interviews with Japanese war veterans who confessed to engaging in cannibalism during the New Guinea campaign. Several autobiographies by Japanese veterans of that campaign also make explicit references to cannibalism. For example, Ogawa Shōji mentioned incidents that occurred between December 1943 and March 1944 when Japanese forces were retreating through the Finisterre Mountains in north-central New Guinea.

> Here I saw something genuinely horrible. There was the body of a soldier lying on the track, and a large part of his thigh had been hacked off. . . . Later I was walking along a track with Y when we were called by a group of four or five soldiers who were not in our troop. They had just finished a meal, and there were mess tins nearby. They said that they had a large cut of snake meat and invited us to join them. But we didn't like the way they were smiling as they said it. We felt that they were not telling us something. It was as if they wanted us to be "partners in crime." There was something unusual about the way they were staring at us, as if they were waiting to see our reaction. Y felt the same way about the situation and said "no thanks; maybe some other time." The situation was very tense. We left hurriedly, but cautiously, scared that they might try to shoot us. After we had walked a while, Y said to me "It's very strange. What do you think they were doing? If that had been snake meat they would never have given any to us. Don't you think they were trying to drag us into the crime they had committed?" . . . In fact we saw many bodies which had had their thighs hacked off.

In a book published in 1992, Ogawa reported that toward the end of the war he was witness to horrific conversations among Japanese soldiers in New Guinea along the lines of "so-and-so has died, let's go and get his body." In another case a friend of his found human flesh in the mess tin of an officer who had become ill and died. The impression left is that the victims of cannibalism were Japanese soldiers who had been killed in battle or who had died of various illnesses.

In his memoirs Nogi Harumichi, the chief of the Japanese naval police force in Ambon, mentioned incidents that occurred in the Philippines and that were reported to him by a Japanese army lieutenant immediately after the war.

> Most of the Japanese forces who were retreating from mountain to mountain were looters. This is a terrible thing to remember. There was absolutely nothing to eat, and so we decided to draw lots. The one

who lost would be killed and eaten. But the one who lost started to run away so we shot him. He was eaten. You probably think that many of us raped the local women. But women were not regarded as objects of sexual desire. They were regarded as the object of our hunger. We had no sexual appetite. To commit rape would have cost us too much energy, and we never wanted to. All we dreamt about was food. I met some soldiers in the mountains who were carrying baked human arms and legs. It was not guerillas but our own soldiers who we were frightened of. It was such a terrible condition.

The Japanese sources give the impression that in most cases Japanese soldiers themselves were the victims of the acts of cannibalism that occurred in New Guinea and the Philippines toward the end of the war when their supplies had been completely cut off. However, incidents also occurred in which Allied soldiers and members of the local populations became victims. For example, Ogawa Shōji noted that toward the end of the war, Japanese soldiers referred to the Allies as "white pigs" and the local population as "black pigs." But such honesty is rare, and so information about the widespread practice of cannibalism during the latter part of the war has long been confined to rumor. The only information on the practice available from the Japanese side has come from autobiographies and memoirs such as Ogawa's.

My recent discovery of extensive reports of the Australian War Crimes Section and records of war crime trials by the Australian military has made it possible to undertake a more comprehensive analysis of the practice of cannibalism committed by the Japanese in New Guinea. I also obtained U.S. National Archives documents that refer to Japanese cannibalism in New Guinea. However, the number of U.S. documents on this subject is very small, which is understandable because at the time the majority of Allied forces operating in this region were Australians.

The victims of cannibalism in the war can be divided into four groups: (1) Allied soldiers, the majority of whom were Australians; (2) Asian POWs who were brought to New Guinea as laborers; (3) the local population of New Guinea; (4) other Japanese soldiers. Not surprisingly, the Australian reports concentrate on incidents in which Australian soldiers were victims of cannibalism and refer only rarely or incidentally to incidents involving Japanese victims, although there is no evidence to suggest that Japanese were victims less frequently than other groups. Indeed, there is the evidence from a number of interviews I conducted with former Australian soldiers who gave eyewitness accounts of many mutilated bodies of Japanese soldiers. U.S. reports contain a number of cases in which Japanese soldiers were victims along with Australians and Americans, despite the overall small number of reports on this issue.

In the transcripts of the Australian War Crimes Section reports and the war crimes trials, the Australian National Archives and the Australian War Memorial have removed all references to the names of Australian victims of cannibalism, the places where the incidents occurred, and the dates of such incidents. This has not been done for incidents in which Asian POWs or members of the New Guinea population were victims. The names of the Japanese soldiers accused of the practice have also been retained in the reports. The U.S. documents contain all the names of the victims as well as suspected perpetrators. However, throughout this chapter, I will use only the initials of the accused, as the purpose of this analysis is to give a more systematic view of the practice of cannibalism and to move away from a focus on particular perpetrators. I do not disclose victims' names that appear in the U.S. documents for the sake of privacy of the victims and their relatives.

Allied Victims of Cannibalism

Among the various reports on cannibalism prepared by the Australian military forces, the most detailed description of the condition of the bodies can be found in cases in which the victims were Australian soldiers. This is probably because the majority of eyewitnesses of such incidents were members of the same squad as the deceased, and they usually reported the incidents immediately after they occurred, when the details were still vivid in their memory. In some cases the bodies were inspected by army doctors, and these reports also contribute to the detailed description of such incidents. In cases in which the victims were Asian POWs or indigenous locals, the incidents were frequently reported by witnesses who did not speak English, and thus many of these reports are more perfunctory and contain much less detail than those of Australian victims.

The following is a typical example of a report on an Australian victim recorded on May 20, 1945:

SX8064 WO II HUGO C of _____ Bn, being duly sworn, states:

On the morning of the _____ at 0900 hours, NX 79420 Cpl GRIFFIN, J, the late Sjt Sewell, and myself recovered the body of

_____ who had been killed by enemy action on the _____. We found the body in the following condition:

(a) all clothing had been removed

(b) both arms had been cut off at the shoulder

(c) the stomach had been cut out, and the heart, liver and other entrails had been removed

(d) all fleshy parts of the body had been cut away, leaving the bones bare

(e) the arms, heart, liver and entrails could not be found

(f) the only parts of the body not touched were the head and feet.

A Japanese mess tin which appeared to contain human flesh was lying four to five yards from _____ 's body between two dead Japanese soldiers.

(signed) C. HUGO WO II
SX 8064

The content of the U.S. reports is quite similar to that of the Australian documents. The following is an example from the U.S. files:

1. On January 24, 1943, Pfc. E.H. was killed in action in an attempt to capture a group of Japanese. The next day the body was recovered by Lieut. William C. Benson, Co. "G," 163rd Infantry Regiment, who certified that it was found in the following condition.

"The abdomen had been opened by two criss-cross slashes. Flesh had been removed from the thighs and buttocks."

The body was examined by Captain Henry C. Smith, M.C., 2nd Battalion Surgeon, 163rd Infantry Regiment, who certified to the following evidence of mutilation.

"A mid-line abdominal incision from the lower rib cage to the pubis. This incision was straight and clear with smooth edges. No examination was made of the abdominal content. A clean strip of skin tissue and muscle approximately 4 x 12 x 2 was removed from the lateral portion of the thigh."

2. Pvt. M.W., 163rd Infantry Regiment, was killed in action 24 January 1943, in an attempt to capture a group of Japanese. On 25 January 1943, the body was recovered by Lieut. William C. Benson, Co. "G," 163rd Infantry Regiment, who certified that flesh had been removed from both thighs.

3. Sgt. H.B. reported missing in action on 19 January 1943 was found in a mutilated condition on 23 January 1943. The body was identified and examined by Pfc. Other [sic] E. Dickson who swore that the body was found in the following condition.

"The flesh part of the thigh and each leg had been cut away. The abdominal cavity had been opened by cutting away the skin and flesh under each lower rib. The face had not been mutilated, thus making identification possible."

Pvt. Dickson further stated that a stew pot in a nearby Japanese bunker contained the heart and liver of approximate size of that [of a] human.

The above statement was also sworn by Cpl. Clinne C. Lamb, 36679399, Co. "F," 163rd Infantry Regiment, who was also a member of the searching party.

Many other cases refer to the fact that Japanese cannibalism extended to the entrails and the genitals of the victims; in some cases the brains were taken out, and therefore in such a case it was difficult to identify the soldier, as the face was disfigured beyond recognition. That intestines were cooked is confirmed by a report dated May 22, 1945, from which the following is an excerpt. This report is about four separate incidents involving a total of six Australian victims. Each incident had between two and four witnesses.

NX14764 Lieut A B Carson being duly sworn states:

_____ , _____ , and _____ , were killed in an attack on enemy positions on the afternoon of _____. My section was sent in to endeavour to extricate the bodies that same afternoon, but accurate sniper's fire forced us to withdraw before reaching the spot where they were reported to have been killed. Enemy resistance made it impossible to get the bodies out before _____, on which day I was again sent out on patrol for this purpose. We found three sets of Aust web equipt, two pairs of boots, two sets of clothing and other odd items which were recognised as belonging to the victims.

Further search revealed scalp which was easily recognised as that of _____, by the _____ . Entrails were strewn across a log and pieces of flesh which had been partially burnt were nearby whilst in one of our own basic pouches were pieces of what appeared to be liver. Evidence such [as] bloodstains and pieces of flesh which had definitely been cut with a sharp instrument, proved beyond doubt that bodies had been butchered, gutted and scalped.

Outside a hut 300 yards further along from this position were found the fresh bones of a burnt foot. Inside this hut we also found fragments of a right thigh bone which had obviously been cooked and broken for the marrow. The size of this bone indicated that it came from a body _____ feet in height presumably _____.

Outside another hut 100 yards away more leg, thigh and shoulder bone were found together with human flesh with _____ on it.

Outside yet another hut the head of _____ was recognised, and the body consisting only of a head which had been scalped and a spinal column lay on the ground. Besides these remains lay a wrist and hand which were charred and burned.

_____ AAB 83 and atebring [sic] roll book were found inside the first mentioned hut.

In all cases the condition of the remains was such that there can be no doubt that the bodies had been dismembered and portions of flesh cooked.

The injuries sustained by these men were not due to high explosive from our arty [artillery] but by rifle fire. The MO of my Sqn examined certain of the above-mentioned remains and concurs fully with my statement. I am quite certain that the remains found were _____, _____, and _____ and the following witnesses will bear out this evidence, themselves assisting in the burial of the remains.

Signed A.B. Carson

Signed before me. Signed. Nisbet Major.

The condition of the scalps indicates that the Japanese soldiers tried to remove the brains of the victims but were interrupted by the advance of the Australian forces. In the cases mentioned here there was neither time nor opportunity for the Japanese soldiers to hide the evidence of cannibalism. In fact, the vast majority of incidents in which Australian soldiers were victims had a similar pattern in that the Japanese soldiers had no time to dispose of the mutilated and cooked remains. The following U.S. report also seems to support such an interpretation:

1st Lieut. H.F. was killed in action 8 January 1943. Statement made by Sgt. Roy G. Mikalson, 20929231, Co. "C," 163rd Infantry Regiment, and S/Sgt. Gordon F. Meager, 20220220, Co. "C," 163rd Infantry Regiment, state that they were within ten and two yards respectively of Lieut. F when he was killed by a Japanese bullet. These witnesses further stated that when the platoon withdrew, Lieut. F's body was not mutilated in any way. At that time it could not be removed as the enemy fire was too intense.

On 11 January 1943, the body was recovered. The left arm had been cut away and was not found with the body. Slices of flesh had been cut from the calves of the legs and the body had been disembowelled, the heart and liver being also missing.

Later, on 11 January, the bones of the left forearm were found in a Japanese perimeter 400 yards north east of the US perimeter Musket.

It seems clear that Japanese soldiers removed the bodies of allied soldiers from the area in which fierce combat was occurring and carried them to a safe area to be cooked and consumed, while others held back the Allied forces in order to prevent them from recovering the bodies. This indicates that these incidents were not isolated or sporadic acts but part of an organized process.

There also appears to have been incidents in which Australian POWs were victims of cannibalism, although there are no Australian eyewitness accounts of mutilated or cooked bodies. Australian military officials interrogated a number of Japanese soldiers after the war, but all denied any knowledge of or participation in the practice of cannibalism, and therefore it became very difficult to establish a reliable account of such incidents.

In November 1944 a Dutch POW, P.W. Wildemar, escaped from the POW camp in Wewak and lived in the jungle nearby. At some time in early 1945 he met a Japanese deserter, Corporal M.T., in this area, and they stayed together for some time. At this time M.T. told Wildemar that he had witnessed the murder and consumption of an Australian pilot POW by Japanese soldiers in January or February of 1945. Wildemar was rescued by the Australian forces, but M.T. stayed in the jungle. M.T. was a member of C Battalion. Toward the end of January 1945 two planes went down in this region, a Royal Australian Air Force (RAAF) Kittyhawk piloted by Warrant Officer R.K. and another RAAF plane piloted by a Corporal F.M. Both pilots were reported missing. Either (or both) of these men could have been the victim of this act.

After the war, the Australian military followed up Wildemar's story and located M.T. in Japan. He was interrogated on June 2, 1947, but denied that he had witnessed the murder of the Australian pilot and claimed he had merely heard about the events secondhand. Australian officials also interrogated members of the Kempeitai stationed in this region and discovered that the Kempeitai had interrogated both of these pilots about troop movements and the like. The pilots had no useful information and were murdered by the police. However, the police denied that they had taken part in acts of cannibalism.

Major H.S. Williams, who investigated this case in Tokyo, sent a letter to the headquarters of the Australian military stating that "as M.T. has been proved to be untruthful, it is proposed to re-open this investigation as soon as any additional leads can be obtained." There is no further information about this case in archive files; presumably it proved impossible to establish a case for prosecution.

What is significant about this alleged incident is that, if true, it is an example of deliberate murder for the purpose of cannibalism rather than the cannibalism of soldiers or civilians who had died in battle or of illness. There are reports of other incidents of a similar nature in the files, but no prosecutions were launched.

Cannibalism of Asian POWs

It is well known that many Allied POWs were forced to work in various parts of Japanese-occupied Southeast Asia during the war, mainly on large-scale construction projects such as the Burma-Thailand railway, where more than 60,000 Allied POWs and 270,000 Asian laborers were exploited. A large number of Indian, Chinese, and Malaysian POWs and civilians were sent to New Guinea and neighboring small islands. Documents in the Australian War Crimes Section report suggest that many such forced laborers became victims of Japanese cannibalism. One of the most shocking cases is that concerning a number of Indian Muslims.

The Indian POWs working in New Guinea were divided into two types of work groups: construction companies and special transport companies in both the Army and the Navy. They were of various sizes; one mentioned in an interrogation consisted of 546 Indian POWs. There were 30 of these companies stationed in the new Guinea region. Given that there were 5,570 Indian POW forced laborers on Rabaul and New Ireland at the end of the war, it can be estimated that there were between 8,000 and 10,000 in New Guinea proper.

Most of these Indians were probably in the Indo-Pakistan forces that formed part of the larger Commonwealth forces and were taken prisoner when Singapore fell in February 1942. The following testimony was given by Hatam Ali, a Pakistani soldier taken prisoner on

February 15. His company was mobilized into forced labor in various places in Malaysia, and attempts were made to recruit members of the company into the Indian National Army, a pro-Japanese force that had been established to benefit from Indian anti-British sentiment. Ali refused to join and was put into a laboring party of about 1,000 prisoners who were sent to Manokwari in New Guinea toward the end of 1943. Soon after they arrived, they were put to work on the construction of an airfield, and in April 1944, 206 prisoners were sent to a new site 300 miles from Manokwari under the supervision of S Unit, one of the construction units. Ali was one of these.

> I was included in this number. We were taken to a place about 300 miles away, we were employed for 12 hours daily on hard fatigues and were given very little to eat. There was no medical treatment and all prisoners who fell ill were immediately killed by the Japanese. Later, due to Allied attacks and activity, the Japs also ran out of rations. We prisoners were made to eat grass and leaves and due to starvation we even ate snakes, frogs, and other insects. At this stage the Japanese started selecting prisoners and everyday 1 prisoner was taken out and killed and eaten by the Japanese. I personally saw this happen and about 100 prisoners were eaten at this place by the Japanese. The remainder of us were taken to another spot about 50 miles [away] where 10 prisoners died of sickness. At this place the Japanese again started selecting prisoners to eat. Those selected were taken to a hut where flesh was cut from their bodies while they were alive and they were then thrown into a ditch alive where they later died. When flesh was being cut from those selected terrible cries and shrieks came from them and also from the ditch where they were later thrown. These cries used to gradually dim down when the unfortunate individuals were dying. We were not allowed to go near this ditch, no earth was thrown on the bodies and the smell was terrible.

Eventually Aki's turn came. He was escorted by two soldiers toward this hut, but he ran away. He was chased by a Japanese soldier and was injured in the left ankle, but he finally escaped. He spent the next 15 days wandering the jungle and was rescued by Australian forces. Investigators located no other witnesses to corroborate his story, but if true it raises certain questions. Why did the Japanese soldiers find it necessary to cut flesh from the POWs while they were still living?

    In the first stage of cannibalism, the soldiers were killing prisoners and then consuming their flesh. But by the time they moved camp, the situation had become desperate. Prisoner numbers were down to less than 100, and there was no likelihood of a conventional food supply being reestablished. It is possible that the Japanese soldiers—faced with the problem of the rapid rate of putrefaction in the Tropics—cut the flesh from living prisoners as a way of ensuring that they would survive for a period and that their internal organs would then be available for later consumption. Hence the ditch in which these prisoners were dumped was not covered with earth. There seems to be no other explanation for the adoption of such hideously cruel methods, unless of course the whole business of systematic cannibalism had brutalized the Japanese soldiers to such an extent that an increasing degree of sadism became incorporated into the process.

This case is a horrifying example of a situation in which POWs were kept alive as a food source for the Japanese guards. However, such cases were comparatively rare. It was far more typical for soldiers to kill and consume POWs who had become ill. Such prisoners were usually shot; however, there are cases in which army doctors would administer lethal injections to the sick prisoners. For example, on April 5, 1943, a Japanese army doctor T.T. administered lethal injections to two Indian army POWs and subsequently cut flesh from their thighs and removed their livers. He ordered another Indian POW—a cook, Rabi Lohar—to prepare the flesh and livers for consumption. But Lohar refused to do this, even after being beaten. Eventually, a Japanese soldier, N.Y., cooked the body parts. In May 1943 another Indian POW was killed by the same method and for the same purpose. T.T. was tried and executed on May 3, 1946, and three Japanese soldiers who participated in the consumption of the Indian POWs were sentenced to ten years' imprisonment.

It is known that a large number of Formosan laborers were also mobilized by the Japanese forces for the construction of military-related facilities in various places in the Pacific region. How many Formosans were sent to New Guinea is unknown, but at least two reports prepared by the U.S. forces clearly indicate that some Formosans also became victims of Japanese cannibalism in this region. One report refers to incidents on Biak Island in the northwest of New Guinea, the other to incidents on Manus Island in the Bismarck Sea, northeast of New Guinea. The following summaries of interrogations conducted on Formosan POWs appear in the Biak report:

PW, JA(USA) 149583, SON, Kei Zun, a FORMOSAN civilian employee of 2 Co, 107 Airfield Survey and Construction Unit, surrendered to US troops at BOROKI, BIAK I, 28 Aug. '44.

Cannibalism 28 Aug. '44, while PW was foraging for food on BIAK I, he heard a rifle shot approx 100 meters away. From concealment he saw two JAP soldiers approach a dead FORMOSAN whom he thought was from 108 Fld Airfield Survey and Construction Unit. JAPS stripped body and used bayonet to hack off a leg. PW became frightened and immediately related incident to other FORMOSANS in his unit. Believing their lives were in jeopardy, they fled to US troops.

PW, JA(USA) 149579, SHU, Kon Tsu, a FORMOSAN civilian employee of 107 Airfield Survey and Construction Unit, surrendered to US troops at BOROKI, 28 Aug. '44.

Cannibalism BIAK I, Jul '44, PW heard from C.Z.R. that he saw JAPS collecting dead Formosans for their meat. 4 Aug '44, PW heard C was murdered by JAPS near WARDO for the same purpose.

14–15 Aug '44, approx six hours march from WARDO toward SORIDO, PW saw the remains of his hometown friend R.H.K. and two others at South agricultural field. Only the head and bones remained but PW noticed each victim had been slashed across the throat. He heard of 15 other FORMOSAN corpses having been stripped of the flesh.

JAP troops and FORMOSANS prepared their meals individually. JAPS always seemed to have meat but FORMOSANS had only the vegetables they grew and the little rice that was allotted them. FORMOSANS often traded with natives but could get meat only from JAPS. JAPS always claimed meat was dog meat but PW suspected it was human flesh, therefore, never bartered. He thought it impossible that there should be a daily supply of dog meat specially when he had rarely seen a dog on BIAK I.

Meat seen by PW had little skin or hair but he knew dog meat to have thick layer of skin and thick stubble of hair. He heard human flesh was too salty to eat if fried, and therefore had to be broiled.

PW, JA(USA) 149826, CHO, Seki Ju, a FORMOSAN civilian employee of 108 Fld Airfield Survey and Construction Unit, surrendered to US troops after reading ALLIED leaflet at WARDO, BIAK I, 7 Sep '44.

Cannibalism Jun '44, on BIAK I, PW and 13 other FORMOSANS decided to surrender to ALLIES after having read an ALLIED propaganda leaflet. En route, group was intercepted by approx 100 u/i JAP troops. Eight of the FORMOSANS were killed and PW felled by a bayonet. While feigning death, PW saw a JAP soldier take the intestines from a dead FORMOSAN and place it in his mess kit. PW did not see more as JAPS left.

Another interrogation summary of a Formosan POW refers to a scene similar to that described in Hatam Ali's testimony about flesh being hacked from live bodies:

> Prisoner of War RI, Shin Te (JA(USA) 149444); Formosan civilian employee of the 107 Airfield Survey and Construction Unit had established the probability of the following acts of cannibalism:
> "During August 1944, prisoner of war saw many corpses lying around Biak with portions of flesh removed by knife, but did not witness such butchery. On 15 August 1944, prisoners of war came across three Formosan bodies that were not dead over few hours. They were lying in a pool of blood approximately 15 feet from a jungle path. Each was bayoneted through the chest and flesh was removed from thighs."

From these interrogation summaries it is almost certain that many Formosans, who were regarded as racially inferior to Japanese despite the fact that they were mobilized as "Japanese Army employees," also became the victims of murder and cannibalism.

Cannibalism of the Indigenous Population

It seems that victims of cannibalism numbered as many among the indigenous population of New Guinea as among Australian or Commonwealth soldiers. Reports of such incidents based on the testimony of members of the local population were made to Australian military officials. In the majority of cases the victims were villagers who were known to be hostile to the Japanese forces and to have actively cooperated with the Australian forces. The following is a typical example of such an incident.

On April 12, 1945, a group of Japanese soldiers attacked a New Guinea village "T," ransacked the houses, and stole yams, copra, and other foods as well as cooking utensils. Most of the villagers hid in the jungle, but two failed to escape and were abducted by the soldiers. In order to rescue these two men, three villagers followed the Japanese soldiers. But when they reached the place where the Japanese soldiers had regrouped, "X," they were attacked by Japanese with submachine guns.

The villagers defended themselves with hand grenades (which had been provided by Australian forces) and retreated. However, one was killed and another who was seriously injured later died in the jungle. The two villagers who had been captured made an escape; one was killed by submachine gun fire. The Japanese remained at "X" for three days and then moved on. A party of villagers, including the two survivors of the earlier incident, returned to "X" some days later. They found two mutilated bodies. One of the three villagers who had followed the Japanese soldiers after the raid gave the following testimony on May 10, 1945:

> I found "W's" body. Flesh had been cut from the chest, thighs, calves, buttocks and back. His shoulders had been cut through and both forearms were missing. The viscera were intact. The top of the head had been cut off, and the brain removed. The flesh had been cut with some sharp instrument. The body of "S" had cuts on it but no flesh was missing. Near a small fire which the Japanese had used for cooking I found the bone from a man's forearm. It had been in a fire and shreds of cooked flesh were still adhering to it. There were scrapings of taro and yam around the same fire.

Manmade Famines
From *Cannibalism: From Sacrifice to Survival*

BY HANS ASKENASY, PH.D.

One tool of war, as forensic clinical psychologist Hans Askenasy points out in *Cannibalism: From Sacrifice to Survival*, is famine. When, a century apart, Napoleon and Hitler each invaded Russia, cannibalism became a brutal reality for soldiers and noncombatants alike.

We have known everything . . .
That in Russian speech there is
No word for that mad war winter . . .
When the Hermitage shivered under bombs . . .
Houses turned to frost and pipes burst with ice . . .
The ration—100 grams . . . On the Nevskey corpses.
And we learned, too, about cannibalism.
We have known everything. . . .
> Daniel Andreyev, quoted in Harrison Salisbury, *The 900 Days*

We can divide manmade famines into two basic types: war-related and those engineered to remove "undesirables." Those that are primarily war-related affect both the enemy's soldiers and civilians. Specifically we have scorched earth policies, prison camps, and sieges. They often overlap.

From the earliest times of warfare, it has often seemed to military strategists that the easiest way to overcome an enemy was to destroy his source of food, primarily crops and livestock. Military campaigns have always left a trail of burned granaries, scorched fields, and confiscated cattle. Related to this is the damage done to transportation routes, vehicles, trains, and ships so that food cannot be moved or imported.

Starvation in prison camps also goes back a long time; occasionally it was a consequence of a general food shortage, but usually it was deliberate policy. No one needed to starve to death at Andersonville, the Confederate prison camp of Union soldiers during the Civil War. In Hitler's opening campaign against the Soviet Union in 1941, approximately 3.8 million Russian prisoners were taken, and great numbers of them were deliberately left to die from hunger or cold in that cruel winter of 1941–42. Prisoners had only one right—the right to die. Of the well over 5 million Red Army soldiers captured, a bare 1 million survived the war. The major commandant of Auschwitz, SS Colonel Rudolf Höss, who was hanged for war crimes in 1947, relates the following in his autobiography:

> On the road to Auschwitz and Birkenau I once saw an entire column of Russians, several hundred strong, suddenly make a rush for some nearby stacks of potatoes on the far side of the railway line. Their guards were taken by surprise, overrun, and could do nothing. I luckily happened to come along at this moment and was able to restore the situation. The Russians had thrown themselves onto the stacks, from which they could hardly be torn away. Some of them died in the confusion, while chewing, their hands full of potatoes. Overcome by the crudest instinct of self-preservation, they came to care nothing for one another, and in their selfishness now thought only of themselves. Cases of cannibalism were not rare in Birkenau. I myself came across a Russian lying between piles of bricks, whose body had been ripped open and the liver removed. They would beat each other to death for food. . . .
> When the foundation for the first group of buildings [at Auschwitz] were being dug, the men often found the bodies of Russians who had been killed by their fellows, partly eaten and then stuffed into a hole in the mud. . . .
> They were no longer human beings. They had become animals, who sought only food.

As for sieges, Julius Caesar, in his *Gallic War*, wrote that the people of Alesia in Gaul, besieged by the Roman army, ate women, old men, and others who could not fight. In 1871, when the Germans encircled Paris, a French butcher shop on the island of Saint Louis sold human flesh. This was not known until much later, after the siege had been lifted; by that time the shop had acquired a great reputation for the quality of its meat.

On June 22, 1812, Napoleon I, emperor of France, crossed the Niemen river on his way to Moscow. Like no man since Caesar he held the reigns of power over most of Europe. All that was left was Russia. Napoleon launched his attack with the Grand Armée—over 600,000 Frenchmen, Germans, Italians, Poles; 110,000 horses; thousands of supply wagons; and vast herds of cattle. Finally he reached Moscow—with only 100,000 men. The Russian territory, typhus, and Field Marshal Mikhail Illarionovitch Kutuzov's Cossacks and scorched earth policy, carried out on an enormous scale, reaped a ghastly harvest. (As in the American Civil War half a century later, many died from their wounds as well as from medical practice.)

In most European countries Napoleon would win one or two major battles, then seize the capital and dictate his peace terms. The gambit didn't work in Russia. Field Marshal Kutuzov, a big, burly man, had only one eye, but it was unusually perspicacious. When others had tried to force him to give battle, he had refused and retreated: "Time and patience; patience and time," he said. Pressured to fight at Borodino, Kutusov held his own—and immediately retreated again. At 2:00 P.M. on September 14, looking down on the glistening golden cupolas of Moscow, Napoleon saw a deserted city. That night Kutuzov set it aflame; the fire raged five days. By that act the French learned something about the Russian character. And so the arrogant little Corsican, who had once boasted that he didn't give a damn about the death of a million men ("A night in Paris will make up for it"), strutted about in the Kremlin for five weeks, not knowing what to do next. He soon found out.

As the endless columns of hungry, exhausted, undisciplined French and allied soldiers struggled back across the same ravished path they had come, their great column stretching for fifty miles, the army of the czar followed on a parallel route. Kutuzov ordered: "Now we will attack. Now we will strike the beast at the flanks." At Borodino they found 30,000 corpses, half-eaten by wolves. At Smolensk, twenty days after leaving Moscow, Napoleon had 36,000 men left. At Vilna, Marshal Ney, commanding the Third Army Group, had a mere twenty. Snow covered the corpses of the rest.

Instead of realistically recalling the anxieties, hardships, immorality and atrocities which his war had brought both to individuals and nations, or having second thoughts about the hundreds of thousands he needlessly sacrificed in the prime of their life, the glorious emperor left his army in the lurch and hurried back to Paris. Arriving at the banks of the Niemen in his miserable sleigh, he inquired of the ferryman whether deserters had come through that way. "No," replied the Russian, "you are the first." It was December 6, and Napoleon assessed the debacle with this grotesque remark: "Perhaps I made a mistake in going to Moscow."

The following account is from *Napoleon's Russian Campaign* by Count Philippe-Paul de Ségur, who "never left the Emperor's side for more than a few feet":

> From now on there existed no fraternity of arms, no society, no human ties. An excess of hardship had made brutes of our men, and hunger, ravenous, devouring hunger, had killed everything in those unfortunate beings but the instinct of self-preservation, sole driving force of the fiercest animals, to which everything else is sacrificed. A harsh, violent, merciless nature seemed to have communicated her fury to them. Like true savages, the strong despoiled the weak: they crowded around the dying, often not waiting to rob them until they had breathed their last. When a horse fell, you would have thought you were witnessing the fatal moment in a hunt, as the men swarmed upon the animal and tore it into scraps, over which they fought like famished hounds! . . .
>
> On the sixth of December, the day following the departure of the emperor, the sky became still more terrible. The air was filled with infinitesimal ice crystals; birds fell to the earth frozen stiff. The atmosphere was absolutely still. It seemed as if everything in nature having movement or life, down to the very wind, had been bound and congealed in a universal death. Now not a word, not a murmur broke the dismal silence, silence of despair and unshed tears. . . .
>
> Before long they fell to their knees, then forward on their hands. Their heads wagged stupidly from side to side for a little while, and a gasping rattle issued from their lips. Then they collapsed in the snow, on which appeared the slow-spreading stain of blackish blood—and their suffering was at an end. . . .
>
> At Youpranoui—the same town where the partisan leader Seslawin had missed the emperor by an hour—our soldiers burned whole houses as they stood to get a few minutes' warmth. The light of these conflagrations attracted some poor wretches whom the intensity of the cold and suffering made delirious. They dashed forward in a fury

[and] threw themselves into those raging furnaces, where they perished in dreadful convulsions. Their starving companions watched them die without apparent horror. There were even some who laid hold of bodies disfigured and roasted by the flames, and—incredible as it may seem—ventured to carry this loathsome food to their mouths!

And this was the army that had issued from the most civilized nation in Europe, that army once so brilliant, victorious over men up to the last moment, and whose name still inspired respect in so many conquered capitals! . . .

Issuing from the white, ice-bound desert were one thousand foot soldiers and troopers still armed, nine cannon and twenty thousand beings clothed in rags, with bowed heads, dull eyes, ashy, cadaverous faces and long ice-stiffened beard.

Two kings, one prince, eight marshals, followed by several generals afoot and unattended, then a few hundred of the Old Guard still bearing arms, were all that remained. . . .

Such were the last days of the Grand Army: its last nights were still more frightful.

Perhaps the most famous of all sieges was that of Leningrad in 1941–43. One hundred and twenty-nine years to the day after Napoleon's crossing the Niemen, at 3:00 A.M. on June 22, 1941, the pale night sky of that shortest night of the year was turned to day by the flash of thousands of guns. Adolf Hitler had invaded the Soviet Union. The basic floorplan was the same, though he had three million men along a front of 1,500 kilometers—one for every foot and a half. It was Hitler's greatest blitzkrieg of them all. He had announced to his secretaries: "In a few weeks I will be in Moscow. There is absolutely no doubt about it. I will raze this damned city to the ground. . . . The name of Moscow will vanish forever." In November the Nazis were within sight of the Kremlin, but the swastika was not to fly over it.

Hitler had also announced: "I have no feelings about the idea of wiping out St. Petersburg [formerly Leningrad]." Hitler's troops had been in the suburbs of Russia's second largest city since early September. Now it was surrounded. Hitler forbad his commanders from accepting any surrender, and so began the greatest siege at least since biblical times. Leningrad would hold—for two and a half years. One million human beings would die from starvation.

Harrison Salisbury, the veteran *New York Times* correspondent, spent twenty-five years studying diaries, memoirs, and archives, and interviewing and corresponding with survivors of the seige of Leningrad. In *The 900 Days: The Siege of Leningrad,* an epic account of human cruelty and courage, he wrote:

"The Haymarket or Sennaya occupied the heart of Leningrad. Some years earlier it had been Peace Square, but no one called it that. The Haymarket it had been since the early days of 'Piter,' and the Haymarket it was in this winter of Leningrad's agony. But sometimes it was called the Hungry Market. . . .

"Ordinary people found they had little in common with the traders who suddenly appeared in the Haymarket. These were figures straight from the pages of Dostoyevsky or Kuprin. They were the robbers, the thieves, the murderers, members of the bands which roved the streets of the city and who seemed to hold much of it in their power once night had fallen.

"These were the cannibals and their allies—fat, oily, steely-eyed, calculating, the most terrible men and women of their day.

"For cannibalism there was in Leningrad. You will look in vain in the published official histories for reports of the trade in human flesh. But the stain of the story slips in, here and there, in casual references, in the memoirs, in allusions in fiction, in what is not said as well as in what is said about the crimes-for-food committed in the city. . . .

"In the Haymarket people walked through the crowd as though in a dream. They were pale as ghosts and thin as shadows. Only here and there passed a man or woman with a face, full, rosy and somehow soft yet leathery. A shudder ran through the crowd. For these, it was said, were the cannibals. . . .

"Cannibals . . . Who were they? How many were they? It is not a subject which the survivors of Leningrad like to discuss. There were no cannibals, a professor recalls, or rather, there were cannibals, but it only happened when people went crazy. There was a case of which he had heard, for instance, the case of a mother, crazed for food. She lost her mind, went completely mad, killed her daughter and butchered the body. She ground up the flesh and made meat patties. But this was not typical. It was the kind of insane aberration which might happen anywhere at any time. In fact, the professor recalled reading of a similar case before the war. . . .

"There was hardly a dog or cat left in Leningrad by late December. They had all been eaten. But the trauma was great when a man came to butcher an animal which had lived on his affection for years. One elderly artist strangled his pet cat and ate it, according to Vsevolod Vishnevsky. Later, he tried to hang himself, but the rope failed, he fell to the floor, breaking his leg, and froze to death. The smallest Leningrad children grew up not knowing what cats and dogs were. . . .

"But no great effort was made to interfere with the grisly trade at the Haymarket. As early as November, according to some accounts, meat patties made from ground-up human flesh went on sale, although many Leningraders refused to believe the meat was human. They insisted it was horse meat—or dog, or cat. . . .

" 'In the worst period of the siege,' a survivor noted, 'Leningrad was in the power of the cannibals. God alone knows what terrible scenes went on behind the walls of the apartments.'

"He claimed to know of cases in which husbands ate their wives, wives ate their husbands, and parents ate their children. In his own building a porter killed his wife and then thrust her severed head into a red-hot stove. . . .

"But if questions were not asked in the markets, there was terrible gossip in the queues where the women waited and waited for the bread shops to open. The talk was of children, how careful one must be with them, how the cannibals waited to seize them because their flesh was so much more tender. Women were said to be second choice. They were starving like the men, but, it was insisted, their bodies carried a little more fat and their flesh was more tasty. . . .

"There was more than one way in which the dead might help the living to survive. Again and again at Piskarevsky and Serafimov and the other great cemeteries the teams of sappers sent in from the front to dynamite graves noticed as they piled the corpses into mass graves that pieces were missing, usually the fat thighs or arms and shoulders. The flesh was being used as food. Grisly as was the practice of necrobutchery there was no actual law which forbade the disfigurement of corpses or which prohibited consumption of this flesh. . . .

"Among the fantastic tales which circulated in Leningrad in the winter of 1941–42 was one that there existed 'circles' or fraternities of eaters of human flesh. The circles were said to assemble for special feasts, attended only by members of their kind. These people were the dregs of the human hell which Leningrad had become. The real lower depths were those occupied by persons who insisted on eating only 'fresh' human flesh, as distinguished from cadaver cuts. Whether these tales were literally true was not so important. What was important was that Leningraders believed them to be true, and this added the culminating horror to their existence. . . ."

In another incident typical of the times, two men "entered a quiet lane and soon came to a good-sized building which had not been damaged by either German gunfire or bombing. Dmitri followed the tall man up the staircase. The man climbed easily, occasionally looking back at Dmitri. As they neared the top floor, an uneasy feeling seized Dmitri. There leaped into his mind the stories he had heard of the cannibals and how they lured victims to their doom. The tall man looked remarkably well fed. Dmitri continued up the stairs but told himself he would be on guard, ready to flee at the slightest sign of danger.

"At the top floor the man turned and said, 'Wait for me here.' He knocked at the door, and someone inside asked, 'Who is it?' 'It's me,' the man responded. 'With a live one.'

"Dmitri froze at the words. There was something sinister about them. The door opened, and he saw a hairy red hand and a muglike face. From the room came a strange, warm, heavy smell. A gust of wind in the hall caught the door, and in the swaying candlelight Dmitri had a glimpse of several great hunks of white meat, swinging from hooks on the ceiling. From one hunk he saw dangling a human hand with long fingers and blue veins.

"At that moment the two men lunged toward Dmitri. He leaped down the staircase and managed to reach the bottom ahead of his pursuers. To his good fortune, there was a light military truck passing through the lane.

" 'Cannibals!' Dmitri shouted. Two soldiers jumped from the truck and rushed into the building. A moment or two later two shots rang out. In a few minutes the soldiers reappeared, one carrying a great-coat and the other a loaf of bread. The soldier with the greatcoat complained that it had a tear in it. The other one said 'I found a piece of bread. Do you want it?'

"Dmitri thanked the soldier. It was his bread, the 600 grams he had planned to trade for the *valenki* [heavy felt boots]. The soldiers told him that they found human hocks from five bodies hanging in the flat. Then they got back into their truck and were off to Lake Ladoga, where they were part of the Road of Life."

As reported in the *Los Angeles Times,* new findings from the Communist Party archives, opened in 1992, confirm Salisbury's contention—widely criticized by leaders of the Soviet era—that murderous gangs roamed wartime Leningrad's streets, killing for ration cards or human meat. Recently discovered documents show that the city police created an entire division to fight cannibals, and some 260 Leningraders were convicted of and jailed for the crime. With the official daily ration of 125 grams of bread, about the weight of a bar of soap, Leningraders supplemented this with anything they could: as historians Ales Adamovich and Daniil Granin wrote in their account of the siege, "with everything from the birdseed to the canary itself." They scraped wallpaper down and ate the paste, which was supposedly made from potatoes. They extracted the same paste from bookbinding or drank it straight from the glue jar. They boiled leather belts and briefcases to make an edible jelly, and plucked and pickled grasses and weeds. They ate petroleum jelly and lipstick, spices and medicines, fur coats and leather caps. Some made face-powder pancakes; others munched grimy crystallized sugar, dug out from under the sugar warehouses leveled by German firebombs.

Historians have recorded twenty-two different dishes made out of pigskin and have collected menus from military cafeterias where choices ranged from fern-leaf soup to puree of nettles and milk-curd pancakes. Scientists at the Vitamin Institute developed diet supplements by extracting vitamin C from pine needles, and swept attics and ventilation shafts at tobacco factories for tobacco dust, which contains vitamin B.

At one laboratory bacteria were also cultivated for study in a medium with meat-broth base. "We had a large stock [of this medium]. It saved many of our staff," said one survivor. "I used to extract a glassful when I arrived at work, then all the staff would sit around and I would give them each a tablespoonful."

But then there also exists something appropriately called the Law of Unexpected Consequences. Moscow had held, as had Leningrad. They were followed by Stalingrad, as we shall now see. Frustrated and furious, Hitler had became obsessed with that city on the Volga bearing the name of his counterpart. It was of little more than tactical significance in the scheme of the war, and all his senior military commanders objected to his plans. Hitler as usual ignored them. If this was to be the showdown, let it be.

This was the showdown between Germany and Russia. The slaughter on both sides was ferocious; it lasted 159 days and nights. From William Craig's *Enemy at the Gates: The Battle for Stalingrad,* we read:

> In five months of fighting and bombings, 99 percent of the city had been reduced to rubble. More than forty-one thousand homes, three hundred factories, 113 hospitals and schools had been destroyed. A quick census revealed that out of more than five hundred thousand inhabitants of the previous summer, only 1,515 civilians remained. Most of them had either died in the first days or left the city for temporary homes in Siberia and Asia. No one knew how many had been killed, but the estimates were staggering. . . .
>
> The German Sixth Army was scattered to more than twenty camps stretching from the Arctic Circle to the southern deserts.
>
> One train carried thousands of Germans from the Volga to Uzbekistan, in Central Asia. Inside each car, stuffed with one hundred or more prisoners, a macabre death struggle ensued as the Germans killed each other for bits of food tossed to them every two days. Those closest to the door were set upon by ravenous soldiers in the rear; only the strongest men survived the weeks-long trip. By the time the train reached the Pamir mountains, almost half its passengers were dead. . . .
>
> Other prisoners, more intent on survival, took matters into their own hands, especially in camps where military self-discipline had broken down. At Susdal, Felice Bracci first noticed it when he saw corpses without arms or legs. And Dr. Cristoforo Capone found human heads with the brains scooped out, or torsos minus livers and kidneys. Cannibalism had begun.
>
> The cannibals were furtive at first, stealing among the dead to hack off a limb and eat it raw. But their tastes quickly matured and they searched for the newly dead, those just turning cold, and thus more tender. Finally they roamed in packs, defying anyone to stop them. They even helped the dying to die. Hunting day and night, their lust for human flesh turned them into crazed animals and, by late February, they reached a savage peak of barbarism. . . .
>
> The Russians shot every cannibal they caught, but faced with the task of hunting down so many man-eaters they had to enlist the aid of "an-

ticannibalism teams," drawn from the ranks of captive officers. The Russians equipped these squads with crowbars and demanded they kill every cannibal they found. The teams prowled at night, looking for telltale flickers of flame from small fires where the predators were preparing their meals.

Dr. Vincenzo Pugliese went on patrol frequently and, one night, he turned a corner and surprised a cannibal roasting something on the end of a stick. At first it looked like an oversized sausage, but then Pugliese's trained eye noticed the accordion-like pleats on the object and with a sickening start, he realized that the man was cooking a human trachea.

In Aleksandr Solzhenitsyn's *The Gulag Archipelago* we read: "At the end of the Civil War [between the Red Army and the czarist forces, beginning in 1917], and as its natural consequence, an unprecedented famine developed in the Volga area. They give it only two lines in the official histories because it doesn't add a very ornamental touch to the wreaths of the victors in that war. But the famine existed nonetheless—to the point at which parents ate their own children—such a famine as even Russia had never known, even in the Time of Troubles in the early seventeenth century."

Later Stalin would deliberately starve millions more to enforce his policies.

In the Nazi ghettos, especially Warsaw, and in both concentration and extermination camps, human flesh was often all that was left for those who still clung to life. Thus, according to the ration scales imposed by the Nazis in Warsaw, Germans there were entitled to 2,310 calories per day; foreigners to 1,700; Poles to 934; and Jews to 183. The following account is given in Nora Levin's *The Holocaust:*

Hunger raged through the Ghetto, more acutely felt than physical pain or the two bitter winters the Ghetto lived through. In May 1940, Ringelblum heard an eight-year-old boy scream madly: "I want to steal, I want to rob, I want to eat. I want to be a German!" Three months later, he wrote: "At a funeral for the small children from the Wolska Street orphanage, the children from the home placed a wreath at the graves with this inscription: 'To the Children Who Have Died from Hunger—From the Children Who Are Hungry.'" There was a day and night obsession with food; women tore at each other for a crust of bread. . . .

Hunger drove some to madness, others to slow death. The corpses of the dead were hidden so that their precious ration cards could be used. . . .

Against these accents of life rose a numbness to death from hunger and disease. As early as February 1941, Ringelblum noted that the sight of people falling dead in the middle of the street no longer stirred people. Naked corpses were laid in mass graves separated by boards. Children began to lose their fear of dead bodies and were seen tickling them to see if they moved. Women who squatted in the streets with their children told Ringelblum they would rather die in the street than at home. . . .

The situation at the Baumann and Berson Children's Hospital was no better. A diary entry by a nurse dated March 20, 1941, records the hopelessness of the staff:

"I am on duty from 3 to 11. I come to my ward. It is a real hell. Children sick with the measles, two or three in one bed. . . . Shaven heads covered with sores swarming with lice. . . . I have no beds, no linen, no covers, no bedclothes. I telephone the superintendent. . . . The answer is terse: where there are two children in one bed, put a third one in and that is the end of it. . . . There is no coal. The rooms are terribly cold. They huddle under the covers, shaking with fever. . . . In the corridor lies a child of five swollen with hunger. . . . The child moves its lips begging for a piece of bread. I try to feed him. . . . but his throat is locked and nothing goes down. Too late. After a few minutes he utters for the last time the words, 'a piece of bread.' "

Smuggling became an absolute necessity and smugglers of all ages, sizes, and kinds, including very small children, crawled through sewers and chinks in the walls. Jews even smuggled openly in carts when the guards could be bribed. Hunger-crazed children who were able to slip through to the Polish Aryan section were often given food; more often they were shot down by Nazi guards. Children reached the Aryan side of Warsaw by digging holes under walls or by hiding near the Ghetto gates and trying to sneak through when the guards turned the other way. Parents would sit at home all day nervously awaiting the return of their only breadwinner. So desperate was the need for food that not even the death penalty for smuggling (decreed in October 1941) could stop it, for strict obedience meant a lingering death by starvation. . . .

Such starvation, the highest Nazi circles believed, would extinguish Jewish life. Before the accelerated exterminations began, it was assumed that this would do the job in the ghettos. But hunger, though a big killer, was not as efficient as the Nazis wished. The governor of occupied Poland, Hans Frank, therefore threatened that, "If the Jews do not die of hunger, the measures will be intensified." They swiftly were.

Postscript. The ghetto in April 1943 measured a thousand by three hundred yards. SS General Jürgen Stroop had 2,090 men, as well as tanks, artillery, flamethrowers, and aerial support; the remaining Jews who refused to be deported to their extermination had decided to fight. They possessed almost no weapons at all. They held out for thirty-seven days.

The Slaughter at Wuxuan
From *Scarlet Memorial:*
Tales of Cannibalism in Modern China

It is a little known fact—and hard for many people to believe—but during the terror of the Cultural Revolution in China in the 1960s, there was "an unprecedented frenzy of cannibalism" in remote areas of the countryside. Worse yet, it was officially sanctioned. Here, Chinese dissident journalist Zheng Yi, author of *Scarlet Memorial: Tales of Cannibalism in Modern China,* describes a visit he made to Wuxuan County, in the southwestern province of Guangxi, to document what had happened there in the early summer of 1968.

Blow the Typhoon

The great battle was undoubtedly an important event in Wuxuan during the Cultural Revolution. It had led to the deaths of nearly one hundred people. Furthermore, along with the "meeting to blow the typhoon," it pushed creative cannibalism to its climax. The hearts, livers, and flesh of four victims had been devoured. The battle at Wuxuan, though, cannot be explained as the key to the outbreak of cannibalism or as its basic cause. In general, I thought I would agree with the view of the Wuxuan locals who believed that the spread of cannibalism was directly related to the cruelty in the battle and to the frenetic revenge mentality it aroused. However, after analyzing most of the cases of cannibalism, I realized that they had nothing to do with the battle or with its reverberations. Besides, many of the incidents of cannibalism cited later had occurred before, not after, the battle. On May 4, 1968, for instance, Qin Hejia and Qin Zhunzhuo were subjected to criticism at Guzuo brigade, Tongwan District. After being shot, the victims were cannibalized. And on May

195

14, 1968, a passerby from a bordering county (Chen Guoyong from Lu village, Phoenix Township, Shilong District, Gui County) met his death at the hands of Wei Changmeng, Wei Changgan, Wei Binghuan, and eleven people from Huama town, Tongwan District. Chen was then cannibalized by his killers. "First, Wei Changmeng chopped the victim to death with a sword. Wei Changgan then cut out the victim's liver and brought it back to the village to serve as an evening snack. More than twenty people sitting at two tables joined in." The case occurred at the same time as the Wuxuan battle, but was not related to it.

I personally think that the outbreak of cannibalism at Wuxuan originated from the movement to "blow a twelve-degree typhoon of class struggle" that was promoted by the local regime of the Party, government, and military. On March 19, 1968, the first death by lynching occurred in Wuxuan County. Far from being punished, the perpetrators were actually egged on. Thus, the killing quickly spread. At the end of May and in early June a meeting to blow the typhoon was called by the head of the Liuzhou Military Sub-District, with Wen Longjun, concurrently the chairman of the Revolutionary Committee and director of the local Armed Police, and Pan Zhenkuai, the chairman of the Sanli District Revolutionary Committee, in attendance. On June 14, the Wuxuan Revolutionary Committee held a conference of high-level cadres from the county, district, brigade, and production-team levels. At this gathering, the spirit of the meeting to blow the typhoon was passed on. At the meeting, Wen Longjun advocated that "a twelve-degree typhoon must be blown in the struggle against our enemies. The method employed should be: to mobilize adequately the masses, rely on the masses to carry out the dictatorship, and hand the policies to the masses. In engaging in class struggle, our hands must not be soft." Thus, Wuxuan, which had been quiet for a month after the great battle, all of a sudden turned into a killing field and a hell of human-flesh consumption!

The killer barber who had cut open Zhou Shian while he was still alive and the injured veteran volunteer soldier, Wang Chunrong, had both been quiet for a full month. During the meeting to blow the typhoon, called by the county Revolutionary Committee, the barber was reborn. Picking up his five-inch knife, he resumed his special contributions to the great enterprise of the proletarian dictatorship. At a criticism rally held in Wuxuan, victim Tan Qiou was beaten to death and Huang Zhenji was beaten into a coma. When Huang Zhenji regained consciousness, he begged Wang Chunrong, "Comrade, forgive me!" Bearing the shiny five-inch knife, Wang Chunrong administered a twist of sarcasm. "We'll forgive you for five minutes," he said. Wang then ordered cadres to drag the victim ahead to the Zhongshan pavilion where, once again, Wang took out his five-inch knife and this time stepped on the victim's chest and cut out his heart and liver. The victim immediately died.

The number of victims killed on that day was not recorded in the official documents that I examined. However, according to a list put together by Du Tiansheng and Chen Shaoquan from the office to handle leftover cases and the Public Security Bureau, "five victims were cannibalized on that day" and several people were killed by Wang Chunrong. This information, however, is not officially documented. But Chen Shaoquan and others from the Party Reform Office verified that when Wang "saw different colors on one liver"—"a spotted liver"—he threw it away and started to cut out the liver of the second victim.

Wang Chunrong was also the one who, on market day in Wuxuan—it was June 17—cut into the body of a temporary worker by the name of Tang Zhanhui (or maybe it was Tang Canwei) right in front of the local Xinhua (New China) bookstore during a street criticism parade (*youdou*). "After Wang Chunrong extracted the liver with his five-inch knife, the crowd pushed forward to get at the flesh. Tang immediately died." Full of excitement and pleasure, Wang Chunrong took the human liver to the pork counter of the food factory, added some spices, and boiled it together with some pork to serve as an appetizer with an aperitif. At that time, it was indeed a situation in which a dry street flowed with men. The people were as numerous as the hills and the seas. It was a great revolutionary festival! In the sea of humanity that had gathered, a former director of the county court, who had already been purged from his position, protested to an army official standing beside him, "Such indiscriminate killing cannot go on. It's time you did something about it." The army officer was Yan Yulin, deputy director of the county Armed Police and deputy director of the county Revolutionary Committee. This patriarchical official, who now held almighty power, simply replied, "This is a matter for the masses. It is out of our control." Naturally, he was not about to stand up and stop the killing and the cannibalism, since he had just come from the meeting to blow the typhoon, where he had occupied a seat on the podium. Now here he was in the crowd, present at the very kind of rally held at the site of the killing that the conference had championed. Hidden among the crowd, he was secretly overjoyed by the immediate results conjured up by the wizard.

In this way, under the general direction of the great helmsman, carried out by an army officer, and acted upon by a veteran soldier with great enthusiasm, an unprecedented and ruthless bloodbath in the history of human civilization came to a climax on the land of Wuxuan. From that point on, all "abstinence from cannibalism" ended. At every criticism rally, the victims were put to death. And each death was garnished with cannibalism. Compared with the big feast of cutting and eating live victims, earlier executions by lynching now seemed generous and merciful.

On the next day, June 18, at least three "feasts of human flesh" were held in three different places. What speedy action!

On June 18, 1968, a rally to criticize Chen Hanning, Chen Chengyun, Chen Chujian, and others was held at Taicun brigade in Sanli District. All the commune members were present as armed militiamen surrounded the site. An atmosphere of killing permeated the entire rally. Director of the Brigade Cultural Revolution Group, Chen Siting, led the rally. After "Chen Dangming, who was in charge of personnel dossiers, read out loud the so-called 'criminal evidence,' it was the masses' turn to give speeches. These lasted for about half an hour. Then Chen Siting called out, 'What should we do with these people?' The masses replied in one voice, 'Kill!' The militiamen immediately pushed the victims from the rally site. Chen Zhiming first chopped the victims to death with a large flat sword and then cut out their livers." Later, the villagers all shared in the boiled human flesh.

On the same day, there was a criticism parade down Huangmao Street. The victim was Zhang Boxun, a man of poor and lower-middle peasant background, who held to Small Faction views, and who was a teacher at the Duzhai village elementary school, Shangwen brigade. Because he could tell that his death was fast approaching, Zhang rushed off in great fear, took the wrong road, and jumped into the river. "Militiaman Guo Lixiang pulled the victim to the riverbank and cut out his heart and liver with a five-inch knife. Guo shared the flesh with Wei Bingliang, who served it up in a casserole. In no time, the victim's skin and intestines were taken away. The consumption of the victims' flesh took place everywhere. The Huangmao Food and Supply Store was among the most prominent sites of cannibalism. A large pot, eight feet in diameter, was used to boil victims, and then about ten people had a feast. The killers also forced others to eat from the pot. Two female workers, who had problems with their 'political standpoint,' were forced to join in. In those two units, 80 percent of the people participated in cannibalism. The masses referred to it as a 'feast of human flesh'."

The ruthlessness of these acts was also recorded in official documents:

> After Zhang Boxun was beaten to death, his liver and flesh quickly disappeared, so that only his small and large intestines were left. The ruthless killer held up one end of Zhang's intestines while the other end dragged on the ground, and with manic glee he yelled, "take a look at Zhang Boxun's intestines! How fat they are!" Then, the killer took the intestines home to boil and eat.

On the same day, "feasts of human flesh" were also held at Wuxuan Middle School. What follows is a simple record in an official document. "On June 18, 1968, after Wu Shufang of Wuxuan Middle School was beaten to death, his liver was baked for medicinal purposes. It is unfathomable that such a ruthless killing could have taken place in a school devoted to cultivating and educating people."

It so happened that before I arrived at Wuxuan Middle School I was able to gain a good understanding of this case; otherwise, the ruthless actions that had occurred there would have remained buried in the simple descriptions in the official record.

In Liuzhou, pursuing a clue provided by Men Qijun, deputy director of the Party Reform Office, I located Wu Hongtai, supervisor of the prefecture Education Bureau. Wu was director of the group handling leftover cases, and he had once served as principal of Wuxuan Middle School; therefore, Wu had a lot to say regarding events in Wuxuan during the Cultural Revolution. I was warmly received by Wu, who originally came from Hubei Province and had been a student in the first graduating class of the Teachers' College of Zhongyuan University (now known as Zhongyuan Teachers' University). Wu had come to Guangxi in 1950 to work in support of the border regions, and thus he was among the first group of educated Communist Party cadres to serve there. Viewed in silhouette, he looked a bit like Zhang Chunqiao, leader of the radical faction in Shanghai. Wu was an extremely kindhearted and straightforward person and a typical teacher. On the second day of my visit, he described some of the major cases of cannibalism that had occurred in Wuxuan. On the first day, he focused primarily on the outbreak of cannibalism at Wuxuan Middle School. He had been a participant in the drama and was later designated to clear up the cases associated with these events, and so the memory of everything was still fresh in his mind.

Wuxuan Middle School was quite famous. It had been chosen in 1960 to participate in a national conference in Beijing. During the Cultural Revolution, Wu was its principal, and naturally he was branded as a capitalist roader. After he witnessed numerous ruthless killings, Wu felt his life no longer had any meaning. So one day he quietly walked out of the school and down to the river. He took off his shoes and neatly placed them side by side on the riverbank. Just at the very moment he was about to jump into the turbulent water, however, an old shepherd happened to shuffle by with his flock of sheep. The old man's dim-sighted yet sage old eyes could perceive what was about to happen. So as the shepherd passed, Wu heard him mutter, "soon it will all be over." The old man's simple, yet wise, observation inspired Wu to abandon his idea of suicide. And so Wu put his shoes back on and returned to the evil world.

Although he had refused to commit suicide, Wu's heavy heart still was not relieved of its burdens. On the evening of June 18, 1968, a certain Wu Shufang, head of the school's Chinese Department and a teacher of geography, was beaten to death. At that time, this case was nothing out of the ordinary, because with the exception of five teachers of poor and lower-middle peasant background whose lives were spared, all of Wu's colleagues had been criticized. What happened next remains beyond belief, however, to this day. A group of armed students ordered Wu Hongtai and three other "old gang" teachers to drag the victim's body down to the riverbank. When they got it there, a few armed students stood behind them, while a larger number of students looked on from a distance:

> Fu Bingkun, a sophomore, took a big knife and stabbed the side of the victim's body, saying, "Spy. Cut out his heart and liver to serve as an evening snack! Don't sever his intestines. If you do, I'll throw you into the river! We only want his heart and liver." The four of us squatted on the ground, and someone threw the knife over to me. I [Wu Hongtai] was trembling so much I was unable to do the cutting. Cursing, the students handed the knife to Qin Chineng. In the torchlight, Qin ground his teeth, forcing himself to complete the job. (Given the bloody atmosphere at that time, if Qin had not succeeded, the students

would have done us all in.) After he had cut out the heart and liver, along with the flesh from the victim's thigh, the crowd took off. They carried some hunks of the flesh away in plastic bags, other hunks they simply slung on their rifles as the blood was still dripping down. They threw the victim's bones into the river.

Wu Shufang's flesh was cooked in three places: One was the school kitchen. Chef Zhang, a female, had let the group in. When the flesh was cooked, seven or eight students consumed it together. The second place was the dormitory room of Huang Yuanlou, deputy director of the school's Revolutionary Committee. There, the flesh was cooked in a casserole. Huang refused to join the dinner party, though four other students did partake of Wu Shufang's flesh. The third cookery was under the roof of the hallway, outside classrooms number 31 and 32. As a result of subsequent investigations, the deputy director of the school Revolutionary Committee was expelled from the Party. His only comment was "Cannibalism? It was the landlord's flesh! The spy's flesh!" He also said that he had offered some to the Party secretary, who now absolutely refuses to admit it. Yet at the time, they were proud of their cannibalism.

After I had arrived at Wuxuan, the first place I visited, in order to show my sympathy, was the middle school. Cannibalism is rare, but students eating teachers is rarer still. I took some pictures of the large kitchen, its big stove, and the hallway outside the number 31 and 32 classrooms. I also took some pictures in a corner of the campus under some lemon trees where the holy fire had been lit. Try to imagine the scene. It's deep night. Thick smoke rises from the chimney into the sky. Outside the classrooms, students cluster around the campus in groups of three and four, perhaps even five, as light from the cooking fire glows on their young faces. Is this a bonfire for some festival? It's a human-flesh barbecue! Bubbling away in their big and small pots, big and small casseroles, and in the "barbecue pot" sitting on top of two bricks and one tile is their teachers' flesh! Respect for teachers, teaching and educating children, moral civilization? The twelve-degree typhoon of class struggle has blown all that Confucian crap away! "Save our children," the great thinker Lu Xun called out at the beginning of the century. For in this China with a "four-thousand-year history of cannibalism" adults had joined in cannibalism, but never children. In its time, Lu Xun's short story "Diary of a Madman," which depicted China's cannibalistic culture, was merely a symbolic literary work, but unfortunately it had been realized under the great and glorious banner of socialism. In the midst of the most glorious idea of mankind, children have started to engage in cannibalism. Children are the hope and the future of the nation. When they are taught to consume their own species, surely the nation has lost all hope and its future.

If teachers could be cannibalized, then so could students. Three days later (June 21), a rally to criticize a Wuxuan Middle School student named Zhang Fuchen was held at Shangjin village in Dongxiang District. Not long after the rally began, a twelve-year-old child named Huang Peigang beat Zhang unconscious with a club.

> The killer then poked his chest with a five-inch knife. Zhang's body twisted in pain. Huang Peigang then picked up a stone and smashed his victim in the head and then stabbed his victim two or three times. Next, Zhang was cut open from his chest to his navel. His heart and liver were removed. Then, Liao Shuiguang cut off the victim's penis. The crowd rushed forward to cut at the flesh.

The documents do not record whether the human flesh was consumed. But at least one point can be confirmed: Since the villagers usually possessed stoves, the cookery must have been handled in a more civilized fashion than that of the students, with their pots and barbecue pits.

Two days later, at Xiangsi village, an incident categorized as "ruthless" in the official documents occurred. It was a case of "wiping out an entire family," in which the husband was killed and his wife raped. According to Du Tiansheng, this act originated with a group of people headed by a production team leader who was implicated in the rape of the wife of a certain Mr. Li. Fearful that other members of the Li family might exact their revenge sometime in the future, the criminals declared that all of Mr. Li's uncles and nephews were four elements and that they had concealed guns in their houses. "If we don't kill them, they'll kill us," the criminals declared. They also decided to cross the Qian River and kill everyone on the other side who had the surname Li. The entire production team was armed with clubs and ordered into action. Those who refused to go would not receive any work points for their labor in the fields. Around noon on June 23, 1968, the villagers from Xiangsi appeared in the center of the market.

> Li Binglong and others bound the feet of Li Mingqi, Li Zhongyuan, and Li Zhongjie (that way, the victims could only drag their feet).

THE SLAUGHTER AT WUXUAN . 203

The victims were also bound around their necks and hands by a rope. Arriving at a vegetable stand, the three brothers of the Li family were ordered to kneel down. Li Binglong read off the so-called evil evidence, screaming: "Should they be killed?" The crowd replied, "Kill!" Li Binglong and others then immediately beat the three victims to death. Thereafter they dragged the dead bodies to the riverbank. Huang Qihuan and others cut open the Li brothers to get at their livers and their reproductive organs, and then they discarded their bodies by the riverside. (Huang Qihuan was a clerk at the county People's Bank. He took one liver back to the bank. Yu Yuerong baked and wrapped it in rice paper. Many people shared it as medicine.)

The murderers had achieved their victory and they returned to the village. That same night, the gang raped Li's widow, confiscated the furnishings of the entire house, and robbed it of everything else. They also slaughtered Li's pigs, cut down Li's vegetable patch, and feasted on these spoils to celebrate the great victory of the "masses' dictatorship." With all the males dead, and the widow subsequently remarried, there is no longer anyone from that village by the surname of Li.

It should be noted, of course, that the cases documented in this book are merely the most prominent examples of what occurred in Wuxuan. They by no means exhaust the list, nor are they even a major part of it. Considering the many incidents of cannibalism that followed within only ten days of the meeting to blow the typhoon of class struggle, the cannibalism at Wuxuan had reached the extremities of terror and insanity. Human blood is not water; therefore, no matter what convincing theories were used to justify these cruel acts, the murderers undoubtedly suffered psychologically when they confronted their own ruthlessness and cruelty. Finally, the murderers themselves could take it no longer. On June 26, the county Revolutionary Committee conducted a study of the ongoing class struggle. After the directors of the various district revolutionary committees and armed police offices had reported their progress (120 dead), they demanded an end to "street criticism parades." In the face of such weakness, Sun Ruizhang, political commissar of the county Armed Police Office and the first deputy director of the county Revolutionary Committee, expressed his discontent. "Don't be so chickenhearted! What is there to be afraid of? Without such an effort we cannot defeat the class enemies and inspire the willpower of the people. Fear not. We must press on." Following this meeting, cannibalism in Wuxuan reached its climax.

The following is a typical case of how a victim was carved up while still alive.

> In July 1968, Gan Kexing of the seventh production team of Dawei brigade, Tongwan District, organized a rally to criticize Gan Dazuo. They pulled their victim to the side of the field and ordered him to kneel down. Gan Yewei struck the victim on the head with a stick, but he did not die. Gan Zuyang then tore off the victim's pants to cut off his penis. "Let me die first, then you can cut it," the victim implored. Gan Zuyang showed little concern and continued to cut. The victim struggled and screamed his lungs out. Gan Weixing and his group then cut off the flesh from his thigh. Gan Deliu cut out the liver. The rest of the crowd pushed forward and stripped the body of its flesh.

The following is a typical feast of human flesh.

> On July 10, 1968, a criticism rally was held in front of the Shangjiang town hall, Sanli District. During the ensuing chaos, Liao Tianlong, Liao Jinfu, Zhong Zhenquan, and Zhong Shaoting were beaten to death. Their bodies were stripped of flesh, which was taken back to the front of the brigade office to be boiled in two big pots. Twenty or thirty people participated in the cannibalism. Right out in the open, they boiled human flesh in front of the local government offices. The impact of this was extremely deleterious.

That day was also a day of bustling crowds rushing to strip the victims of their flesh. Someone saw an old gray-haired woman struggle to grab a piece of a human liver. How gleeful she was. On her way back home it began to drizzle. The raindrops, together with the blood from the liver, stained the road she was walking along.

I also heard about another bizarre case involving escape. Chen Jinwu, a rightist and a teacher at the Sanli Middle School, was locked in an empty room on campus so that the next day he could be killed. But he was dramatically saved by the wife of the school chef, Yang Guanghuai (also a rightist). In great fear, Chen hurried to escape. Unfortunately, a "cross" had been shaved on top of his head to mark him as a rightist. Thus imprisoned within the proletarian net, he had no way out. Indeed, as he tried to leave Wuxuan, Chen was arrested by the militiamen. The director of the commune armed police, Xie Kainian, a veteran army officer who had fought in the Korean War, originally from Liling, Hunan Province interrogated the prisoner. Chen had heard that Xie was from Hunan, and claiming that he, too, was from Hunan, he kneeled down and begged Xie to let him go. This aroused Xie's sympathy, and he came up with an idea: They would falsely claim that Chen was a "parachute spy" and put him in the county military prison. This was a brainstorm because by the time this case of a parachute spy was cleared in the courts, the wave of cannibalism had subsided. Chen was thus saved. Surely Chen would forever remember his rescue by Xie with special gratitude, especially since it was rare indeed that a victim escaped being cannibalized during those times. [. . .]

During the frenetic wave of indiscriminate killing and cannibalism, three social dregs with the surname Diao from Dongxiang Township, who held fast to Small Faction views, managed to escape up Hema Mountain. On July 10, 1968, Qin Zhonglan, director of the district armed police, ordered three squads of militiamen from his own district and another squad from nearby Jinggang Township to go up to the mountain to "defeat the bandits" and to arrest the renegades. Diao Qishan managed to escape, but Diao Qiyao fell into a cave and died. Diao Qitang was shot to death. "Luo Xianquan cut out Diao Qitang's heart and liver. He then loaded the remains of the body in a basket. When Luo Xianquan returned to the canteen of the district office, Diao Qitang's flesh was boiled and eaten. Squad member Wang Wenliu also brought two pieces of flesh back home to her mother. Once Wang had achieved renown for consuming human flesh, she got one promotion after another. Eventually, she became the vice director of the Wuxuan Revolutionary Committee.

When contemporary liberal intellectuals in China dispute the vicious means by which military men get promoted, they generally use the phrase "painting the crown with human blood." However, that phrase cannot be used to describe Wang Wenliu and her ilk, for they earned their promotions not only by helping to kill people, but also by eating them.

Messrs. Li, Yang, Zhou, and He from the county Party Reform Office once tried to defend Wang. They argued that "while there were incidents in which people consumed reproductive organs, Wang could not have taken part in them because she was only eighteen years old at the time and unmarried. It is true that she consumed human flesh and for that reason she has been removed from the Party and has lost her position as cadre. She is now a worker at the county reservoir." Should I believe the words of these officials, who refused me access to the official documents? Or should I believe the rumors? Emotionally, I cannot force myself to believe the officials. To conclude merely that it sounds impossible that Wang could have dined on reproductive organs is indefensible.

Various cases of cannibalism have been confirmed only after thorough investigations. The very few unconfirmed rumors are indicative of the absurdity and cruelty of cannibalism. For instance, when I first arrived in Guangxi, I heard one rumor that fat out-of-towners are drugged with a special medicine, cut open alive, and shown the entire procedure with a mirror. Initially, it seemed like a rumor, but, later, I unintentionally discovered that this "rumor" consisted of figurative language that actually informed the prototype for the brutal cases of cannibalism that were taking place. *Drugging the victim with a special medicine* was simply an exaggerated way of describing how a victim was knocked unconscious with a stick or stone. The word *fat* simply indicated someone who wasn't appallingly lean, as most victims were, beset by poverty. (In a certain school, a decision had to be made about whether the Party secretary or the principal should be selected for execution. After some discussion, it was decided to kill the fat one—the principal. Thus, the Party secretary survived. However, if a blow the typhoon campaign breaks out in China again sometime in the future, the "thin ones" will be victimized first, because all the fat people have already been done in.) *Out-of-towners* refers to the innocent. (Case in point: Wei Changmeng and others from Huama village killed a passerby named Chen Guoyong for no reason whatsoever and served him up as a "midnight snack.") *Cut open alive* simply implied fierce and brutal acts, of which there were numerous cases. Finally, *show the victim the entire procedure with a mirror* also refers to the ruthless and cruel torture. (For instance, forcing Zhou Weian's widow to kiss her dead husband's face and caress his decapitated head.)

We know that in ancient times rumors supplied a basis for comparing, symbolizing, and exaggerating the existing reality. Modern rumors are no different, especially in modern totalitarian countries where the masses can only spread important news via rumors and the social grapevine. Legends, stories, and rumors are a form of special rights enjoyed by the masses who are deprived of the rights of news, publication, speech, assembly, association, and so on. Not only can rumors not be suppressed, they can be spread extremely rapidly, poisoning the entire province and the entire country. This itself shows that rumors are believable. Not only do the masses believe in and spread the rumors, they also perfect and exaggerate them so that they reach a state of qualitative abstraction. Isn't the aforementioned seemingly absurd rumor the most representative generalization of the killing and cannibalism that took place in Guangxi? I myself think so. In a country where rumors and lies permeate official broadcasts, newspapers, movies, television, conferences, advertisements, official communiqués, university podiums, courts, economic reports, "internal reference materials restricted to top leaders," and bids for projects, only two things are believable: the date of publication and the rumors reported in the newspapers. Up to this point, I had not believed the "rumored account" of Wang Wenliu's consumption of the male organ, especially when I realized that she was only eighteen years of age, a time of life when I myself had been full of fascist frenzy. I also realized that she was being singled out for blame through the rumor mill because she was a woman. I even hesitated to describe her case in this book. But the pen in my hands was very heavy. I was deeply aware—I will be held accountable in both the legal and the moral realms for every word added or deleted in this book. Thus, I have only one choice, and that is to write down verbatim everything I have learned. I can only hope that in reading the rest of this book, the reader will develop some sort of understanding or sympathy toward people like Wang Wenliu, and others.

★ ★ ★

[. . .] Let me summarize what I had learned in Wuxuan. An unprecedented frenzy of cannibalism in human history had occurred. Even uglier than the mere fact alone was that the frenzy was not caused by some uncontrollable defect in human nature. It was a violent act, caused directly by the very same class struggle advocated by Marxism-Leninism-Mao Zedong Thought, armed by the theory of proletarian dictatorship, silently agreed upon and directly organized by the power organizations of the Chinese Communist Party. After my intense interviewing in Wuxuan, I had put together a general picture of the cannibalism in Guangxi. Based on the characteristics of the people's emotions at that time, I categorized the process into three phases.

Phase one was the beginning, characterized by secretive and frightening actions. The numerous cases in Shanglin County were rather typical: In each case, the murderers made their way secretly to the killing fields late at night to secure the hearts and livers of victims shot some hours earlier. Out of fear, disorganization, and lack of experience, in almost all cases the murderers ended up puncturing a bowel or cutting open a lung by mistake. Once they discovered their error, despite their fear the murderers would return to the site to get what they wanted. After they had boiled the parts, dozens of people surrounding the fireplace would hasten to consume them in silence. The next morning, the murderers would call their pals and invite them over to share the leftovers. Afraid these associates would refuse their invitation, they pretended that the food consisted of the hearts and livers of cattle. Only after the pals had finished eating did the killers gleefully announce that they had just consumed so-and-so's liver.

Phase two was the high tide. This was characterized by blatant expressions of enthusiasm. By this point, the act of cutting out hearts and livers while the victims were alive had evolved into a rather skilled technique. Based on the rich experience handed down by veteran guerrilla fighters who years earlier had engaged in cannibalism, the method was honed nearly to perfection. For instance, if you ever decide to cut a victim open while he's still alive, simply make a cut underneath the rib cage in the form of the Chinese character for *person (ren)* with a sharp knife, then step on the stomach with one foot and immediately squeeze out the heart and liver. (If the victim happens to be tied up to a tree, push on the stomach with one knee.) The leaders assumed the privilege of cutting out the heart, liver, and genitals, and everyone else was free to scramble for all the other parts. Red flags fluttered and slogans were changed. Altogether the scene had a certain disgusting magnificence about it. At some "get-together" parties in certain villages, a unique practice of boiling human flesh and pork together in a pot was indulged by the locals. When done, villagers would line up and take turns getting a single chunk.

After I had suffered the terrible shock of hearing these horrid scenes described in detail, I realized that it was an interesting psychological phenomenon. The collective frenzy that emerged from CCP labels and phrases such as "class hatred," "a firm political standpoint," and "drawing a line between enemy and comrade" had driven the people to cannibalism. The moral conscience, however, could not be completely suppressed and so a compromise had been worked out. People would join in the collective act of cannibalism, but each conscience was appeased by the random selection of a piece from the pot mixed with human flesh and pork. This random selection reconciled two conflicting drives among the cannibals: on the one hand the drive to participate in the struggle against the victims and on the other the drive to shrink from the act of eating human flesh. Such was the supreme form of the swindling, and self-swindling, compromise that was stitched between a beastly mentality and human instinct, one which ensured some measure of psychological compatibility between collective frenzy and individual conscience. Naturally, this was not something invested by the folks in Guangxi. There had been similar cases during the Land Reform period (1849–1953), when the practice was devised of a collective act of killing that permitted each person to strike a blow with a knife or stone. Such scenes of "class struggle," along with the techniques of collective execution, sprouted forth from a domineering psychological mentality no different from the collective cannibalism of Guangxi. The only nuance to the collective cannibalism was that it represented the zenith of such thinking. And it ended up generating rather dramatic styles of the technique.

Phase three could be summarized as the mass movement of cannibalism. In Wuxuan, for instance, the masses simply went berserk in their cannibalism, like a pack of hungry dogs who feed on the dead after an epidemic. Every so often, some victims would be singled out "to be criticized." Each criticism rally was followed by a beating, and each death ended in cannibalism. Once the victim fell to the ground—whether the victim had stopped breathing was irrelevant—the crows rushed forward, pulled out their cutting knives and daggers, and started cutting at whatever piece of flesh was closet to them. After the flesh had been cut away, they targeted the large and small entrails, along with the broken bones. I was told that a certain elderly woman, who had heard that a diet of human eyes helped to restore eyesight, used to wander from criticism rally to criticism rally with a vegetable basket over her arm. She would hover about for the opportune moment to rush toward a victim. Once the victim had been beaten down onto the ground, she would quickly pull out her sharp, pointed knife and use it to dig out the victim's eyes. Mission accomplished, she would scurry away.

There were also a few elderly men who made a specialty of eating the human brain. Because it was hard to smash open the skull and get at the brain, they developed their own unique method of feeding on the brain. Each one procured a medium-sized steel pipe, with one end sharpened to a point. Once the crowd had finished cutting away the victim's flesh, they would then slowly advance toward the victim (at that point they had no competitors). After they had pierced the victim's skull with their steel pipes, they would kneel on the ground and suck the brain through the pipe, rather resembling a small group of people in the act of sharing a jar of yogurt with straws. At the scene, women with children on their backs rushed in to grab a piece of flesh to show off to their parents. Not only common people, but everyone, even innocent young boys and girls and teachers, joined in the delirious wave of cannibalism. The very last sense of sin and humanity was swept away by the mentality of following the crowd. The frenzied wave spread like an epidemic. Once victims had been subjected to criticism, they were cut open alive, and all their body parts—heart, liver, gallbladder, kidneys, elbows, feet, tendons, intestines—were boiled, barbecued, or stir-fried into a gourmet cuisine. On campuses, in hospitals, in the canteens of various governmental units at the brigade, township, district, and county levels, the smoke from cooking pots could be seen in the air. Feasts of human flesh, at which people celebrated by drinking and gambling, were a common sight.

Part Five
Serial Cannibals

Cruelty Amid Chaos
From *Cannibal Killers: The History of Impossible Murderers*

BY MOIRA MARTINGALE

After World War I, a crushing depression fell upon Germany. Anarchy reigned in the street, streams of refugees from the wasted countryside poured into large cities like Berlin, and—as Moira Martingale writes in her *Cannibal Killers: The History of Impossible Murderers*—"an atmosphere of godlessness" prevailed.

Not only were the seeds of Nazism sewn during this period, but there also arose a horror unlike any other previously seen: serial cannibal killers who preyed upon the dispossessed for meat and profit. Following is the story of four such men: Fritz Haarman, George Grossmann, Karl Denke, and, perhaps most terrible of all, Peter Kurten, the "Dusseldorf Vampire."

If you were to destroy in mankind the belief in immortality, not only love but every living force maintaining the life of the world would at once be dried up. Moreover, nothing then would be immoral, everything would be permissible, even cannibalism.
Fedor Dostoyevsky, *The Brothers Karamazov*

Cannibal killers are few and far between. While the twentieth century abounds with murderers—and indeed, statistics show that there are now more instances of serial killings than ever before in civilization's history—the crime which, because of its primitive bestiality, evokes the most horror and revulsion in all of us is, thankfully, uncommon. How curious, then, that Germany—a small country in comparison to the USA—has thrown up at least four cannibalistic murderers this century, with three of them operating between the wars, during the 1920s.

After the First World War anarchy reigned, law and order had collapsed, thieves and confidence tricksters abounded and the rest of the people got by as best they could. The economy was at an all-time low and the country was in chaos. There was an atmosphere of godlessness. Streams of refugees roamed through the cities looking for jobs, begging on the streets and sleeping on pavements. A backwards glance at the way Nazism was due to flourish and gain primacy over the next decade or so makes one wonder what exactly was happening to German society during this period which, perhaps, predisposed the population to tolerate the atrocities which were in store. One answer immediately springs to mind. When the population of any species hits rock bottom, the law of the jungle dictates the survival of the fittest. But that does not necessarily mean the survival of the best.

Into this desperate society one morning in 1918 walked a newly-liberated Fritz Haarmann: the prison gates slammed shut behind him and he breathed the free fresh air once more. Recognizing Hanover as being riddled with crooks and villains who exploited those weaker than themselves, Haarmann felt at home. He liked the world he now found himself in. He had been serving a five-year gaol-term for fraud and theft, the latest in a long history of imprisonments imposed as punishment for stealing, picking pockets or indecently assaulting small children. He was thirty-nine in 1918 and had little to show for his life, having spent it as an itinerant hawker and thief, devoted to his mother who had been incapacitated after his birth and remained a lifelong invalid, but filled with hatred for his father, a bitter, miserable railway worker with the revealing nickname Sulky Olle. Fritz's father had beaten him and made his childhood desperately unhappy. As Fritz grew older it became apparent that his IQ was lower than average and he showed signs of the uncontrolled violence which was to make him one of the worst mass murderers of all time. With what turns out in hindsight to have been commendable astuteness, Fritz's father had tried to have him committed to an institution when he sensed the potential dangerousness of the boy, but doctors declared him to be safe and refused Herr Haarmann's request. Had they thought otherwise, a great many lives would have been saved. As a child, Fritz used to enjoy dressing up in his three sisters' clothes—his sisters had drifted into prostitution when they were comparatively young—and as a teenager he was sent to a mental institution for a spell after attacking small children. He escaped to join the Army, but was soon dismissed as an "undesirable" and it was then he devoted himself to a career of theft and sex attacks.

A fleshy man with superficial charm, he was blatantly homosexual and made his mark on the criminal underworld, where he was well liked but thought to be rather stupid, if harmless. Whether he would have been quite so popular had they realized he was also a police informer is something to speculate about, yet this was another string to Haarmann's bow. The police also liked him because of his "it's a fair cop" attitude: he never resisted arrest, appeared to enjoy the discipline of gaol life and joked with them as they pulled him in. The Hanover police nicknamed him "Detective" because he told them of so many crimes and plots that were afoot, and he was even paid a small salary and given a badge—something which provided excellent cover for him to commit his dreadful crimes. Moving among the swindlers at the market in Hanover, Haarmann began gravitating to the nearby railway station where wretched people arrived from all over the country to huddle around stoves in the station's waiting area and beg from passersby. Among them were scores of homeless youths, some not even teenagers, most of whom had run away from home. They were nameless, untraceable. Over the next five years these boys proved easy prey for Haarmann . . . literally. A smiling Haarmann would flash his police badge and invite a youth to accompany him home. Coupled with his charm and apparent sympathy for their plight, the promise of a good meal tempted these lost and hungry youngsters to return with him to his apartment as easily as the witch persuaded Hansel and Gretel to enter her gingerbread cottage. And Haarmann had exactly the same thing in mind.

The apartment which he shared from 1919 with his young lover, twenty-year-old Hans Grans, was in Hanover's ghetto area, on the third floor of a crumbling block overlooking the River Leine. After getting the youths home, Haarmann would seduce or attack them, use them for his own sexual gratification and then kill them by tearing their throats out with his teeth, after which he would drink their blood and indulge in necrophiliac activities. Then he would drag the body up to his attic where the walls were crimson with encrusted blood. There, sometimes helped by Grans, he would dismember the body and slice it up, transferring the pieces of flesh to buckets. Then Haarmann donned his other vile identity: that of market meat-trader. Taking his buckets of human flesh, he sold it, along with secondhand clothes, at his stall in Hanover's marketplace, telling the hungry German citizens that it was horsemeat. The clothes of his victims also found their way on to his stall. His blackmarket meat business was highly successful—after all, his prices were lower than anyone else's—and the police, who needed spies like

Haarmann to enable them to monitor underworld corruption, turned a blind eye to the illegal trading activities of their paid nark and asked no tricky questions.

Haarmann's first victim among the starving and penniless boys who fell prey to his bribery and charm was seventeen-year-old Friedel Roth, who disappeared in 1918 after being seen with Haarmann. The police investigation led them to Haarmann's door, but their enquiries were half-hearted; Haarmann was, after all, very useful to them. Many years later, when he was finally caught, Haarmann bragged that when police visited his room, "the head of the boy was lying wrapped in newspaper behind the oven." The police did not look too closely on that occasion—or on others. When Haarmann met the psychopathic Hans Grans (who, curiously enough, was a runaway who escaped the lost boys' usual fate) the slim, elegant youth was to incite him to further outrages. Grans, a librarian's son, was Haarmann's social superior and tormented Haarmann with his sarcastic remarks and insults. He selected victims and ordered their murder, often simply because he wanted their clothes. Haarmann sold clothes from victims only days after having killed them and on one occasion, someone saw Grans wearing a suit that he had seen a few days earlier on a boy at the railway station.

Haarmann's neighbours had no idea what was going on, although they were later to recall that they often saw a large number of young men entering the apartment, but never saw them leaving. They heard chopping noises through the walls but thought nothing of it; after all, this man *was* a butcher so it was only to be expected that he chopped up carcasses. Even when one neighbour bumped into Haarmann in the hall when he was carrying a bucket of blood downstairs, she suspected nothing. Another neighbour, meeting Haarmann after he had been butchering a body in his attic, asked him cheekily: "Am I going to get a bit?" Haarmann merely laughed and promised her some meat next time. Occasionally he would supply meat to people in the other apartments. His main problem—disposing of the skulls and bones of his victims— was somewhat solved by giving the bones to the neighbours, who would make soup with them, believing them to be from animals. But eventually, people began to harbour suspicions. These bones were too white, they murmured. What sort of animal did they come from? Haarmann stopped handing the bones out and tossed them, with the skulls, into the river which flowed close by. One customer who bought some meat from Haarmann's market-stall was so worried about it that she went to the police to ask what it was. Pork, she was told.

If the police really suspected the true horror of Haarmann's activities—and perhaps one can understand why such a terrible idea never entered their heads—it was in their interest to ignore it. Time and again, parents in search of their lost sons found the trail of clues led to Haarmann, who had been the last person with whom their sons had been seen; time and again the police declared themselves satisfied that he was innocent and had had nothing to do with the youths' disappearances. By 1923, Haarmann was greatly valued by the police and under their protection. He was helping them to recruit people for a secret organization trying to combat French occupation of the Ruhr and had even joined forces with a prestigious police official to run a detective agency. But thankfully the newspapers were under no obligation to protect a killer or draw a veil over police corruption. It was they who eventually pressured the police into taking some action by drawing attention to the number of youths who arrived in Hanover and then instantly disappeared. One newspaper suggested the figure could have been as high as six hundred in one year. With publicity, the very name "Hanover" began to induce a chill and rumours began to circulate that there were such things as werewolves after all—and that one was at large in the town, eating the children. The police and the authorities pooh-poohed such suggestions and dismissed them as hysteria . . . and then the skull was washed ashore beside the River Leine. It was May 1924 and the frightened public began harassing the police and demanding action. A second skull—a small one—was discovered a few days later, and more were found in the months to come, together with sackfuls of human remains. Dredgers were brought in to dig in the riverbed; more than five hundred human bones were found.

The horrified citizens of Hanover were defying their own disbelief and putting two and two together. Haarmann was their prime suspect. Knowing public opinion was against him, the chief of police had no alternative but to have his valued informer watched. At the end of June 1924 in Hanover railway station, Haarmann tried to pick up a boy who then called the police, objecting that Haarmann had sexually interfered with him. Haarmann was arrested and, with him in custody, officers went to search his apartment. They found the bloodstained room, together with piles of clothes, but when confronted with this Haarmann protested. He was a butcher, he said, and a clothes-trader. What did they expect to find? It was the mother of a missing boy, who said her son's coat was being worn by one of Haarmann's neighbours, that prompted the killer's full confession. He instantly implicated Grans in the murders.

At the trial on 4 December 1924, Haarmann, now forty-five, and Grans, twenty-five, were charged with the murder of twenty-seven teenage boys, but this was believed to be an under-estimate. One policeman believed that during the previous year or so, Haarmann and Grans had been killing two boys a week. When asked how many youths he had murdered, Haarmann shrugged carelessly and replied: "It might have been thirty, it might have been forty. I really can't remember the exact number"—and this ghoulish contempt was evident throughout the trial. Fame was his at last and he regarded the court as his stage. Although Grans remained silent throughout, Haarmann behaved like a callous showman, admitting his guilt, showing no remorse but instead making vulgar asides to Grans. Despite there being heartbroken relatives of his victims in court, he interrupted proceedings at will, often making jocular remarks and claiming that he was a selective killer, choosing only to kill good-looking boys and denying three of the charges. One parent whose son was missing showed a picture to the court and Haarmann objected indignantly, cruelly saying: "I have my tastes, after all. Such an ugly creature as, according his photographs, your son must have been, I would never have taken to . . . Poor stuff like him there's plenty . . . Such a youngster was much beneath my notice." One distraught mother broke down weeping while testifying and Haarmann, finding this tiresome, interrupted to ask the judges if he could smoke a cigar. Amazingly, he was given permission.

The newspapers, which had been so instrumental in bringing Haarmann to justice, were revolted at the way he behaved and did not conceal their revulsion. One report described the pitiful scenes "as a poor father or mother would recognise some fragment or other of the clothing or belongings of their murdered son . . . And with the quivering nostrils of a hound snuffling his prey, as if he were scenting rather than seeing the things displayed, did he admit at once that he knew them." People in court paled when Haarmann was asked how he killed his victims and he replied without emotion: "I bit them through their throats."

He became furious when it seemed to him that Hans Grans might be found innocent. "Grans should tell you how shabbily he has treated me," he protested. "I did the murders—for that work he is too young." But he told how Grans knocked on the attic door after he had just finished dismembering one body, and said, on entering: "Where is the suit?" Cold and unmoved, Grans remained unnervingly silent, which the crowds in court found equally horrifying. Haarmann was anxious not to be found insane and sent to a mental hospital, instead pleading with the court to behead him in public, on the spot where he had dealt in his evil trade. "I want to be executed in the marketplace," he demanded excitedly. "And on my tombstone must be put this inscription: 'Here lies Mass Murderer Haarmann' On my birthday Hans Grans must come and lay a wreath upon it." On the last day of the trial he shouted at the court: "Do you think I enjoy killing people? I was ill for eight days after the first time. Condemn me to death . . . I am not mad. It is true I often get into a state when I do not know what I am doing, but that is not madness . . . I will not petition for mercy, nor will I appeal. I just want to pass just one more merry evening in my cell, with coffee, hard cheese and cigars, after which I will curse my father and go to my execution as if it were a wedding."

Two psychiatrists declared that Haarmann was mentally sound. He was found guilty of twenty-four murders and beheaded. Grans was sentenced to life imprisonment but was released after twelve years, to walk the streets once more. He may still be alive today.

Haarmann was proof that given the right social conditions, a killer who is careful and cautious enough can get away with his crimes for years. And between-the-wars Germany with its catastrophic inflation rate and mass unemployment evidently provided the right climate in which the usual restraints of civilization were removed and perverts and psychopaths were enabled to flourish. Just as primitive peoples who have practised cannibalism and brutishness abandon this practice when touched by civilization, the reverse evidently applies. Poverty was rife in Germany at this period and self-interest was the dominating motivator, so maybe we should not be so surprised that "dog-eat-dog" became a byword. And it seems in many cases, people ate people, too.

Haarmann had two cannibal contemporaries. George Grossmann, like Haarmann, butchered an unknown number of people during the years after the First World War. Unlike Haarmann, his primary urge for killing was said to be fuelled by mercenary greed rather than sexual deviation, although one might doubt the truth of this, for even the most avaricious villain would blanch at Grossmann's method of getting rich illegally. The *modus operandi* was startlingly similar to Haarmann's. A pedlar, he hung around Berlin's railway station and picked out women who were particularly plump. He took them home, killed them and chopped up their bodies into cuts of meat to sell to the hungry people of Berlin. With inflation running so high that armfuls of money were needed to buy so much as a loaf of bread (at one point the German mark stood at 19 million to the British pound), Grossmann's cut-price joints proved popular and highly lucrative. He lived in a Berlin rooming-house and it was 1921 when tenants in adjoining rooms reported hearing sounds of a struggle coming from his room. When police burst in, they found the trussed-up corpse of a girl on the bed, waiting to be butchered by Grossmann. Grossmann hanged himself in jail.

Meanwhile, in Munsterberg, Silesia (now Ziebice, Poland), Karl Denke ran a boardinghouse, offering free accommodation for the many homeless tramps who passed through the city during the dire years between 1918 and 1924. They should have known there was no such thing as a free lunch. Unless, of course, one was Karl Denke. If one mark of a maniac is a glib exterior and the ability to charm one's associates, then Denke, like so many other psychopathic killers, had it. He was known as "Papa" among his neighbours and tenants and was regarded as a God-fearing, law-abiding man. Every Sunday he went to church, where he played the organ, and his kindness to the homeless was admired.

But as a landlord, he had his tenants at his mercy—and since many were vagrants about whom no one asked any questions, they made easy prey for Denke. Between 1921 and 1924 he killed at least thirty strangers, male and female, in order to eat their flesh bit by bit. Then, as a chilling postscript to abhorrent crime, he methodically entered the victims' names, weight, date of arrival at the boardinghouse and date of death in a ledger before pickling parts of the bodies in brine to eat later. Just before Christmas 1924, his crimes were discovered. A man who lived on the story above Denke heard terrible screams from the lower floor and rushed downstairs to find a young man bleeding profusely from a wound on the back of his head, caused by a hatchet. The man, who was one of Denke's tenants and did not at the time appreciate his luck in escaping from his landlord's clutches, soon lost consciousness, but before doing so, he managed to say that Denke had attacked him from behind. The police, thinking it was a routine assault case, were staggered to find pots of bones and the pickled remains of thirty bodies in Denke's flat. Denke admitted his crime and said he had eaten nothing but human flesh for three years. Soon after his arrest in 1924 Denke committed suicide by hanging himself with his braces in his prison cell.

But if these cannibal-killers escaped justice for so long, the infamous Peter Kurten, who was also busy instilling terror into the folk of Düsseldorf at around this time, outlasted them, managing to avoid detection for seventeen years, from 1913, when he committed his first murder, to 1930. Kurten was inspired by his own madness, rather than anything as mundane as financial expedience during an economic slump. His insanity was portrayed by Peter Lorre in Fritz Lang's movie of 1931 about Kurten's crimes, *M*.

The "Düsseldorf Vampire," as he came to be known, was born in 1883, one of thirteen children of a family steeped in crime and violence. His brothers all served jail sentences for theft and his father and grandfather were both alcoholics. His father was cruel and violent to both his wife and his children. He would take his violent sexual impulses out on his wife by having brutal intercourse with her as the children watched her pain and indignity, and he regularly raped his thirteen-year-old daughter. Kurten followed his example and raped the girl too.

As a child of only nine, Kurten was drawn into the sordid world of yet another individual who would help with his conditioning into the life of blood and violence which he was to enjoy. The man was the local council's dog- and rat-catcher who had a penchant for torturing animals; part of his sickness was to do it while the young Kurten watched. Kurten found the sight of suffering animals stimulating, and since the rat-catcher also committed sexual acts as part of his attacks, yet again the coupling of sex and sadism reinforced the child Peter's sexual predilections. Kurten soon graduated to committing his own acts of torture, stabbing sheep and other docile farm animals. He particularly found the sight of blood stimulating and often tore the heads off swans to enable him to drink their blood, a taste he never outgrew; when he was an adult and murdered many people, he often indulged in brutal sadism and necrophilia, sometimes drinking the blood of the corpses.

At the age of sixteen he met an older woman whose masochistic tendencies complemented his sadistic desires. During sex, she would enjoy being half-strangled and beaten and she even drew her daughter—who was the same age as Kurten—into their sexual acts. But despite their apparent carnal compatability, the relationship failed. Soon after this, Kurten attacked a girl in a wood and left her for dead, but she survived. Then came an attack on another girl whom he tried to strangle, for which he was arrested and sent to prison for a derisory four years. Altogether, Kurten spent twenty-seven years in prison out of the forty-seven years of his life, during which time he contented himself by fantasizing about performing sadistic acts upon the helpless, or killing schoolchildren by giving them chocolate laced with arsenic. He also obtained sexual pleasure from imagining setting fire to buildings, causing people inside to perish and upon release he began to act out his fantasies for real. Fortunately, no one died during the fires which he caused, but his sadism claimed many victims. Several women and children who were attacked escaped over the years, but just as many were slaughtered.

His violence first exploded into murder in 1913 when he broke into a tavern and raped the ten-year-old daughter of the innkeeper as she lay asleep in bed. Kurten recalled the killing in detail at his trial, showing no emotion, other than enjoyment at the recollection. "I discovered the child asleep. Her head was facing the window. I seized it with my left hand and strangled her for about a minute and a half. The child woke up and struggled but lost consciousness . . . I had a small but sharp pocket knife with me and I held the child's head and cut her throat. I heard the blood spurt and drip on the mat beside the bed . . . The whole thing lasted about three minutes." The day after the murder, Kurten went to a cafe opposite the inn to drink a glass of beer, read about the murder in the newspaper and listen to the shocked locals discussing the crime. "All this amount of horror and indignation did me good," he said.

Called up for the army, Kurten showed himself to be a coward and deserted the following day—presumably the sight of blood and death only held appeal when he was not at personal risk. He ended up in jail once more for arson offences and volunteered to work in the prison hospital, to enable him to lay out prisoners who had died. Kurten's appearance belied his blood-lust. He was a fastidious, charming, smartly-groomed, well-spoken man with impeccable manners, able easily to persuade his victims to walk with him in a park, or otherwise meet him alone. Children, too, warmed to him and trusted him, which made his grisly acts that much easier to perform—and lends them an added dimension of abomination. In fact, he appeared to be a gentle man to all who knew him—or thought they knew him—including his wife, whom he married in 1921 in Altenburg and to whom he was always kind and loving. When Kurten finally confessed his crimes to her, she would not at first believe him. Within his marriage, Kurten appeared to try to suppress his sadistic instincts, restricting himself to fantasy and exciting himself by reading about Jack the Ripper, who had caused a frenzy of fear in London a few decades previously. He even took a normal job as a molder in a factory and became an active trade union member—although he did take mistresses with whom his sexual activities became increasingly violent. He enjoyed beating and half-strangling them. But a few years after his marriage he returned to Düsseldorf because he had started a new job. "The sunset was blood-red on my return to Düsseldorf," he told a psychiatrist many years later: "I considered this to be an omen symbolic of my destiny." It was 1925 and from indulging in occasional bloodletting, he began to commit more and more crimes of arson and attempted murder, leading to a campaign of murder so intense that from February 1929 the city was in a state of terror for a full sixteen months until Kurten was caught. Indeed, it was a great irony that Kurten's wife was so afraid of the "Düsseldorf Vampire" that her husband had to accompany her when she came home late at night from the restaurant where she worked.

Men, women and children were stabbed and horribly mutilated in frenzied attacks, their bodies sometimes tossed into the river. Kurten cunningly varied the style of his attacks in order to confuse the police: sometimes his victims were stabbed, sometimes strangled, sometimes bludgeoned to death. All they were certain of was that many, many crimes had been committed by someone who enjoyed drinking the blood of his victims. On occasions he returned to the graves of those he had killed and dug up the bodies. Once when he did this, he intended crucifying the corpse, but then abandoned the idea. "I caressed the dead body . . . experiencing the tenderest emotions that as a living woman she had failed to arouse in me earlier," he was to confess later. As Kurten's defence lawyer said at his trial when trying to encourage the jury to proclaim Kurten insane: "He unites nearly all perversions in one person . . . he killed men, women, children and animals, killed anything he found." And in addition to the murders, there were many more attacks in which the victims, miraculously, escaped.

His last murder victim was a five-year-old girl, Gertrude Albermann, whom he slaughtered with a thin-bladed knife, slashing thirty-six wounds on the child's body—yet he was captured by chance after he inexplicably let a potential victim go. Meeting twenty-year-old Maria Budlik in May 1930, he took her back to his flat for coffee and then offered to walk her home. On the way he dragged her into a wooded area and began to strangle her and try to rape her. Suddenly, he stopped and demanded: "Do you remember where I live, in case you ever need my help?" Smartly, Maria lied, saying she did not remember—which probably saved her life. Kurten escorted her to her tram and she returned to her dwelling, whereupon she contacted the police and led them to Kurten. When Kurten knew that the police were on his trail, he told his wife the truth about his Jekyll-and-Hyde life, urging her to tell the police he had confessed to her, so she could claim the reward which was being offered for his capture. She did so.

At his trial in 1931 he admitted sixty-eight crimes, pleading guilty to nine charges of murder and seven of attempted murder. Standing inside a cage to prevent him escaping, Kurten confessed his crimes in detail, admitting being a sex maniac, rapist, sadist, arsonist, murderer . . . and vampire. Clearly deriving pleasure from the recollections, he described his crimes in depth—even down to his sexual attacks on animals—and admitted drinking blood from the cut throats, hands and other wounds of both his male and female victims. Calmly he told of his repetitive dreams of sex, death and blood, his obsession with Jack the Ripper and of his desire that one day he would deserve a place in a waxworks chamber of horrors. He blamed his childhood and his spells in prison for twisting his mind and turning him into a killer—and he also blamed his victims for "asking for it," a notion that is sadly still prevalent today in some male-dominated circles, notably among misogynistic high court judges. "I do feel that I must make one statement: some of my victims made things very easy for me. Manhunting on the part of women today has taken on such forms that . . ." Kurten began pompously to say, before the judge's disgust exploded and, outraged, he silenced the killer. Kurten was found guilty and sentenced to death, which was by the guillotine. As the day dawned, Kurten's perverted blood-lust took on a new twist. He asked his psychiatrist, curiously: "After my head has been chopped off, will I still be able to hear, at least for a moment, the sound of my own blood gushing from my neck?" He added: "That would be the pleasure to end all pleasures."

Deranged
From *Deranged: The Shocking True Story of America's Most Fiendish Killer!*

BY HAROLD SCHECHTER

For sheer evil, probably the worst American cannibal killer was an old man named Albert Fish, who killed and ate children out of an insatiable sexual sadism. Following, from Harold Schechter's *Deranged: The Story of America's Most Fiendish Killer,* is an account of how he was captured and brought to trial after the 1928 kidnapping/murder of young Grace Budd.

In the years since Albert Corthell had been captured and released, the police had been unable to come up with a single plausible suspect in the Budd kidnapping. Officially, the case was still open. But no one in the Bureau of Missing Persons had much faith that it would ever be solved. No one, that is, except William F. King.

For over six years, King had continued to pursue the case. During that period, he had been involved in other investigations, including the search for Joseph Force Crater, the New York Supreme Court Justice whose disappearance in August, 1930, was one of the major mysteries of the Depression (and remains unexplained to this day).

But King had never abandoned his hunt for the missing Budd girl and her elderly abductor. By the fall of 1934, he had traveled over fifty thousand miles on that quest, running down rumors, following deadend leads, chasing phantoms. He had done everything possible to flush his quarry out of hiding.

One of his ploys was to plant phony news items about the Budd case in the New York City papers. He didn't want the public to forget about the case. Each time one of these stories appeared, the police would receive dozens of phone calls and letters from people who claimed to know something about the missing girl. None of these tips had ever panned out. But there was always the chance that someone might yet come forth with a key piece of information. The newspaper gambit was a long shot, King knew. But he was willing to give anything a try.

The main outlet for King's plants was Walter Winchell's enormously popular gossip column, "On Broadway," the pride of William Randolph Hearst's brassy tabloid, the New York *Daily Mirror.* Winchell was unquestionably the most influential newspaper columnist of his time and on close terms with everyone from J. Edgar Hoover to the mobster Owney Madden. He was always happy to do the police a good turn.

On November 2, 1934, the following newsflash appeared in Winchell's column:

> I checked on the Grace Budd mystery. She was eight when she was kidnapped about six years ago. And it is safe to tell you that the Dep't of Missing Persons will break the case, or they expect to, in four weeks. They are holding a "cokie" now at Randall's Island, who is said to know most about the crime. Grace is supposed to have been done away with in lime, but another legend is that her skeleton is buried in a local spot. More anon.

There was no factual basis at all for this story—no cocaine addict on Randall's Island with inside knowledge of Grace Budd's death. But by a strange turn of event, this fabrication would prove to be uncannily prophetic and come to be chalked up as another major coup for Winchell.

*   *   *

Ten days after Walter Winchell reported an imminent break in the Grace Budd case a letter arrived at the home of the missing girl's family. It had been mailed the previous night, November 11, from the Grand Central Annex post office in Manhattan and was addressed to Delia Budd.

Though Mrs. Budd was functionally illiterate, she could make out her name—written in a neat, bold script—on the front of the envelope. Seating herself at the kitchen table, she carefully tore open the top of the envelope and removed the folded sheet inside. But she had trouble reading what the letter said.

It was the one time in her life that her illiteracy proved to be a blessing.

Her son Edward was at home, relaxing in his bedroom. Mrs. Budd called him into the kitchen and handed him the letter. The young man began to read it silently. Almost immediately, the color drained from his face.

Mrs. Budd stared at him, alarmed. "What's wrong?" she demanded. "What does it say?" Edward Budd didn't answer; he was already on his way out the front door.

★   ★   ★

By 10:30 that morning, the letter was in Detective King's possession.

Over the years, King had read countless pieces of crank mail—inhumanly cruel letters full of vile taunts. But for sheer viciousness and depravity, nothing he had ever seen could begin to match the letter that Edward Budd had just delivered into his hands:

My dear Mrs. Budd,

In 1894 a friend of mine shipped as a deck hand on the Steamer Tacoma, Capt. John Davis. They sailed from San Francisco for Hong Kong China. On arriving there he and two others went ashore and got drunk. When they returned the boat was gone. At that time there was a famine in China. *Meat of any kind* was from $1—to 3 Dollars a pound. So great was the suffering among the very poor that all children under 12 were sold to the Butchers to be cut up and sold for food in order to keep others from starving. A boy or girl under 14 was not safe in the street. You could go in any shop and ask for steak—chops—or stew meat. Part of the naked body of a boy or girl would be brought out and just what you wanted cut from it. A boy or girls behind which is the sweetest part of the body and sold as veal cutlet brought the highest price. John staid there so long he acquired a taste for human flesh. On his return to N.Y. he stole two boys one 7 one 11. Took them to his home stripped them naked tied them in a closet. Then burned every-

thing they had on. Several times every day and night he spanked them—
tortured them—to make their meat good and tender. First he killed the
11 yr old boy., because he had the fattest ass and of course the most meat
on it. Every part of his body was Cooked and eaten except head—bones
and guts. He was Roasted in the oven (all of his ass), boiled, broiled,
fried, stewed. The little boy was next, went the same way. At that time, I
was living at 409 E 100 st., near—right side. He told me so often how
good Human flesh was I made up my mind to taste it. On Sunday June
the 3—1928 I called on you at 406 W 15 St. Brought you pot cheese—
strawberries. We had lunch. Grace sat in my lap and kissed me. I made
up my mind to eat her. On the pretense of taking her to a party. You said
Yes she could go. I took her to an empty house in Westchester I had already picked out. When we got there, I told her to remain outside. She
picked wildflowers. I went upstairs and stripped all my clothes off. I
knew if I did not I would get her blood on them. When all was ready I
went to the window and Called her. Then I hid in a closet until she was
in the room. When she saw me all naked she began to cry and tried to
run down stairs. I grabbed her and she said she would tell her mamma.
First I stripped her naked. How she did kick—bite and scratch. I choked
her to death, then cut her in small pieces so I could take my meat to my
rooms, Cook and eat it. How sweet and tender her little ass was roasted
in the oven. It took me 9 days to eat her entire body. I did *not* fuck her
tho I could of had I wished. She died a *virgin*.

So monstrous was this letter that it was hard to conceive of the mind
that could have produced it. Still, it had a strangely authentic quality.
Though clearly deranged, it was far more coherent than the foul ravings
of most hate letters. And the details it described—the strawberries and
pot cheese, for example—were completely accurate.

True, those details had been reported in the papers. But there
was a piece of information that hadn't. The writer had supplied a specific address—409 East 100th Street, located in the very neighborhood
where the police had concentrated their search in the weeks immediately following the abduction.

Was it possible that Grace's kidnapper had decided, for whatever
insane reason, to communicate with her family after all this time?

There was one way to find out.

Fetching his file on the Budd case, King dug through it until he
found what he was looking for—the photostat copy of the handwritten

message that "Frank Howard" had sent to the Budds on June 2, 1928, informing them that he would be delayed by a day.

Placing it beside the letter, King compared the two. He was no graphologist. But it didn't take an expert to see that the writing was exactly the same in both.

At that moment, William King could hardly have helped feeling that, after six and a half years of bitter frustration, the solution to the Budd mystery was finally—and quite literally—within his grasp.

*   *   *

With Fish's trial date set for March 12, James Dempsey had to move fast, and one of his first steps was to secure the services of two psychiatrists of his own. The men he engaged were an impressive pair. Smith Ely Jelliffe was one of the country's most distinguished neurologists. A tireless champion of Freud's revolutionary ideas, Jelliffe was a pioneering figure in the history of American psychoanalysis (though Freud himself had a somewhat disparaging view of him, as he did of the United States in general). Jelliffe had already served as a psychiatric expert in a number of sensational cases, including the trial of millionaire playboy Harry K. Thaw. (In June, 1906, Thaw shot and killed architect Stanford White on the roof of Madison Square Garden, a building that White himself had designed. Thaw committed the crime after discovering that his wife, former showgirl Evelyn Nesbit, had been White's mistress. He was declared criminally insane and institutionalized for nine years.)

The second psychiatrist Dempsey retained was Dr. Frederic Wertham. Born in Nuremberg in 1895, Wertham was educated in Germany, London, and Vienna (where he had a brief but memorable encounter with Freud). Emigrating to the United States in 1922, he joined the Phipps Psychiatric Clinic at Johns Hopkins, authored a standard textbook on neuropathology called *The Brain as an Organ,* and began a long and at times controversial career that would make him one of the best-known psychiatrists of his day.

Among Wertham's proudest achievements was the establishment of the LaFargue Clinic in Harlem. Created with the support of such prominent figures as Ralph Ellison, Richard Wright, and Paul Robeson, the clinic offered psychological counseling to the disadvantaged for the nominal fee of twenty-five cents per visit.

A few years after the clinic was established, in the early 1950s, Wertham gained widespread renown (and underlying notoriety in certain circles) for spearheading a national campaign against comic books, which he saw as a major cause of juvenile delinquency. His bestselling 1954 diatribe, *Seduction of the Innocent,* led to a Congressional investigation of the comic-book industry and the creation of the Comics Code Authority, a strict self-regulatory agency that remains in force to this day.

Comic-book devotees still regard Wertham as a sort of boogey man and lump him together with more recent, right-wing proponents of media censorship. In fact, Wertham was a political liberal and humanitarian, whose anticomics crusade was only one manifestation of a life-long obsession with the social roots of violence.

At the time that Dempsey approached him, in mid-February, 1934, Wertham had been senior psychiatrist at Bellevue for two years, as well as the director of the psychiatric clinic for the Court of General Sessions, a pioneering program which provided a complete psychiatric evaluation of every convicted felon in New York City.

Of all the psychiatrists who interviewed Fish in the weeks leading up to the trial, Wertham came to know the old man best, partly because they spent the most time in each other's company—more than twelve hours in all during Wertham's three visits to Eastview (Vavasour and Lambert together had traveled to the prison only once and examined Fish for a total of three hours). Moreover, though Fish seemed indifferent to Wertham at first ("Some *Doctor* came . . . last night and asked about a million questions," he sneered in a letter to Anna on February 14), he warmed up to the psychiatrist when he realized that Wertham had a sincere, scientific interest in understanding the workings of Fish's baroque psychology.

As Wertham later wrote in a published reminiscence of the case, Fish began to show "a certain desire to make himself understood and even to try to understand himself." The old man conceded that he might be suffering from some psychological problems. "I do not think I am altogether right," he declared at one point in their conversation.

"Do you mean to say that you are insane?" Wertham asked.

"Not exactly," answered Fish. "I compare myself a great deal to Harry Thaw in his ways and actions and desires. I don't understand it myself. It is up to you to find out what is wrong with me."

Accepting Fish's challenge, Wertham probed into every aspect of the old man's sordid past, grotesque fantasy life, and appalling sexual history. So many of Fish's assertions seemed incredible that, in an effort to verify them, Wertham spent hours checking the old man's medical and psychiatric records, interviewing his family members, and studying criminological literature for comparable cases.

In the end, Wertham was forced to conclude that there *were* no comparable cases. Fish's life had been one "of unparalleled perversity," Wertham later wrote. "There was no known perversion that he did not practice and practice frequently." Wertham determined that all these depravities had been fueled by a single, monstrous need—an unappeasable lust for pain. "I always had a desire to inflict pain on others and to have others inflict pain on me," Fish told Wertham. "I always seemed to enjoy everything that hurt. The desire to inflict pain, that is all that is uppermost."

Wertham was the first to learn another significant fact from Fish, too—a piece of information that the doctor promptly transmitted to James Dempsey, who saw it as a key to the insanity defense he was preparing. Fish told Wertham that, after decapitating Grace Budd, he had tried drinking her blood from the five-gallon paint can he had shoved under her neck. The warm blood had made him choke, however, and he had stopped drinking after three or four swallows.

Then he had taken his double-edged knife and sliced about four pounds of flesh from her breast, buttocks, and abdomen. He also took her ears and nose. He had wrapped the body parts in a piece of old newspaper and carried them back to his rooms. Simply holding the package on his lap as he rode the train back to New York put him in a state of such acute excitation that, before he had traveled very far, he experienced a spontaneous ejaculation.

Back in his rooms, Fish had cut the child's flesh into smaller chunks and used them to make a stew, with carrots, onions and strips of bacon. He had consumed the stew over a period of nine days, drawing out his pleasure for as long as he could. Later, Fish would tell Dempsey that the child's flesh had tasted like veal, though he had found her ears and nose too gristly to eat.

During all that time, he had remained in a state of absolute sexual arousal. He had masturbated constantly. At night he would lie in the darkness, savoring the lingering taste of the meat, and masturbate himself to sleep.

The next morning he would awaken, hungry for more.

Issei Sagawa
From *Cannibal Killers:*
The History of Impossible Murderers

Cannibalism as art? The case of the Japanese student Issei Sagawa is one of the strangest in recent history. Found mentally incompetent to stand trial after killing and eating a young Dutch woman, he is out of an asylum and currently a celebrity in his native Japan. Moira Martingale's *Cannibal Killers* takes up the tale.

If there is one cannibal killer who would in all likelihood applaud the beauty of Swinburne's poetry together with the notion that you can eat someone to prove you love them, Sagawa would probably fit the bill. He, too, is an artist and he particularly admires tall, generously-proportioned, beautiful girls. He enjoys painting them, reproducing the tones of their flesh and the plumpness of their buttocks on the canvas. Now in his early forties, the tiny Japanese artist says he contents himself with such depictions to fulfil his fantasies. But in Paris in 1981 he did not restrict his sensuous pleasure to the external beauty of the female form. Unlike Swinburne, who restrained the most shocking desires of his imagination within his writing, Sagawa allowed his frighteningly deviant fantasies off their leash. His longing was for soft flesh and hot blood, for complete, exploratory knowledge of those big, beautiful women—and in Paris he found satisfaction with a 25-year-old Dutch woman, Renee Hartevelt, with whom he fell in love "at first sight."

Renee was beautiful, blonde and well built, a serious-minded, independent woman who spoke three languages and was in Paris studying for her Ph.D in French literature at the Censier Institute. She supported herself by teaching languages and encountered Sagawa when he asked her to teach him German and offered to pay her handsomely. The son of Akira Sagawa, the wealthy and influential president of Kurita Water Industries, a prestigious Tokyo company, Issei had been a precocious child, enjoying Impressionist paintings from the age of five and being a prodigious reader from an early age. Like Renee, Sagawa was an intellectual, also working on his doctorate—in comparative literature—at Paris University. He already had his MA in Shakespeare Studies.

When he sat next to Renee Hartevelt in a classroom one day, he saw in her the living stuff of his fantasies. "I couldn't keep my eyes off her. Out of her short T-shirt I could see her white arms," he wrote later in his book *In The Fog,* in which he described what he called his Parisian "affair." He and Renee talked about literature together. They went to concerts and dances. Issei wrote her love letters. She should have been suspicious when he spoke of his love of raw meat, but she evinced no surprise. When he held her to dance, he envisaged her nude body with its "white flesh." So far, not an uncommon normal male fantasy, one might think. But Sagawa was no normal male. In fact, he was wildly abnormal in enjoying the dark avenues down which his imagination took him.

"I admire very much beautiful girls, especially Occidental girls who are healthy and tall. On the other hand, I also have this aspiration, this strange desire for cannibalism," he calmly told reporter Peter McGill in the British newspaper the *Observer* in 1992, as if it were for all the world just a quirk of taste, an antisocial habit. He recalled the childhood nightmare which he blamed for his "strange desire." He and his brother were boiling inside a pot. "It was my first nightmare of cannibalism, first, not to eat someone, but to be eaten." By the age of fifteen, the child was regularly fantasizing about cannibalism. "In my case it is just sexual desire. Sexual fetishism," he explained to McGill. "For Japanese girls I haven't any sexual desire. I am feeling as if she is my own daughter, no, sister, so it would be incestuous. For Occidentals though, I have a big adoration. The style, physically, I find very sexual . . . I prefer big women, but they are also repulsive."

Sagawa had studied for his degree in English literature at Wako University in Tokyo. While he was there he attacked a German woman, who, like Renee, was teaching him German. "In my head there was always a fantasy of cannibalism, and when I met this German lady in the street, I wondered if I could eat her," he explained to McGill. With "a mischievous smile" he related how he had climbed through the window of her ground-floor apartment on a summer's afternoon. "She was sleeping and almost naked. I wanted to attack her with an umbrella, but I was a little scared, and when I got close to her, she woke and screamed. She was stronger than me, I fell down, and tried to escape. I couldn't tell people it was because of cannibalism. I was too ashamed." After the attack, he saw a psychiatrist who declared that Sagawa was "extremely dangerous," but the incident was hushed up and in the late 1970s Sagawa, supported by the wealth of his father, went to live in Paris. He at once bought a rifle—as self-protection, he would later tell the police. There were, he explained, many murderers in Paris.

Renee apparently liked Sagawa. She wrote to her parents telling of her friendship with "a brilliant Japanese student" and invited the slightly-built, strange-looking oriental man to her room to discuss literature and have tea with her. He was not a threatening-looking man: less than five feet tall, weighing only six stone and with a limp, he was soft and rabbit-like. His lisping voice was gently plaintive and feminine: his hands and feet were tiny and childlike. Renee would tease him about his French, saying that it was so execrable that she would have to teach him French as well as German, and when, in turn, he invited her to visit him in his apartment to continue their discussion of literature, she willingly went. He served tea and his own special whisky brew. The two were kneeling on the floor, facing each other Japanese-style when Sagawa told Renee he loved her and asked her to go to bed with him. She dismissed his declaration of love and told him she would not sleep with him, for she saw him as a friend—that was all. Sagawa appeared to take her refusal placidly, nodding and indicating his assent. Standing up, he reached for a book of poetry and asked Renee to read it aloud to him. While she was preoccupied with this, he fetched his rifle and shot the girl in the back of the neck.

Sagawa told what happened next in *In The Fog,* the book he wrote when he was incarcerated in a French mental hospital and in whose pages he enthuses about eating human flesh. But before Sagawa dined on Renee's corpse, he indulged in what to him was a little foreplay: after undressing he had sex with the body. Then he cut off the tip of Renee's nose and part of a breast, which he devoured raw. "I touched her hip and wondered where I should eat first. After a little consideration, I ate right in the centre of the abundant, bouncing part of the right hip . . . I took a meat knife, and when I stabbed it went right in . . . When I started cutting, I could see some cornlike yellow stuff. I thought it was probably a white woman's own peculiar thick and soft fat. Beyond that I could see a red colour, it looked like beef, red meat . . . a little came out and I put it into my mouth . . . it had no smell or taste, and melted in my mouth like raw tuna in a sushi restaurant. Finally I was eating a beautiful white woman, and thought nothing was so delicious!"

With an electric carving knife, Sagawa cut up Renee's body carefully, removing strips of flesh to store in his refrigerator, and keeping the other parts he wanted to eat later. Some pieces he ate raw, others he fried with salt, pepper and mustard. Those parts in which he had no interest he cut into pieces small enough to be easily discarded. In between his butchering, Sagawa took photographs of his handiwork. He also took time off to go and watch a film with his friends. After a supper of raw flesh, Sagawa went to bed to sleep well in preparation for the busy day ahead. The next morning he went out and bought a luggage trolley and two large suitcases, together with a carpet-cleaning machine. He placed the remains of Renee Hartevelt in black plastic bin-liners and then put them into the suitcases, called a taxicab and tried to find a suitable place to dispose of the suitcases. He failed.

In fact, he made three attempts to get rid of them, but there were always too many people about. It was the following day when he finally dragged his wheeled trolley to a pond in the picturesque Bois de Boulogne where he intended to dump the cases in the water. It was hardly surprising that he was spotted by passersby. Sagawa was such an unnaturally small, slight person that the suitcases weighed more than he did and dwarfed him. Diners at a restaurant watched with interest as a little Japanese man puffed and panted his way across the grass with his heavy load. He was about to push them into the pond when he saw a couple watching him. Sagawa panicked and ran away, leaving the cases. Curiously, the couple approached the cases. They were heavily blood-stained, but what horrified them more was the hand which protruded from one . . .

The police were greatly puzzled when they found the butchered female remains, together with Renee's clothes and shoes, in the suitcases. The purpose of this dismemberment seemed only to be to make the body fit into the cases. Most murderers would mutilate a body in order to prevent identification, yet here were the young woman's head and hands almost intact, apart from the missing nose-tip, and together with her belongings this would make it easy to find out who she was—which they discovered within days. And they were soon to solve their murder mystery. A taxi driver remembered collecting Sagawa from his apartment and the police closed in on him within forty-eight hours.

The 33-year-old man greeted the officers pleasantly and confessed freely to the murder, but claimed he had a history of mental illness. When the police opened the refrigerator door and discovered Renee Hartevelt's breast, one of her lips and both buttocks on the shelves—and when Sagawa said he had eaten the other missing parts of her body "sliced thin and raw" and that it was as satisfying as he had always imagined it would be—they were inclined to agree that they were dealing with a madman.

While waiting for his trial to begin, Sagawa was confident that his influential father could do something to help him. He expressed no regret for his victim, but he did say he had learned a lesson from his experience of murder. He was quoted as saying: "I know now what to do when killing a girl, how not to be arrested." It was 1983 before a judge decided that Sagawa was mentally incompetent to stand trial, that criminal charges would be dropped because Sagawa was in a "state of dementia" at the time of the murder and that he should be placed in a secure mental hospital—the Paul Guiraud asylum in a Paris suburb—indefinitely. Hospital psychiatrists said that he was an untreatable psychotic.

And there the story should have ended. Unhappily ever after for Sagawa. But that is to disregard the curious appeal that this man held for the Japanese people. Sagawa had described Renee Hartevelt's raw, dead flesh as tasting "like raw tuna in a sushi restaurant," and those Westerners whose stomachs turn at the Japanese predilection for sushi—raw fish—can only feel even more disgust at what happened next to "insane" Issei Sagawa: he became a star. No sooner had he arrived at the Paul Guiraud hospital than a Japanese film company was looking at his story in just the way Sagawa had regarded Renee: in terms of consumer appeal. This could be a hit, they told Japanese playwright Juro Kara, who immediately began exchanging letters with Sagawa, which were then published in the form of a fictional novel called *Sagawa-kun kara no Tegami (Letters from Sagawa)* in 1983. In it, with a distasteful—and entirely inappropriate—picturesquesness, Kara described French women as having huge breasts "swinging to and fro like monsters, with blue veins running through them like Martian rivers." The book was a sell-out and won a literary prize for its "interesting intellectual approach." The Rolling Stones wrote a song about the case, called "Too Much Blood," and recorded it on their album *Under Cover*. Meanwhile, Sagawa was writing his first of five books, *Kiri no Naka (In the Fog)*, which contains lavish and intricate descriptions about the murder and cannibalization of Renee, written in a way that reveals the erotic fetishism which dominated Sagawa's psyche. The blurb on the cover includes a quotation from Sagawa describing Renee as "the most delicious meat I ever had" and the book was an instant success in Japan, where the newspaper *Tokyo Shimbun* declared it to be "beautifully done, and outstanding among recent Japanese literature, which has become boring." Sagawa also began making plans for directing a film of his experience, with himself in the starring role.

One would think that these offerings and plans were proof enough that Sagawa was a hopeless and dangerous case of a sexual deviant who should remain incarcerated until the breath has left his body. As Dr. Bernard Defer, one of Sagawa's psychiatrists in France, remarked in 1991: "Sexual desire, especially perverse desire, is something lasting, something permanent. It forms part of the personality. He can still have the desire to eat a woman. It is preferable that he still be in an institution." But Issei Sagawa is not still in an institution. Following approaches from his father shortly after his hospitalization, within a year Sagawa was removed from the French hospital and taken back to Tokyo where he was placed in the Matsuzawa Hospital "by the agreement of his parents," rather than being officially committed. Fifteen months later, in 1985, Akira Sagawa decided that his son should leave the hospital. Unable to object, they let Issei Sagawa out, whereupon he became an exciting celebrity with a story that combined sex, violence and fetishism and commanded untiring fascination. He was feted by the popular press and on television, a real-life Hannibal Lecter to whet the strange appetites of the Japanese masses. One interviewer fawningly told Sagawa: "Human beings like you are very rare. You act as a prism. You are Sagawa, who ate a human being." Sagawa was featured on the gourmet page of a magazine, eating barbecued food at a restaurant.

The Japanese, more than most nationalities, have always shown a peculiar appetite for the bizarre, especially if there is a macabre element of suffering or pain to spice up the entertainment value. Arguably the most successful Japanese writer of all time, Yukio Mishima, who died in 1970, was a homosexual sadist who was stimulated by the sight of blood and only joined the army in order to be able to observe blood, agony and death at first-hand. His dreams, according to his biographer Henry Scott Stokes were of "bloodshed—massacring youths, preferably Circassian [white] on large marble tables and eating parts of their bodies." Obsessed with strong young male bodies, Mishima himself was unattractive, short in stature, weak and thin—something which may find an echo in what we know of Issei Sagawa—and later in his life he became obsessed with bodybuilding to improve his physique. Yukio Mishima was his penname; he was originally named Kimitake Hiraoka and was a descendant of the *samurai*. His fascination with their ritualistic suicide tradition, *hara kiri,* was unsurprising since one of his favorite erotic images—seen graphically time and again in his work—was of a knife being thrust into an abdomen, which was then ripped asunder.

In the 1960s he became a right-wing political activist. He and his Imperialist sympathizers would swear allegiance by dripping blood from a cut finger into a cup, which would then be passed around for drinking. His public behaviour became more and more bizarre. He appeared in a trashy film and posed for a series of narcissistic photographs, one of which depicted him as St. Sebastian during his execution, his flesh pierced by many arrows. Death, he declared, was "the only truly vivid and erotic idea" and in November 1970 the stuff of his erotic imagination entered into reality. He and his small army stormed the headquarters of the Eastern Army in Tokyo and took the commander hostage. After notifying the media of his actions, he emerged from the building to speak out against democracy, but receiving only jeers he went back inside, knelt down, drove a dagger into his own abdomen and ripped it sideways to disembowel himself. He was forty-five.

Issei Sagawa grew up during a time when Mishima's genius was being lauded and Mishima's pervertedly "erotic" act can be compared with Sagawa's attempt to bestow artistic values upon his act of murder and his unstable sexual proclivities. He likes to speculate about whether the murder of Renee was one of exquisite and pure love, of crime redeemed by art. In the world of normal sexuality, the debate over where erotica ends and pornography begins may be argued by defining the erotic in the beauty of expressiveness of words or images, where coarseness or exploitation is absent. But this argument concerns images of "normal" sexuality. What of the abnormal—and what of "flawed genius"? There are those who say that with true genius also comes instability—that creativity cannot co-exist with normality—which is why many of the world's greatest artists and writers have displayed mental, emotional or sexual trauma in their lives. So what if the talented artist—like Mishima or Swinburne—can bring all his wonderfully positive literary or expressive devices to bear in his creation of "erotica," acknowledging that for him, the erotic is that perversion which he finds most arousing, but disgusts the normal human being? Deviant desires like sadism, murder, necrophilia, cannibalism? Is it still art?

Issei Sagawa clearly regards himself as an artist. Under an assumed name, he now lives in a third-floor apartment in a suburb of Tokyo where the walls are hung with his own oil paintings—mostly of Western women, with particular attention paid to their fleshy pink buttocks. He is unsupervised, despite the fact that Dr. Tsuguo Kaneko, the superintendent of the Japanese hospital where Sagawa was kept prior to his release, believes that he is a dangerous psychopath who should be prosecuted for his crime. "I think he is sane and guilty. Maybe he is a danger to foreign females. He must be in prison." Dr. Kaneko is reported as saying. Instead, Sagawa has become an established media figure, a role in which he delights and for which he is prepared to do and say just about anything. In 1989 he was announcing his intention to open a vegetarian restaurant in Tokyo; by 1992 he was planning his autobiographical film with Juro Kara and wondering who to choose to play the victim.

There is a complete absence of moral concern from both the media and Sagawa himself. He now says he is "no longer a cannibal," that he was sick during his Parisian period, but has recovered and would not repeat his crime. But the books he has written about cannibalism have all been best-sellers—an anthology of short stories on cannibalistic fantasies he describes as "a little bit comical"—and he writes regular articles for pornographic magazines, repeating in gory detail the story of his cannibalistic exploits. He writes film reviews for another magazine, revealing that he thought *The Silence of the Lambs* movie lacked psychological depth but he liked very much a German film called *Trance* "about the very beautiful girl who kills her boyfriend when he wants to leave her, and ate him up." In 1992 there was much outrage—particularly from the Netherlands embassy in Tokyo—when the Japanese authorities issued Sagawa with a passport to enable him to travel to Germany to appear on a chat show and talk about how he killed and ate Renee Hartevelt.

Contrasting with the shocked disbelief with which most Westerners regard Sagawa's celebrity status, there is, in addition to the tabloid-and-TV support he receives, a nucleus of intellectuals in Japan who, astonishingly, sympathize with Sagawa, regarding him as an anti-establishment outsider who should be admired for the fulfilment of his fantasy and for his "artistic insanity." High-flown debate rages in respected artistic circles concerning the "artistry" of Sagawa: whether he showed the purest form of love by devouring his girlfriend or whether it was simply a bizarre fetish. Morality does not enter into it. The artistic circles claim Sagawa's "crime" had to be committed, otherwise his "art" would have suffered. Detached, they speak philosophically about Sagawa's enjoyment of Renee Hartevelt's body, for all the world as if this was an imaginary learning experience rather than a real horrific sex murder. "Eating human flesh is the same thing as assimilating yourself to the body you are eating," coolly explains psychologist Shu Kishida. "In the Western world there are many historical cases in tribes, that you eat the flesh of the man you respect. In Sagawa's case it is an extreme form of the inherent admiration of every Japanese for the white race. His admiration of the white race took the extreme form of killing and eating that white woman's flesh."

Yasuhisa Yazaki, the editor of a magazine which carried a flattering article about the cannibal killer describes him as "a human being who has undergone a very special experience." He elaborates: "We have to say that in this world some human beings want to eat the flesh of other people. We have to admit their existence and accept it in the future." Other magazines carry pictures of his paintings. Sagawa believes he is artistically stimulated by "tall and robust" Western women and declares: "I'm essentially a romantic." Some women have been persuaded to pose nude for him. One of them, a young Dutch model, Ingrid, whom he contacted when he saw her photograph in a magazine, returned to Holland without ever knowing his real name or anything of his past. A British reporter, Joanna Pitman of the *Times,* actually went and took tea with Sagawa—not unaccompanied, of course—and was alarmed when he handed out cups of the special tea-and-whisky brew he had given to Renee before killing her:

> He welcomed us to his cramped and dingy home with fawning hospitality, displaying an ominous and hair-raising delight at the sight of a foreign female visitor. "I still adore the sight and the shape of young Western women, particularly beautiful ones," he said, his wolfish eyes staring out from behind dark glasses. "I was a premature and unhealthy baby, I am ugly and small, but I indulge in fantasies about strong healthy bodies."

Most alarmingly, Sagawa still talks with enthusiasm about cannibalism being an "expression of love" and seems unwilling to admit to the perversity of his peculiar passion. "Cannibalism has been my obsession since I was very young, it is a pleasure lying deep in the human spirit," he says. In magazine interviews he outlines his various sensual aims. "My long-cherished desire is to be eaten by a beautiful Western woman," he said on one occasion—and then admitted that he still fantasizes about eating a woman's flesh . . . although, he hastened to add, without murdering her and only with her consent. Such irrationality is evidence of the unbalanced mind of Sagawa, who is basking in the Japanese limelight thanks to his heinous deeds. But how will he react when the limelight fades? One of his former friends said she was afraid of what may happen when the media loses interest in him. "It's like a protective wall for him," she says. "He lives now in a type of world that he knows really well how to work."

And although he tries to make clear that artistic fantasy now substitutes for his very real desires, Joanna Pitman observed his "disturbingly carnal" paintings and said: "One of the most distressing aspects of this solitary man is the fact that he believes he is normal." Sagawa told her: "My time in the mental ward was like hell. Everyone else in there was crazy, but the doctors saw that I was not like them, that I was cured. I am normal. I eat an evening meal with my parents every day and spend my spare time painting and writing." In a magazine article entitled "I Ate Her Because of Fetishism" he explained that he recognized that he was sick in Paris, because he had allowed himself to become consumed by his fetishes and fantasies. "I think everyone has a curious fantasy. But they can't realize it, that's all. My fantasy of cannibalism is not crazy. Everyone has fantasies. The special thing about me is that I acted upon mine."

Jeffrey Dahmer
From *Cannibal Killers:*
The History of Impossible Murderers

BY MOIRA MARTINGALE

Jeffrey Dahmer, more than any other serial killer, has captured America's horrified imagination—his slaughterhouse of an apartment in Milwaukee contained, among other things, a refrigerator wherein resided three human heads. How could an ordinary American suburban boy become a twisted monster? Moira Martingale seeks answers in *Cannibal Killers.*

He has an awful lot of love for me . . . He always wanted to do things for me. He's a boy who likes things I like. He loves flowers, roses. He doesn't hesitate to show his love for me.

A doting grandma is describing her grandson, a man who has just been arrested for an abominable series of crimes. The man's stepmother is talking to a British journalist and says: "If you could meet him he would wring your heart out. He is such a sad person, he brings out all your maternal instincts." "Sit down and talk with him," says his lawyer, "and you'll say he's as nice a young man as you could meet." The man's neighbour recalls: "We used to hear sawing coming from his apartment at all hours . . . I said [to my husband] one night at about two in the morning, 'What in the world is he building at this hour?' " And . . . "He seemed like a regular guy," says the frightened individual who narrowly avoided becoming the regular guy's eighteenth victim—and supper. Tracy Edwards had fled the man's apartment in panic after being drugged, handcuffed and threatened with a knife. He gibbered out his story to two passing bored police officers—who sighed deeply and offered to check out his tale, all the time assuming it would be just a routine rapping of the regular guy's knuckles.

Their first glimpse of Jeffrey Dahmer certainly would not have indicated that he was anything other than a normal, somewhat serious young man. The good-looking 31-year-old who opened his front door to them on that night in July 1991 was skinny and blond, with a gentle, unhurried manner and a calm voice. Perhaps this makes it more understandable why three other police officers, two months previously, had returned to Dahmer a 14-year-old boy who had escaped his murderous clutches and, bruised, bleeding, naked and near-catatonic, had wandered out on to the street where the policemen found him after being called by a neighbour. Dahmer had turned up and, in pacifying tones, had explained that the young man was a friend who was staying with him and had had too much to drink. The officers had been convinced. They had allowed Dahmer to take Konerak Sinthasomphone back into his apartment, where the uncomprehending boy had watched the door close on his last chance of survival.

But in July these police officers, Robert Rauth and Rolf Mueller, knew nothing of that incident as they asked Jeffrey Dahmer if they could look around his apartment, having received complaints from Tracy Edwards, the 32-year-old black man who stood at their shoulders, that from being a friendly, normal guy one minute, this man had suddenly become crazy and tried to kill him the next. Dahmer quietly acquiesced and offered to go and fetch the key to the handcuffs from his bedroom. Edwards loudly told the officers that Dahmer's knife was in the bedroom, so Mueller went to search instead. What he found jolted and revolted him. In a drawer were gruesome Polaroid pictures of bodies at different stages of mutilation and dismemberment, photographs of skulls and skeletons . . . and a picture of a severed human head. As soon as the horrific importance of his discovery dawned on Mueller, Dahmer was handcuffed and arrested and Mueller showed Edwards the awful picture of the severed head. "This could have been you," he told him grimly with barely controlled revulsion. Edwards, in a state of high excitement by now, remarked to Mueller that Dahmer had freaked out when he had gone to open the refrigerator earlier in the evening. "Maybe there's a head in there?" he cried. Mueller smiled nervously at this outlandish idea—fuelled, no doubt, by Edwards' hysteria. "Yeah, maybe," he laughed, pulling open the door. There was a head in there. In fact, there were three heads in there.

Mueller screamed.

The question everyone wanted answering was: what turned Jeffrey Dahmer into a monster who cannibalized the bodies of those he murdered?

And the answer is simply: nobody knows. People who like to claim that early environment—perhaps an unhappy childhood, severity of punishment or being starved of affection—is to blame for a man's later heinous crimes, would scratch their heads over Dahmer, who fails to fit any bill of deprivation. Born in 1960, Jeffrey was the elder son of Lionel and Joyce Dahmer, who led a comfortable middle-class life in Bath, Ohio. Lionel Dahmer told a reporter that Jeffrey was an ordinary little boy. He recalled how his son would become excited when his grandparents came to visit, just like any normal kid. He denied a story, which was circulating at the time of Dahmer's arrest, that his son had been sexually abused by a neighbour when he was eight years old—as, indeed, did Jeffrey Dahmer himself. And although another journalist turned up a schoolteacher's report which said that the 6-year-old Jeffrey Dahmer seemed to feel neglected after the birth of his brother David, this is a common enough occurrence in families.

There seems little in the way of childhood trauma to explain adequately why this small boy grew up to be a sick cannibalistic serial killer who would shock the world. One psychiatrist suggested that it might have been because he had had a hernia operation at the age of four; a suggestion born, one feels, of desperation rather than real in-depth analysis. The home was not without affection; Jeffrey was adored by his grandmother in particular. True, there were problems between his parents and soon after David's birth they moved into separate bedrooms—friends even claimed that Lionel Dahmer had a string of bells outside his room to warn him of his wife's imminent arrival—but the couple stayed together for the sake of their sons until Jeffrey was eighteen and David twelve. Jeffrey Dahmer would later tell a probation officer that if there was anything he would have liked to change about his childhood, "it would be the way my parents behaved towards each other," but again, thousands of children from broken homes endure far worse. But while David developed normally, Jeffrey's peculiar interests and fantasies began to evolve early. The child was only eight when his interest in dead bodies began to manifest itself. He was fascinated by the insides of bodies, the bright colors, Dahmer's lawyer was to tell the court at his trial—when it was also revealed that Dahmer preferred to have sex with the viscera of the young men whom he had killed.

Lionel Dahmer, a chemist, may have thought his son would follow in his footsteps when he bought little Jeffrey a chemistry set. The worst use to which most children put their chemistry sets is creating flashes and bangs. Jeffrey's experiments were more sinister. His early interests lay with insects which he preserved in jars, but later he moved on to mammals, impaling cats and frogs on sticks. He would collect animals which had been run over and skin them, using the substances in his chemistry set. Dried-out animal skins and their decapitated heads impaled on spikes were scattered around the woods at the back of his home and he was fascinated with the innards of animals, cutting them up to see how they worked. Dahmer later told the police that when he was young he and a friend would drive around looking for dogs which were walking along the road, and run them over. He recalled hitting a beagle puppy and relished the look of terror on its face as it hit the windshield of the car.

At age fourteen, he said, he had his first homosexual experience and confessed that he regularly fantasized about using a corpse for sex. Necrophilia became an obsession and like other sadistic killers he had a fertile imagination. As his lawyer Gerald Boyle was to remark after Dahmer's imprisonment, "When you're fourteen and you want to make love to a dead body, you've got a hell of a problem." Schoolmates cast back their minds and described the teenage Dahmer as an isolated, lonely individual with a peculiar sense of humour. One girl remembered, "I felt uncomfortable around him because he was so weird and so emotionless," and another recalled that he had an established drinking problem by the time he was sixteen, which led to him drinking neat Scotch during class. Gerald Boyle said that by this age Dahmer was "a desperately lonely person with no friends" and claimed, "If Jeffrey Dahmer had gotten help when he was sixteen he'd be a free man today."

Dahmer's home life was obviously far from perfect at this time, but it was not until he was eighteen—an independent adult, according to the law—that his parents sorted out their divorce, which involved a wrangle over custody of Jeffrey's younger brother, then aged twelve. Lionel and Joyce accused each other of neglect and cruelty and Lionel alleged that Joyce should not be awarded custody of David because of "extreme mental illness." However, Joyce did win custody and a month later, in August 1978, she left Jeffrey in the family home and took off with her younger son to settle firstly in Chippewa Falls, Wisconsin and later in Fresno, California. Lionel, robbed of his regular meetings with his younger son, applied to the court again for custody—and this time it was granted. Meanwhile, throughout all these family battles, during that summer of 1978 Jeffrey was left very much to his own devices.

The month before his parents' divorce hearing, Jeffrey Dahmer murdered the first of his seventeen victims. "One night," Gerald Boyle was to tell a packed Milwaukee court, "he is driving around and he sees a hitchhiker, and the hitchhiker doesn't have a shirt on, and Jeffrey Dahmer wants his body." Boyle was to pause before repeating significantly: "His *body*." Dahmer picked up 18-year-old Steven Hicks, who was hitchhiking from a rock concert, took him home, got drunk, had sex with Steven and then killed him, hiding the corpse in the crawl-space beneath the house. "The guy wanted to leave and I didn't want him to leave," he said later. Then, as he had done with the animals ten years previously, Dahmer dismembered Steven Hicks' body with a kitchen knife, placed the pieces in plastic bags and carried them around in his car with him. Much later he scattered Steven Hicks' remains around the wood at the back of his home. The murder was not to come to light until thirteen years later when Dahmer made a confession to Milwaukee police, although he could remember the hitchhiker only as Steve. When shown a photograph of Hicks, he said: "Yeah, that's him," displaying no emotion at all.

But back in 1978, Dahmer's family had no clue to the teenager's unspeakable fantasies or his awful secret. Jeffrey went off to Ohio State University to study business but dropped out after one term, his drinking problem increasingly hard to handle. In December that year Shari Jordan married Lionel Dahmer. Jeffrey was eighteen and she remembers him as "practically an alcoholic." Like his father, she was to express bewilderment at Jeffrey Dahmer's dreadful crimes. "None of us know why, out of two children with a similar upbringing, one should become a killer," she said. Dahmer enrolled in the army where he was to spend the next two years. The following July he was posted to Baumholder, West Germany, as a combat medic. Unlike many soldiers he did not join in the "buddy culture" and remained a loner, on the periphery of his fellow soldiers' social interactions. Occasionally he drank heavily and hurled racist abuse at black soldiers and in the course of duty it seemed he was squeamish. He was afraid of needles and could not bear to take anyone's blood—which makes it even more curious to consider that, only a year after his discharge for alcohol abuse, he got a job at the Milwaukee Blood Plasma Center, doing exactly that.

But his first job on leaving the army was in a Florida sandwich bar where he worked for a time before moving back to the home of his father and stepmother. Lionel Dahmer, unable to cope with his son's heavy and frequent drinking at the local bars, decided to send him to his grandmother's house to live, on the grounds that Catherine Dahmer and Jeffrey had always been very close. It was true that there was a loving bond between the two of them. But a stable home life over the next five years did not alter Dahmer's lifestyle. At the end of this period he was working at a chocolate factory during the daytime and in the evenings he cruised around the gay bars. He was arrested a couple of times for exposing himself and masturbating in public, and on one occasion he was accused of drugging people at a gay bathhouse, but predictably enough no man wished to stand up and be counted by pressing charges against Dahmer. There was nothing and no one to stop Dahmer. Towards the end of 1987, and still living with his grandma, he began his killing spree in earnest.

Steven Toumi, one of the few white males who became a Dahmer victim, shared a hotel room for a night with Dahmer after meeting him at a gay bar in Milwaukee. Dahmer claimed in his later confession that he woke up the next morning to find Toumi dead and bleeding from the mouth. Experts, puzzled as to why he should give graphic accounts of other murders but insist he remembered nothing of this one, are inclined to believe that for some reason he has blocked out all memory of the events that night. However he clearly recalled his actions the following morning: he bought a big suitcase, put the corpse inside and took it back to Catherine Dahmer's house where, after having sex with the body in his basement room, he mutilated the corpse and then dismembered it, putting the pieces into the dustbin.

Two months later he repeated his actions with a 14-year-old boy, James Doxtator, whom he had picked up outside the same club. This time, Dahmer avoided the cost of a hotel room by bribing the boy with cash in return for posing naked for him, and taking him straight home. After having sex with James, Dahmer gave him a drink with some sleeping pills in it—a technique which was to become a routine part of his killing method. When the drugs had the required effect, Dahmer strangled James and dismembered his body, throwing it out with the rubbish as he had done with Toumi. The scenario was repeated after another two-month period of abstinence. This time the victim was Richard Guerrero, aged twenty-five.

Dahmer did not keep any "mementos" of these three victims, unlike later in his killing career when he began preserving their heads, genitals, bones or other organs. At his later trial, Dahmer's attorney Gerald Boyle said Dahmer viewed the act of mutilation as "just making a human being disappear"—as if he was driven to dispose of his victims in this way by sheer expedience. That was certainly not the case towards the end of his murderous spree—and judging by what we know of Dahmer's perverted childhood interests, it was probably not his prime motivation at the time of these murders. His behavior with corpses was, however, going to become more and more extreme to meet his necrophiliac desires. Eventually he demanded greater stimulation to gain the same sexual satisfaction, and would achieve it in a number of ways, including cannibalism.

Jeffrey's drunken behaviour was becoming as intolerable for his grandmother as it had been for his father. In summer 1988 she asked him to move out and he found an apartment in Milwaukee. Almost immediately, he intercepted a 13-year-old boy on his way home from school and offered him fifty dollars to go home with him and pose half-naked for photographs. The boy obliged and Dahmer made homosexual advances to him, kissing him and touching his penis. He also gave the boy some drugged coffee, but perhaps he misjudged the quantity of drug required to knock out the teenager because, although dopey, the youth did not fall asleep. Instead he went home where, after behaving in a disoriented way, he eventually passed out and his family took him to hospital. The drugs were discovered, the story was told and Dahmer was soon under arrest.

His family rallied round. Catherine Dahmer took her grandson into her home again and Lionel Dahmer put up bail and hired a top lawyer, Gerald Boyle, to defend him. At first Dahmer denied the events, explaining away the drugging as an accident—because, he claimed, when he took his sleeping tablets, he always drank them from the cup which he had given to the child. Obviously, he said, there must have been some residue left in there. But when the case was heard the following year, he pleaded guilty to second-degree sexual assault and to enticing a child for immoral purposes.

While on bail, Dahmer was seeing a psychologist from the probation department. These consultations had, declared one report, been most useful. Dahmer was more amiable and relaxed and more willing to talk about himself, the report said optimistically. The probation department did not know that Dahmer had been busy during those months when it was supposedly monitoring him. A matter of weeks before he was due to be sentenced, he picked up 20-year-old Anthony Sears at a gay bar, took him home to his grandmother's house for sex and killed and disposed of him in his customary way. This time, he kept a souvenir: Anthony's head, which was to be discovered when police raided Dahmer's apartment two years later. After boiling the head to remove the skin, he painted the skull grey, so it would appear to be like a medical model such as doctors or medical students might use. Later he would admit that he enjoyed masturbating in front of this skull, and other skulls.

In court for sentencing on the enticement charge, the Assistant District Attorney Gale Shelton pleaded that Dahmer be imprisoned for many years—on the grounds that although he was superficially co-operative he had "deep-seated anger and deep-seated psychological problems." Two psychologists agreed with her, between them offering opinions that Dahmer was manipulative, had problems with his sexuality and was a schizoid personality who needed intensive treatment. His defending attorney Gerald Boyle, unaware that the man in the dock had already killed five people, the last one only weeks previously, pleaded for lenience, citing Dahmer's sense of responsibility in holding down a job and his belief that Dahmer was "semi-sick"—that he had not reached the stage where he was a chronic offender. "I believe that he was caught before it got to the point where it would have gotten worse—a blessing in disguise," he said and added that as far as he was aware, there had been "no recurrence of this type of conduct." In an ironic sense, this was true; Dahmer had made sure that things were different with Sears, his most recent victim, giving him such a hefty dose of drugs that he was too sedated to get up and leave Dahmer's room to blow the whistle on him.

But Dahmer was the very model of contrition in court, blaming alcohol for his misdeameanors, saying he had never before done anything as awful as this assault on the boy and that it had shocked him out of his bad behaviour pattern. He pleaded that the court allow him to continue his job. "Please don't destroy my life," he begged piteously, knowing all the time that he had destroyed five other lives more completely than this court could ever hope to damage his. But the judge was convinced of Dahmer's wish to reform. He sent Dahmer to a correction center for a year, with day release so he could continue his job, and gave him suspended prison sentences on both the charges, together with a five-year probation order and an order to get counselling and treatment for his drinking problem. Three years later, Gerald Boyle was to say that this sentence was appropriate at the time, no one having had any idea of Dahmer's dark secrets: "He fooled a lot of people." When Dahmer was released from the correction center ten months later, he moved into the apartment which was to become the most infamous in Milwaukee. In only a matter of months Dahmer turned it into a human abattoir.

In just over a year, Dahmer murdered twelve people in that apartment, typically luring them there for sex, photographic sessions or to watch homosexual videos, with the promise of payment. The murders were part of his weekend entertainment; before he left to cruise the gay bars and select a victim, he would shift the furniture to make more room to carry out the murder when he returned later. He was preoccupied with the horror film *The Exorcist III* and would often play the video of it to his potential victims. He would sedate them, strangle or stab them, have anal and oral sex with the corpses and then dismember them, always doing this in the nude to avoid messing up his clothes. Before dismemberment he would frequently wait until the bodies were stiff with rigor mortis, then he would stand them up, cut them open and take Polaroid pictures, which he put in an album. He would remove the genitals, preserving them in formaldehyde and would decapitate his victims, usually boiling the heads to keep as trophies and sometimes painting them grey. He saved the penis of one victim and painted it a "natural" flesh colour. Dahmer told police he disposed of six victims' torsos by soaking them in acid until they became "slushy" and then flushing them down a toilet.

Dahmer ate the flesh of three victims and performed sex acts on two of the several heads. He admitted experimenting with various culinary seasonings in order to make the flesh taste better and kept human-meat "patties" in the freezer.

During his later confession to the police, he was reluctant to give details about which victims he ate, but admitted to cutting flesh from one man's thigh and eating it, to saving a heart in his freezer "to eat later" and to frying and eating the biceps of 24-year-old Ernest Miller "because they were big" and he "wanted to try it." Ernest Miller, a dancer, evidently held many attractions for Dahmer—he also flayed this man's body, removed the flesh from the bones and discarded it, saving the skull and skeleton, which he hung in his apartment. A photograph was found of the skeleton hanging in the shower.

As time went on, even this horrific behavior became inadequate to satiate Dahmer's lust. He began to perform experiments on his sedated victims. Testimony at his sanity trial showed Dahmer drilled the skulls of some unconscious victims and poured acid into the holes in a crude attempt to lobotomize the men and create zombie-like sex partners for himself. Needless to say, the experiments failed. Sometimes, in a further twist of cruelty, Dahmer would anonymously telephone the families of his murder victims and tell them their sons were dead and that he had killed them.

The majority of Dahmer's victims were non-white, which makes their murders at the hands of Dahmer unusual in terms of serial murder statistics. FBI profiles of serial killers show that they usually only attack people within their own ethnic group—and serial killers are almost always white. Dahmer also was unusual in that he didn't have a car and killed most of his victims at his home. Since Dahmer's arrest, many people have come forward to declare that Dahmer was a racist who frequently made anti-black remarks. At Dahmer's trial, however, Dr. Frederick Fosdal, a forensic psychiatrist hired by the state, said that in his interview of Dahmer he found no evidence that the killings were racially motivated, although he established that Dahmer was homosexual.

All Dahmer's known victims were gay—a fact which Dahmer was keen to point out at the time of his confession, as if he thought it might exculpate his murders. Why should he draw attention to this when he was himself gay? There are clues to be found to this puzzle. All the time that Dahmer was committing these dreadful crimes, he was turning up—fairly regularly, at least—for his monthly appointments with his probation officer Donna Chester, who noted his depression and his problem with his sexual identity. He admitted being gay but said he felt guilty about it. This attitude is borne out by a 21-year-old single mother who, in 1992, under banner headlines of "The Only Woman Who Loved Hannibal the Cannibal" told a British newspaper, *Today*, about Dahmer's hatred for homosexuals and his preoccupation with God and religion.

She met Dahmer in 1988 when he was living with his grandmother before his arrest on the indecency charge—about which the young woman knew nothing until Dahmer's atrocities were made public—and they became friends. She even helped him to choose the apartment in which he later butchered countless victims. The young woman would sit in Dahmer's room for hours and he would sometimes recite the Lord's Prayer or preach passages from the Bible to her. Sometimes, she revealed, he would ask her what she thought about homosexuals and he made plain his own opinion. "He couldn't stand them," she said. "He said sex between men and men or women and women was wrong . . . that they were committing a sin."

Dahmer's antipathy towards homosexuals is interesting in that it provides a possible shred of insight into his behavior. This knowledge tells us that he must necessarily have been filled with self-disgust at his own homosexual desires, and possibly, wishing to deny the homosexual act in which he indulged, he projected this disgust on to his partners. By eradicating them, in some twisted way he may have believed he was attacking himself and destroying the evidence of his "shameful" actions. However, while this internal conflict might offer a "reason" why a person with a severe personality disorder would wish to kill, it fails to explain why they would indulge in the sordid cannibalistic and necrophiliac activities which so delighted Dahmer.

In May 1991, two months before the full horror of what had gone on in Jeffrey Dahmer's apartment was discovered, the police had a telephone call from Sandra Smith, one of his close neighbors who, with her mother, Glenda Cleveland, was alarmed to see a naked boy, his legs covered with blood, running down the street, having fled from Dahmer's apartment. By the time officers Joe Gabrish, Richard Porubcan and John Balcerzak arrived, so had Dahmer, on his way back from a bar. Dahmer had already had oral sex with 14-year-old Konerak Sinthasomphone while the drugged boy was inert and unconscious and he had left his flat only briefly to buy some beer, relishing the thought that his next blood-sacrifice was drugged into oblivion and would be there when he returned to do with as he pleased. Instead his plan was going wrong, for he was alarmed to see this boy standing stark naked in the company of three police officers. But Dahmer was gratified to observe that the drugged coffee *had* taken effect: the boy was dazed and incoherent. Having summoned up a surge of strength and courage to run, he now slumped into glassy-eyed silence. In the glib, manipulative way which Dahmer had practised before and was to display again, he quietly told the police that their charge was a 19-year-old friend who was staying with him and had had too much to drink.

The three officers were clearly fooled by Dahmer but decided to check out his apartment anyway. There they found Konerak's clothes neatly stacked on a chair with no apparent sign of any struggle. Konerak

sat on the sofa and said nothing, no longer trying to escape, and the officers put the incident down to a lovers' tiff. Had they investigated a little
further, they would have discovered the decomposing corpse of Tony
Hughes spread out on Dahmer's bed, where it had been since Dahmer
had killed him three days previously. Sure, the police officers noticed the
appalling, blocked drains-type smell in Dahmer's apartment—as did
everyone else who visited it—but they had no reason to conclude that
this was because the pleasant, polite, sandy-haired chap before them had
several rotting corpses in a fifty-gallon container in his bedroom. As Balcerzak said later: "Dahmer was a straightforward, calm, convincing person
who voluntarily came forward with information with no hint of stress
and no hint that he didn't want us to continue with our investigation."

Nevertheless, they were glad to leave the stench of the room and
the squalor of the Milwaukee building and be on their way. In flippant
mood they radioed in to HQ "The intoxicated Asian naked male was
returned to sober boyfriend," Balcerzak reported amid much laughter,
adding, "my partner's going to get deloused at the station" as a graphic
comment on the unsanitary conditions of the apartment. As soon as
the police had gone, Dahmer is said to have drilled into Konerak's
head and poured acid into his brain in one of his attempts to create a
zombie sex slave. Then he strangled Konerak, sexually violated his
corpse and dismembered it, taking photographs and keeping the boy's
skull.

When Dahmer was eventually arrested and tried for murder, the
details of this bungled incident emerged and the three officers found
themselves "in the dock" too. As Janie Hagen, the sister of victim
Richard Guerrero said: "Jeffrey Dahmer will get what he deserves—life
in prison. The three police officers are next." Joe Gabrish and John Balcerzak were fired almost instantly; Richard Porubcan was suspended. In
retrospect it is easy to blame these officers for failing to carry out their
duty to the hapless Konerak and no one doubts that they should have
been more suspicious of Dahmer. But Dahmer, as a psychiatrist was later
to declare, was "a formidable liar." He had already shown, at the indecency trial where he had deceived everyone from his attorney to the
judge, that if you're smart enough, you *can* fool all of the people all of
the time.

Tracy Edwards, the man who lived to tell the tale of his encounter with Milwaukee's most infamous murderer—and who put a
stop to his slaying of young men—claimed that there was no mention of

homosexuality when he went back to Dahmer's apartment with him on 22 July 1991 (although Dahmer claimed that Edwards was there for a "photo session") but that he went merely for a drink. However, he told the court at Dahmer's trial, he suspected that his rum and Coke had been drugged when he began feeling dizzy. In the bedroom, where the walls were plastered with pornographic pictures of gay sex acts, Dahmer handcuffed Edwards and pulled out a knife. The horrified young man said he saw a large bloodstain on the bedspread and later said that there was a human hand sticking out from under the bed—although he does not appear to have mentioned this to the police at the time they rescued him. Dahmer, claimed Edwards, told him he intended to eat him. "You'll never leave here," he said and pulled a skull out of a filing cabinet saying: "This is how I get people to stay with me—you will stay with me too." Then he listened to the terrified Edwards' heart beating and announced, "Soon it will be mine. I'm going to cut your heart out." (It must be noted that doubt has been cast on Edwards' claims regarding these threats; such killers do not usually announce their intentions in advance, say some psychiatrists.) Seizing an opportune moment—when Dahmer was rocking manically back and forth and chanting, "It's time, it's time"—Edwards said he punched and kicked him and fled the apartment to flag down officers Rauth and Mueller, who exposed the bloody slaughterhouse which was Jeffrey Dahmer's home. The remains of eleven victims were found there. Most were identified by dental records.

Meanwhile, officers investigating his past discovered other unsolved murders in places where, coincidentally, Dahmer had lived. While Dahmer was in the army and stationed in Baumholder, Germany, there were five unsolved murders involving mutilation of the victims in the area. The Baumholder connection was abandoned as theoretically unlikely because there were females among the victims. When Dahmer left the army he lived for a time in Miami. Four months after his arrival, a 6-year-old boy named Adam Walsh was abducted in Hollywood, Florida and two weeks later his head was found in a canal 120 miles away. No other remains were found. Dahmer refused to admit any involvement in this murder and police appear to have ruled out any connection.

Dahmer confessed to killing seventeen young males, sixteen in Wisconsin and one in Ohio, but when he came to trial on 13 January 1992 he was only charged with fifteen. One of the Wisconsin murder cases was abandoned because of lack of evidence and Dahmer's first victim, Steven Hicks, was killed in Dahmer's home town of Bath, Ohio, where he was due to stand trial separately. Dahmer pleaded guilty but insane to the fifteen murders. When the jury was selected, Dahmer's attorney Gerald Boyle cautioned that the trial would include "human carnage, killing, mutilation, cannibalism—everything you can possibly imagine." Two women who said they couldn't endure it were excused. After the trial the jury were offered counselling to help them cope with the gruesome details they had heard.

Jurors had to decide whether Dahmer suffered from a mental illness which prevented him from knowing his crimes were wrong or which made him unable to stop himself from committing them. District Attorney Michael McCann reminded them that the case was about Dahmer's state of mind when he killed, not about the carnage surrounding the deaths. "This is about responsibility for killing fifteen men," he advised. "Not responsibility for dismemberment. Not responsibility for having sex with a dead body." Dahmer sat silently during most of the jury selection, looking at the floor or at the judge, although he occasionally looked at potential jurors with sideways glances. If found insane, he would be sent to a mental hospital and could petition for release every six months. If judged to be sane, he would receive a mandatory life prison sentence for each murder. Wisconsin has no death penalty.

One of the officers who had taken down Dahmer's confession described to the court how calm and composed the killer was as he talked for hours about how he had mutilated his victims, smoking cigarettes and drinking coffee as he went over the details. Detective Murphy said that Dahmer told the police he "would have preferred that the victims stayed alive. However, he felt that it was better to have them dead than to have them leave," he added. "He became more relaxed as conversations went on. At the beginning there was no eye contact. Toward the end he would look at us and occasionally smile." Officer Murphy said he was like someone who had been caught doing "something wrong and was a little embarrassed about it." He said Dahmer told him of taking the bicep of one of his victims and frying it, using meat tenderizer on it and then eating it. "He said it tasted like beef."

Gerald Boyle argued that Dahmer's craving for sex with dead bodies and his fear of loneliness escalated into a killing spree that he couldn't control. Dahmer's acts were not those of a normal man, he said, but a man who was caught up in the "personification of Satan." Dahmer's early dabblings in necrophilia had involved an attempt to dig up a body from a cemetery but he had failed because the ground was frozen, said Boyle. He said that although Dahmer had tasted blood while working at the plasma clinic in Milwaukee in 1983, he didn't like it and had never tried it again. However, later in his killing spree he did perform acts of cannibalism. There were two occasions confirmed, but up to ten reported by Dahmer, it was said. Boyle expanded on the idea that Dahmer was "keeping" his victims with him to prevent them abandoning him—a grisly attempt to fulfil a need for human contact. "He ate body parts so these poor people he killed would become alive in him," said Boyle, claiming that the fact that Dahmer's victims wanted to leave drove him to kill them to keep them with him out of loneliness and out of his desire to have their bodies and enjoy them sexually in numerous ways. Dahmer could not perform sexual acts with men when they were awake, so he would drug them and then kill them. He said that after sex Dahmer missed feeling the heartbeats of his partners—and that was when he began experimenting with lobotomies to turn his victims into "Zombies or sex slaves . . . people who would be there for him." After Dahmer had drilled holes in the skulls of his unconscious victims, he injected muriatic acid into their brains. Some died instantly, but one victim, Jeremiah Weinberger, walked around for two days after being "lobotomized."

One clinical psychologist, Dr. Judith Becker, revealed that Dahmer had planned to build a magical shrine which would enable him to receive "special powers." Dahmer had drawn a picture of this shrine, which featured a black table and chair, incense burners and the skulls and skeletons of his victims. He had already bought the base of the table and planned to illuminate it with blue lights directed on to a backdrop curtain featuring a goat. Dahmer had also bought a statue of a mythical monster, the griffin, which—like the goat—is sometimes used in Satanic ceremonies. Dahmer told the psychologist that the griffin captured the way he felt, in that it represented evil.

Throughout the terrible evidence offered during the trial Dahmer's father and stepmother listened intently, sometimes hugging relatives of Dahmer's victims. "They knew that we were hurting too," Lionel Dahmer told reporters and Shari added: "It's tragic. And what do we say to those families out there who don't even have the child to bury in many cases?"

"I don't think I'll ever come to terms with it," Mr. Dahmer said. "Nothing will ever be the same again."

Dahmer spoke at the end of the trial, issuing an elaborate apology to the families of his victims and begging to be forgiven for his "holocaust" of evil. "I hope God can forgive me," he said. Lionel Dahmer, a religious man who could never have imagined that when he bought his small son his first chemistry set all those years ago, it would one day lead to this horror, listened in sorrow, saying later that Jeffrey would willingly have chosen death as punishment. But Dahmer was not to get his wish. He was declared to be sane and sentenced to fifteen consecutive life sentences and was sent to the Columbia Correctional Institution at Portage, about eighty miles northwest of Milwaukee, where he lived in an isolated glass cage reminiscent of that which contained Hannibal the Cannibal in the movie *The Silence of the Lambs*. The high-tech equipment and design made it one of the most secure and safe prisons in the country, but it ultimately didn't save Dahmer, who was killed in 1994 in an attack by fellow inmates.

Those people who had seen *The Silence of the Lambs* realized, watching Dahmer, that charming, powerful psychopaths like Hannibal Lecter exist mainly in fiction. The courtroom crowds in Milwaukee may have been disappointed to see, not the wild-eyed Devil incarnate, but an untidy, somewhat insubstantial young man who kept his eyes downcast and remained passive throughout the trial. His manner changed only once, to display a grisly sense of humor. The day that the case went to the jury, he brought into court a copy of a supermarket tabloid with his picture on the cover. The headline read: "Milwaukee Cannibal Kills His Cellmate." The story said Dahmer also ate the cellmate. Dahmer flashed the paper around in disdainful amusement. "Isn't it amazing what they come up with?" asked the man who may not have eaten his cellmate but *had* killed and partially eaten seventeen other people. The irony of his words was lost on him.

Part Six
The Taste:
Human Flesh as a Delicacy

The Gourmets
From *Cannibalism: From Sacrifice to Survival*

BY HANS ASKENASY, PH.D.

Although many people might like to avoid the subject, human flesh as food is a topic much debated among aficionados. Does it taste like chicken, pork, veal? Depends on who you talk to and, apparently, just who is being eaten. . . . Hans Askenasy provides some refreshing culinary details in *Cannibalism: From Sacrifice to Survival*.

> *"Do not enter the Kitchen, sir . . . tonight or on any other evening of your life: never enter Shirro's Kitchen!"*
>
> Stanley Elin, *the Kitchen in the Restaurant Robinson*

The Latin Proverb *De gustibus non est disputandum,* literally translated, means "one cannot dispute tastes." More freely it means: "Thank God I am not like other people." Cannibalism is a gruesome subject, but in this chapter we will look at it in a lighter vein, tongue in cheek so to speak. Fortunately not everyone finishes up in someone else's stomach, but a notable number of those who do seem to be considered gastronomic delicacies (and sometimes dietary ones), and prepared accordingly. In short there seem to be those who like human flesh for its own sake. And there is no accounting for taste, as those who believe they are blessed with it never cease to emphasize. The relevant literature is full of examples, and we have already come across many. Surprisingly I have found almost no actual description of exactly *how* we taste. One I have found is this: the Fijis compare us to pork, and favorably at that—given a choice, they prefer the "long pig," *puakabalaua,* to the short one.

To caution yet again: not all reports and tales that follow are necessarily the truth, let alone the whole truth; the subject lends itself to fancy and gratuitous elaboration. The ferocious Caribs, for example, became heir to numerous legends, constantly improved upon; thus they were said to have split captured men into two, eaten their guts and limbs, and salted and dried the rest "like our hams." As the saying goes, we interrupt this fantasy to bring you a message of reality: as it happened the Caribbean people knew nothing about the process of salting until they learned it from the Europeans. With all this in mind let us see what can be done with our earthly parts, and peruse some original (or is it aboriginal?) recipes.

Humans were considered delicacies by men other than the Fijis, for example, by the Baja, Sande, Pambia, Manjema, Wadai, Haussaland, and Gerse, all of whom preferred humans to anything else; by tribes on the Solomon and other islands, such as New Caledonia, Fate, Erromango, and New Zealand; and by numerous others. When cows were given to the Basuto in order to make them give up cannibalism, they tasted them and declined the beef.

Specific preferences deal with sex, age, and race. A New Zealand chief, living in London for some years in the early nineteenth century, confessed that what he missed most about home was "the feast of human flesh . . . he was weary of eating English beef . . . the flesh of women and children was . . . the most delicious." The Bele in Liberia, however, ate only men, given their belief that the flesh of women was bitter. Certain Maoris preferred a man of fifty, and a black over a white one. They also never ate the flesh raw, "and preserved the fat of the rump for the purpose of dressing their sweet potatoes." The Fijis, by all accounts among the experts in the field, also disliked the taste of white men; preferred women to men in general; and considered the arm above the elbow and the thighs the tastiest joints. Their fondness for human flesh was such that the greatest praise they could bestow on any delicacy was to describe it "as tender as a dead man."

The Tartars were especially fond of females, and succulent young girls became officers' fare, "while the common soldiers had to make do with tough and stringy matrons." Breast meat, the greatest delicacy, was preserved for the princes' tables. The Baja king ate only women and girls. The chief of the Aoba had young girls slaughtered every few days, but dined only on their breasts. The Tangale, a confirmed headhunting tribe, specialized in the preparation and consumption of enemy women's heads. On the Gazelle peninsula a chief preferred the flesh of unborn children, and therefore hunted pregnant women. In eleventh-century China eating people became commonplace, and in human-meat restaurants, dishes made from the flesh of old men, women, and children all had special names, "and presumably special tastes." In sum, then, it seems that the consensus went something like this: women and children are better than men; blacks are better than whites (though at least one source stresses a preference for Chinese—perhaps because their diet was largely vegetarian); and in general the young are tastier than the old.

As for body parts, many have already been mentioned in other contexts. Nigerian tribes praised the palms, fingers, and toes, and incidentally felt that monkey meat was almost as good as man. A liking for brain and bone marrow is, as we have seen, age-old, as is the drinking of blood. Ibo cannibals favored the knuckles. The Jincang Dyaks ate only the head. The Nigerian Bafum-Bansaw tortured their prisoners before killing them by using bellows to pump boiling palm oil into their bowels and stomachs to make the meat juicier; at other times they pumped the oil into a carcass and left it to marinate. Indonesian cannibals were partial to the soles. Roasted over hot ashes the penis was regarded as a great dish by some.

A few other local preferences include: heart and liver—south and east Africa, Mexico, Fiji; kidneys—Dar For; kidney fat—Australia; navel—Bechuana; genitals—Herero; brain—New Guinea and many headhunters; eyes—Polynesia and New Zealand; cheeks—Torre; hands—New Caledonia; feet—Warega.

One description of a major dietary implication is the following from the 1972 Andes crash:

> On the other hand they all took to the marrow. When the last shread of meat had been scraped off a bone it would be cracked open with the ax and the marrow extracted with a piece of wire or a knife and shared. They also ate the blood clots which they found around the hearts of almost all the bodies. Their texture and taste were different from that of the flesh and fat, and by now they were sick to death of this staple diet. It was not just that their senses clamored for different tastes; their bodies too cried out for those minerals of which they had for so long been deprived—above all, for salt.

Additional culinary details in preparing "the long pig": In 1610, in the new colony of Virginia, a hungry settler murdered his wife, then salted/powdered her, and was eating a portion when he was discovered. He is said to have remarked that, "Now whether she was better roasted, boyled, or carbonado'd, I know not." We have already met the notorious Grossmann, who transformed out-of-work peasant girls into sausages in Germany in the 1920s. The Maori of New Zealand, who keep appearing in the relevant literature, also cut the bodies of their victims into pieces, and then cooked them in holes made in the ground into which hot stones were dropped. Some Australian tribes smoke-dried the corpses of tribesmen, consuming those portions rendered liquid by the heat.

Smoking the flesh is common, and the Badinga cut off arms, legs, and heads before placing them into the smoke. The result was described as especially delicious. The Tuari of Brazil burn their dead and preserve the ashes, mixing them with daily meals. The Hamatsas also appreciated smoked meat, but believed that eating hands or feet would cause their immediate death. The Banalas broke a slave's arms and bones and lowered him into a river for three days, apparently allowing the skin to come off more easily and tenderizing the morsels. The Manjema put flesh into water for three days so it would rot and gain a strong smell. The Bassange laid a slain enemy into water overnight, and on the next day cut off the head and thighs and placed these in an anthill; if the ants ate from it, "it was good." Eating cadavers in various stages of advanced decomposition is said to have been fairly widespread, and if true seems to have been a matter of taste without any other significance. Buried carcasses were unearthed after two weeks and then eaten by the Tanna. Tribes in New Guinea followed in style. The Tarianas and Tucanos in the Amazon jungle buried their dead in special houses, at the same time preparing a large batch of caxiri (an alcoholic mixture), which was left to ferment; a month later the corpse was dug up, much decomposed, and burned. The remains were powdered and mixed with the caxiri.

The following house specialty was created by Vlad, the original Dracula. Boyars who had offended him were beheaded, and the heads fed to crabs; these crabs were in turn served at a feast attended by the victim's relatives and friends. But then again, perhaps this menu is as apocryphal as Adlai Stevenson's story (related in Peter Ustinov's delightful biography, *Dear Me*): "The work of the Catholic missions in New Guinea is beginning to pay dividends. Statistics have shown that on Fridays the staple meat is fishermen."

One Man's Meal
From *Jungle Ways*

BY WILLIAM B. SEABROOK

William B. Seabrook, author of *The Magic Island* and *Jungle Ways*, is not much remembered today, but in the 1920s he was a celebrated author/explorer, a man of cultivation willing to venture where few others would set foot. In 1929, he was the guest of cannibals in French West Africa and in this section from *Jungle Ways* he provides that rarest of narratives: a first-hand account of eating human flesh.

The occasion was one which would probably never be repeated, so that I felt in duty bound to make the most of it. In addition, therefore, to a portion of stew with rice, sure to be so highly seasoned with red pepper that fine shades of flavor might be lost to an unaccustomed palate, I had requested and been given a sizable rump steak, also a small loin roast to cook or have cooked in whatever manner I pleased.

It was the meat of a freshly killed man, who seemed to be about thirty years old—and who had not been murdered.

Neither then nor at any time since have I had any serious personal qualms, either of digestion or conscience, but despite time, distance, and locale, I feel that it would be unfair, unsporting, and ungrateful to involve and identify too closely the individual friends who made my experience possible.

Fortunately such identification will not be necessary to establish authenticity. When a man has actually done a special thing of this sort, he need never worry about whether it will be accepted as authentic. Some millions of people will sooner or later read these lines in one language or another. No matter what phrases I choose, whether I write well or awkwardly, the authenticity will take care of itself, for I propose to set down details as full, objective, and complete as if I were recounting a first experience with reindeer meat, shark meat, or any other unfamiliar meat experimented with for the first time.

The raw meat, in appearance, was firm, slightly coarse-textured rather than smooth. In raw texture, both to the eye and to the touch, it resembled good beef. In color, however, it was slightly less red than beef. But it was reddish. It was not pinkish or grayish like mutton or pork. Through the red lean ran fine whitish fibers, interlacing, seeming to be stringy rather than fatty, suggesting that it might be tough. The solid fat was faintly yellow, as the fat of beef and mutton is. This yellow tinge was very faint, but it was not clear white as pork fat is.

In smell it had what I can only describe as the familiar, characteristic smell of any good fresh meat of the larger domestic animals. I am not expert in the finest shades of odor. When various meats begin cooking, there are special odors, easily distinguishable once they begin sizzling, as for instance beef, mutton, and pork. But in the raw state meats even so different as the three I have mentioned smell exactly alike to me, and this present meat smelled the same.

Having at hand my portion of highly seasoned stew, prepared in the classic manner (and not yet tasted because I was anxious to get the clearest first impression possible of the natural meat, and feared that excessive condiments would render it inconclusive), I had determined to prepare the steak and roast in the simplest manner, as nearly as possible as we prepare meat at home. The small roast was spitted, since an oven was out of the question, and after it had been cooking for a while I set about grilling the steak. I tried to do it exactly as we do at home. It took longer, but that may have been partly because of the difference between gas flame and wood coals.

The cooking odors, wholly pleasant, were like those of beefsteak and roast beef, with no special other distinguishing odor. By "other distinguishing odor," I mean that if you go into a kitchen where they are cooking game or mutton or fish or chicken, there is in each case something quite special which you can distinguish with the nose alone.

When the roast began to brown and the steak to turn blackish on the outside, I cut into them to have a look at the partially cooked interior. It had turned quite definitely paler then beef would turn. It was turning grayish as veal or lamb would, rather than dark reddish as a beefsteak turns. The fat was sizzling, becoming tender and yellower. Beyond what I have told, there was nothing special or unusual. It was nearly done and it looked and smelled good to eat.

It would have been obviously stupid to go to all this trouble and then taste too meticulously and with too much experimental nervousness only tiny morsels. I had cooked it as one would any other meat for my regular evening dinner, and I proposed to make a meal of it as one would any other meat, with rice and a bottle of wine. That seemed to be the way to do it. I wanted to be absolutely sure of my impressions.

I sat down to it with my bottle of wine, a bowl of rice, salt and pepper at hand. I had thought about this and planned it for a long time, and now I was going to do it. I was going to do it, furthermore—I had promised and told myself—with a completely casual, open, and objective mind. But I was soon to discover that I had bluffed and deceived myself a little in pretending so detached an attitude. It was with, or rather after, the first mouthful, that I discovered there had been unconscious bravado in me, a small bluff-hidden unconscious dread. For my first despicable reaction—so strong that it took complete precedence over any satisfaction or any fine points of gastronomic shading—was simply a feeling of thankful and immense relief. At any rate, it was perfectly good to eat! At any rate, it had no weird, startling, or unholy special flavor. It was good to eat, and despite all the intelligent, academic detachment with which I had thought I was approaching the experience, my poor little, cowardly and prejudiced subconscious real self sighed with relief and patted itself on the back.

I took a good big swallow of wine, a helping of rice, and thoughtfully ate half the steak. And as I ate, I knew with increasing conviction and certainty exactly what it was like. It was like good, fully developed veal, not young, but not yet beef. It was very definitely like that, and it was not like any other meat I had ever tasted. It was so nearly like good, fully developed veal that I think no person with a palate of ordinary, normal sensitiveness could distinguish it from veal. It was a mild, good meat with no other sharply defined or highly characteristic taste such as for instance goat, high game, and pork have. The steak was slightly tougher than prime veal, a little stringy, but not too tough or stringy to be agreeably edible. The roast, from which I cut and ate a central slice, was tender, and in color, texture, smell as well as taste, strengthened my certainty that of all the meats we habitually know, veal is the one meat to which this meat is accurately comparable. As for any other special taste or odor of a sort which would be surprising and make a person who had tasted it not knowing exclaim, "What is this?" it had absolutely none. And so for the "long pig" legend, repeated in a thousand stories and recopied in a hundred books, it was totally, completely false. It gives me great comfort here to be able to write thus categorically. A small helping of the stew might likewise have been veal stew, but the overabundance of red pepper was such that it conveyed no fine shading to a white palate; so I was glad I had tried it first in the simpler ways.

If I had begun, despite my objective intentions, with a certain unconscious trepidation, I finished well enough, able after the first sensation of relief had passed to consider the meat as meat, and to be absolutely sure of the correctness of my impressions. And I felt a great satisfaction in having learned the empiric truth on a subject concerning which far too many books and pieces have been written and rewritten, filled with almost nothing but speculation, hearsay, legend, and hot air. A sense of pride also in having carried something through to its finish. And a longstanding personal curiosity satisfied at last.

Permissions Acknowledgments